Volume 3

Parent/Teacher Handbook

Teaching Children Ages 10 to 12 Everything They Need to Know About

The Bible

Dr. Edward A. Buchanan

Dear Phyllis,
May God bless you!
Ed Buchanan

ISBN-10: 0805427139
ISBN-13: 9780805427134

Published by Broadman & Holman Publishers
Nashville, Tennessee

Dewey Decimal Classification: 649
Subject Heading: CHILD REARING \ CHURCH HISTORY \
CHRISTIAN EDUCATION OF CHILDREN

1 2 3 4 5 6 7 8 9 10   10 09 08 07 06 05

*In memory of Mr. and Mrs. Clair Heichel and
Mr. and Mrs. Osborne Buchanan, Sr., who
taught my wife, Gladys, and me to study
and love God's Word.*

ACKNOWLEDGEMENTS

In preparing this handbook, I have deeply appreciated the help of my student assistant, Tiffany W. Ferrell and my secretary, Phyllis C. Keith. I would like to express special thanks to my editor, Kim Overcash, and to Broadman & Holman Publishers. Without their help this project would not have become a reality.

Edward A. Buchanan
March 2005

Table of Contents

General Introduction
for Parents and Teachers

Similar to the first two books in this series, this book was born out of a conviction that children need to know and understand the Word of God, if they are to live their lives in accordance with the will of God. They also need to know about the great civilizations of the past that have held allegiance to God's spiritual and moral precepts in life. Current research shows that we are living in a world that is growing increasingly hostile to the Christian faith. We need to become more deliberate about the way in which we guide our children through those busy preteen years of childhood. Rather than being caught up in the milieu of a materialistic, violent, and sex-crazed culture, our children must understand and commit themselves to Christ and to enduring Christian values. We want these principles and values to become integrated into their lives. Our hope does not reside in this world. We are only pilgrims in this world. Our hope lies in Jesus Christ and the salvation that He purchased for us at Calvary. Our hope lives in the eternal world.

NINE TO TWELVE YEAR OLDS

Children are heavily involved in soccer, baseball, basketball, music, martial arts, gymnastics, swim teams, scouting, and a host of other busy activities that go well beyond their classroom involvements. Even church sponsored groups preempt a good share of their time and energy through programs like Team Kid, AWANA, RAs, GAs, children's choir, summer camping programs, and even Sunday school. Parents are caught in the flurry of activity, and their time and energy is spent transporting their children from one activity to another. It is even a greater problem for parents with two or more children in the same age range.

Children's lives are further complicated by the changes in our culture that have occurred in recent years. Researchers at one of our major state universities have discovered that some girls of age eight have already reached menarche, or the onset of their menstrual cycle. In the past this did not begin until at least age twelve. These are extremely busy and difficult years for both children and their parents.

Beyond the busy routines of these years, children are in a very critical spiritual stage in their development. It is essential for parents to give careful consideration to determine whether all of the frantic energy is expended in the right direction. If a firm foundation in the Chronological Bible Story and an understanding of our Christian heritage was put into place through volumes 1 and 2 of this series, what do we do next? If you are new to this series, you might want to obtain volumes 1 and 2 that provide the base for this series. We will briefly review the Old and New Testaments in this volume. In any event, the preteen years are a crucial period when the majority of conversions to Christ take place. Adequate preparation must be made for the children to make this decision. It is not a decision that parents can contrive or manipulate. It is not a decision that can be based on mere emotional experience. It cannot be one that comes solely from peer pressure. It must come from a heart-felt desire to become a child of God and live as God would have him or her live in obedience to Him.

Several years ago it was possible for a child in the nine- to twelve-year age range to grow-up in a relatively safe and healthy environment. To be sure, children had problems. But the nature of those problems in later childhood was epitomized in a sitcom like *Leave It to Beaver*. The episodes were devoted to working out the problems faced by an average American child in his life in a typical family. Today more than half of the children under age eighteen in America will spend at least three years in a single-parent family. For many, the problems of making sense of their world are much more complex than in the past. In addition to the typical problems of how to get along with siblings, how to deal with school, and how to relate to parents, many children must also cope with the added burden of parents who live on opposite sides of the country. They may have to learn to relate to a new step-parent and to newly acquired siblings.

Each year the Gallup organization polls teachers about the most significant problems they face in their classrooms and schools. During the era of *Leave It to Beaver,* the problems included chewing gum, talking without permission, putting feet in the aisle, littering, and not conforming to dress-code standards. Today teachers report that the problems are much more serious. Problems today include drug and alcohol abuse, pregnancy, rape, suicide, violence among students, and violence against teachers.

We live in an increasingly hostile culture for children. There appears to be a rise in the exploitation of children by self-centered adults. The filth of pornography exploits children. Even the ban on the use of four-letter words in the mass media has been lifted. Advertising on television exploits children by creating wants among children for material goods that would not otherwise have been likely there. Evolution degrades our children by telling them that they are nothing more than a product of the evolution of one animal species to another and encouraging low morals. Children in New York City public schools cannot be exposed to the nativity at Christmas because the New York School Board has determined that the manger is a Christian symbol. However, they can be exposed to the *menorah* of Judaism and the *crescent* of Islam, because the school board has arbitrarily decided that these are secular symbols.

The research is clear that in the past moral decisions were made during the teenage years. Today, however, moral decisions and commitments are made during the preteen years, ages nine to twelve. This is the last period of years in which you as a parent or teacher will have for significant impact upon your child's moral development. You can help him or her determine right from wrong and determine how your child will live their lives for years to come. Jesus said, "For what does it benefit a man to gain the whole world yet lose his life? What can a man give in exchange for his life?" (Mark 8:36–37).

While this is an extremely busy period of life, it is necessary to take inventory of the ways in which you and your child are using your time and energy. Is all of the frenetic activity justified by the results that accrue from these actions? As a parent or teacher, this may also be the last time you will have the opportunity to have a significant spiritual impact on your child before he or she enters the traumatic years of adolescence. It is essential to plan together for time spent in deepening spiritual commitments. Learning activities, such as the ones in this book, are worth the time and effort to do together as a family. They will help prepare your child for a life-long commitment to Jesus Christ and a Christian lifestyle.

CHILDREN AND LEARNING

The Bible states emphatically that parents are to teach their children and pass the wisdom of past generations to the future generations. Solomon stated it this way, "Listen, [my] sons, to a father's discipline, and pay attention so that you may gain understanding, for I am giving you good instruction. Don't abandon my teaching" (Proverbs 4:1–2). The psalmist also indicated that fathers must tell their children and future generations about the works of God and the wisdom that is generated from the lessons of redemptive history (see Psalm 78). The purpose of this teaching is to help children not to make the same mistakes as their forefathers made. It is also designed to inspire confidence in God and His purposes for His people. *Repetition* and *review* are important learning tools for rehearsing God's dealings with His people. The Israelites used these learning tools effectively. The same principles need to be applied to Christians today.

The single most important principle of learning for acquiring new knowledge is that we must operate from a foundation of *prior knowledge.* This means that what we have stored in our minds in the past provides the basis for what we can learn in the future. Therefore, it is essential for a child to learn how to please God and how God has dealt with persons in the past. This knowledge lays a firm foundation for future learning about God and His Son, Jesus Christ. Building upon this prior knowledge base is very important during these childhood years. Some educators would like the child to construct his own meaning in life, but the Scripture indicates clearly that we are to teach our children to build a firm Christian orientation to life.

During the preevangelism phase, before a child is ready to make a personal commitment to Jesus as Lord and Savior of his life, he needs to have a knowledge base and an understanding that will prepare him for committing his life to Christ. After conversion, or in the postevangelism phase, the child now has the indwelling Holy Spirit to guide him into a deeper knowledge of Christian truth. The Holy Spirit is also active in deepening the child's personal relationship with God. Learning about the Christian faith in the childhood years helps to build the prior knowledge base that will lead toward integrating and internalizing core Christian values to guide him throughout the rest of life. The Holy Spirit can use that learning to deepen Christian faith. The young person must develop what has been termed a Christian-world-and-life view. While it will not be fully formed in childhood, significant strides may be made in the formation of that view.

May I encourage you to read the text material with your child and then to engage your child in the learning activities from the lesson plans. The text and the learning activities comprise a total learning package. The activities are intended to help your child deepen his understanding through repetition and review. They will assist the process of moving from just the biblical and other factual content toward internalization and development of a Christian view of life. In the past decade we have come to appreciate that at least eight intelligences need to be developed. Most of these are included at several places in the learning activities. We have also come to understand that each person processes information through one of four different learning styles. Activities are designed to help a learner find meaning in the material for whichever personal learning style is applicable to him.

BASIC CHRISTIAN LEARNING

The concept of Basic Christian Learning connotes more than learning the content of Scripture. Since the Scripture comes from a different time and place from our vantage in the twenty-first century, it is important to know the persons, places, events, time lines, terms, symbols, and customs of Bible times. Scripture is foundational to everything else we believe. Every Christian needs to be firmly rooted in Scripture. Just as the first volume in this series began with the chronological story of the Bible, this book continues with a study of books of the Bible that were not included in the history of redemption. In the Old Testament that means the poetic and wisdom literature, and in the New Testament that means the letters of Paul and the general epistles. There will be a brief introduction to both the Old and New Testaments.

Basic Christian Learning begins with the foundation of Scripture. This is bedrock to anything else. But it is also important for a Christian believer to have a basic understanding of theology. What do we believe and why? It is impossible to witness to faith in Christ without some rudiments of theology. *Theology* is literally the study of God. A basic understanding of elementary apologetics is also needed for a Christian believer who will witness to faith in Christ. The term simply means that one can defend the truth of Christian beliefs. Along with these topics are Christian practices of worship and education and their roots in Jewish worship and education. The church was called by Jesus to mission. Our mission extends beyond the borders of our community, state, and nation. To fulfill the Great Commission, the church must carry the gospel to the ends of the earth. There are still people groups in other parts of the world that have never heard the name of Christ. They need to hear the gospel in their own heart language.

Basic Christian Learning extends to many of the practices that we have in the church today, which are different from those of the early church. For example, Sunday school is one of the most important groups of the church for reaching and teaching. Yet Sunday school had its origin in 1780 in Gloucester, England. The history of the church is a fascinating tale of the ways men and women of past centuries, who had commitment to Christ and His Word, were willing if necessary to give their lives to maintain their faith. This kind of exemplary courage and dedication can help us today to maintain our allegiance to Christ and His kingdom as well. The story of the growth and development of our denominations also needs to be told. In America, where there are so many diverse ethnic backgrounds, we seek to find our rich cultural heritage as it gives us an identity. The same is true for our spiritual ancestry, as it helps us to understand who we are and how we came to hold the beliefs we cherish today.

Basic Christian Learning includes art, music, literature, and scientific discovery of past generations. Many of the geniuses of the past held a more Christian outlook than is true of our present culture. Our children and youth need to be exposed to good science, like that of Galileo, who clearly intended his scientific discoveries to support the greatness of God. Thomas á Kempis, a medieval German monk from the fifteenth century, wrote what has been the most widely read work of religious literature *Imitation of Christ,* outside of the Bible. It teaches that the believer today needs to follow the example of Jesus if one is to find God's grace through life. Yet the book also draws from the Greek and Roman philosophers and writers. Johann Sebastian Bach from the seventeenth century came from a line of church musical directors that extended back over one hundred years. He was one of the world's most prolific writers of religious and some nonreligious music. His complete works in today's world may be found on a total of seventy-two CD-ROMs. Much of the world's greatest art has also come from Christian sources as well. Giotto painted in the 1300s. Among Giotto's religious paintings were those of Jesus' family, the life of Francis of Assisi. He was the architect for the Duomo, the great Cathedral in Florence, Italy. His realistic pictures revolutionized painting and greatly influenced the Renaissance.

Scripture is essential to our Christian faith and hence to Basic Christian Learning. Scripture must first be known and understood. People have wrestled with great themes of life, such as suffering, in past generations that help us understand the problems of life from a Christian perspective. The church has grown to become what it is today through the martyrdom of many of its saints, who would rather give their lives for their faith than live a life apart from Jesus Christ. Inspiration for great works of art, music, literature, and scientific discoveries came from their personal faith in Jesus Christ. Our children need to learn about this rich reservoir of Christian knowledge and its meaning for their lives today. Basic Christian Learning is a means to help them grow in their knowledge and understanding of Christ and this rich Christian cultural heritage in which we share today.

ABOUT THIS BOOK

This handbook is designed as a resource tool for teachers and parents who would like to get more depth and understanding into the lessons they are teaching. Some of the foundation materials are part of volume 3, and they have been carried over into volume 4. This volume will help you and your ministry to older children by providing Basic Christian Learning to bring the Bible to life.

The content of this volume includes everything from examination of selected Scriptures to ancient Bible history and customs from Bible times. You'll understand more about the context of the Bible and how the lives of people in the Bible have influenced our lives down through the ages. You will get a glimpse of travel in Paul's day. You will explore the Tabernacle in the Wilderness and the Temple. You will discover how the Hebrews and later Jews educated their children in their faith.

Volume 4 will provide you with more materials to share in the education of children in Jewish times. Volume 3 will also help you learn about life in Bible times. You'll discover the fascinating story of the ancient Empires of Egypt, Assyria, Babylonia, and Persia. This will provide background for the events that occur in Iraq and Iran today. You'll discover the wonders of ancient Rome and the caesars who conquered the world. You'll be inspired by the martyrs who suffered and gave their lives for their faith in Jesus.

As the church continues to grow and develop, your students will develop a better understanding of the changes in the church through the centuries. You'll come to understand the rise of the variety of denominations. You will have opportunity to explore the medieval church and compare it with the church in today's world. This volume will equip you with the tools for greater understanding of what we believe and why we believe as we do.

Once your children and preteens are grounded more thoroughly in their faith, they'll appreciate the diverse ways that Christianity is shared in our culture. We'll give you a glimpse at missions and a greater understanding of the Great Commission.

Since we're surrounded by fine religious art, we'll give you and your students a better sense of how that magnificent artwork developed over the centuries and what inspired the masters to create the works that we still stand in awe of today. And finally, we'll take a little peek at Christianity and science and how the two are not necessarily at odds with each other. We live in a world where many scientists admit their work only enhances their faith in God. Our mission is to enhance and instill that faith in our children. We thank you for the part you play in getting that work done.

INTRODUCTION TO THE CHILDREN'S BIBLE STUDY

The word *Bible* comes from the Greek word, *biblia*, which means a paper scroll or book. It was first used in the period between the Old and New Testaments to refer to the "holy books" of the Jewish Scriptures. It was later used by the early church fathers, like Clement of Alexandria, to refer to the collection of the Old and New Testaments. It was later used in Latin, *bibliotheca*, for the Scriptures. The name has continued through the centuries to refer to the Old and New Testament Scriptures.

The second name given to the Bible is Scripture. It comes from the Latin word, *scriptura*, which simply means "writing." In 2 Timothy 3:15 the apostle Paul used the term to refer to the "Holy Scriptures" that Timothy had known from his early childhood. *Scripture*, like *Bible*, refers to the writings from the Old and New Testaments.

A third designation for the Scripture is the Word of God. It comes from the Hebrew word, *debar*, which would usually be given by word of mouth through the prophet. This means a divine command or proclamation. Occasionally, it described the written Word as stated in Psalm 119:105. The Greek word, *logos*, appears many times in the

New Testament to refer to the gospel that was given by God in Christ.

Through the centuries the Bible has been read and reread. It is still the world's most read book. Its principles stand at the center of our culture. The history of Western culture has been affected by the Bible. Until just recently, it has provided the basis for our laws of right behavior. It has provided and continues to provide answers for persons who are seeking God. For children, the Bible is able to fire their imagination and inspire the ideals of a godly heritage.

The Bible is more than a mere collection of stories. The Bible is a special book because God Himself guided the writing. The Bible was composed by thirty-five different authors, and the books were written across many centuries. Yet, there is a unity of the Scripture that is unlike any other book. The uniqueness of the Bible lies in the power of the Holy Spirit, who superintended its writing across the centuries. Even today the Holy Spirit guides the reader of Scripture into understanding the Bible and introduces the reader to the God of the Bible.

On one hand, the Bible is a simple book so a child can appreciate its truths and, yet on the other hand, the Bible is a very complex book that can tax the mental ability of the most erudite theologian. It is an exciting book to read. In the past, people read the Bible in their search for God. People still read the Bible in their search for God. But as they read the Bible, they discover that the God of the Bible is reaching out to them. God wants all people to come to know Him. He wants people to know that He loves them. God wants people to enter into a relationship with Him.

The stories of the Bible tell about the lives of real people. These people are both good and bad. Some have experienced success, while others have failed. Some have been persons who have expressed love, and others have expressed anger. The Bible still has the power to stir our feelings as well. But most important, the Bible tells of persons who have found God in their quest for meaning in life. The Bible demonstrates the love of God for a lost humanity. This has continued over the past millennia, and it continues today to all who will respond to Him through faith.

Technology changes across the centuries. Civilizations change as time passes. Today we watch television, drive automobiles, fly in airplanes, listen to music CDs, and type on computers. Life in the ancient world had none of these things. The truths of the Bible remain constant. The heart of man has not changed. Even though we live in a very different culture from that of the first century after Christ, the inner longings, dreams, hopes, and desires of people have not changed. The Bible is just as relevant to us today as it was for our grandparents or their ancestors before them.

The difficult questions about life are addressed in the Bible. What is the meaning of life? Does God exist? Does the great God, who created the universe, care about us today? Why do good people suffer? How can a person find happiness? How can a person find peace with God? How can a person live to please God? How can a person tell right from wrong? How can a person come to know God? The Bible addresses these questions and many other questions that people ask.

In volume 1 of this series, we examined the chronological events of the Bible as they unfolded through the centuries. These action stories began with the drama of creation to the fall of mankind. Humanity continued to sink deeper into sin and alienation from God until God called Abraham. From the call of Abraham to the time of Christ, the Bible tells of God's personal relationship with His people Israel. Then the Bible continues with the story of God's Son, Jesus. He came, ministered, taught, healed, and was sacrificed for the redemption of fallen humanity. The gospel now came not only to the Jews but also to the Gentiles. The Book of Acts tells of Paul's ministry of the gospel throughout the ancient world.

In volume 3 we return to the Old Testament and review its events. We will examine the literature of poetry and wisdom. The books of Psalms, Proverbs, Ecclesiastes, Song of Solomon, and Job are included. In the New Testament we return to review the life and ministry of Jesus and the missionary journeys of Paul. We will examine the thirteen letters he wrote to the churches to correct their problems and give them guidance. These include Romans, 1 and 2 Corinthians, Galatians, Ephesians, Philippians, Colossians, 1 and 2 Thessalonians, 1 and 2 Timothy, Titus, and Philemon. In addition, we will look at the general letters, written by other authors. These include Hebrews, James, 1 and 2 Peter, 1, 2, and 3 John, and Jude.

Since the target audience of nine to twelve year olds for volumes 3 and 4 are better able to read, we will take a different approach in these pages. We have selected passages for study. We have selected passages on the basis of their immediate application in the lives of the nine to twelve year olds. Explanations of the text will enlarge on its meaning to help older children gain understanding from their reading.

Review of the Old Testament

You will recall from the *Parent Teacher Handbook Vol. 1: The Bible*, that we followed the chronological teaching approach to the story of the Bible from Genesis to Revelation. In the Bible section of this handbook, we will review the Bible history through the Old Testament. Then we will look at the poetry and Wisdom literature of the Old Testament. You will want to return to the review of the Old Testament, and the timelines before you study the poetry and Wisdom literature. Each of these—the poetry and the wisdom literary pieces—comes from a particular time period. It will be interesting to see how each of these relate to a particular person from the Old Testament. You will want to refer back to these time lines and charts as you look at specific Old Testament passages.

THE BEGINNING OF THE HUMAN RACE
GENESIS 1–11

Genesis is an important book. It tells us that God created the heavens and earth. Then He created our first parents, Adam and Eve. Adam and Eve were living in beautiful surroundings In the Garden of Eden. They had everything they could ever desire. But Satan tempted Eve, and together with her husband Adam, they both disobeyed God and ate of the tree of the Knowledge of Good and Evil. The result was that all people from that point to this have been born in sin and will eventually die. God drove Adam and Eve from the Garden of Eden.

In those days the evil on earth grew much worse. God finally decided that He must destroy all human beings from the earth. But God chose to spare Noah and his family. Noah was a righteous man and did what God wanted. God told Noah to build an ark that would hold pairs of animals and Noah and his family. When the ark was ready, God shut the door of the ark. For forty days and forty nights, it rained on the earth. All living creatures, except those in the ark, were destroyed in the flood. After living in the ark for a long period of time, the flood waters began to recede. It was now possible for Noah, his family, and the pairs of animals to leave the ark. Noah and his family worshipped God. God made a covenant with them that he would never destroy the earth by flooding it again. The seal of that covenant was the rainbow.

Sadly sin was still in the human heart. The flood waters had not erased sin. Sin again continued to grow worse. Humans tried to build a tower to the gate of God, known as the Tower of Babel. God saw their evil purpose. He scattered their languages. Since different people groups could no longer speak the same language, they began to migrate to places where they could be understood. The story of the first eleven chapters of Genesis tells us of God's creation and how sin came upon the human race through Adam and Eve. The rest of the story of the human race is one of continuing rebellion against God. God had to bring judgment upon the human race.

Listing of Events before Abraham
(Dates unknown)
1. Creation of the universe (Gen. 1:2–3)
2. Creation of Adam and Eve (Gen. 2:4–25)
3. The Fall of Adam and Eve and driven from the Garden (Gen. 3)
4. Cain kills his brother, Abel (Gen. 4)
5. Noah and the Flood (Gen. 6:5–9)
6. The Tower of Babel (Gen. 11:1–9)

TIME LINE FROM ABRAHAM TO SOLOMON

2000 BC	1800 BC	1600 BC	1400 BC	1200 BC	1000 BC
Abraham called by God	Israel goes to Egypt	Slavery in Egypt	Exodus and conquering Palestine	Period of the Judges	Kingdom Period—Saul, David, and Solomon

THE PATRIARCHS THROUGH THE JUDGES
GENESIS 12–RUTH

It all looked very dark until God chose to make a covenant or promise with Abraham and his family. This began the period of the patriarchs.

PATRIARCHS

The word patriarch refers to the fathers of the nation of Israel. It comes from two Latin words, which mean "father" and "rule." The patriarchs were Abraham, Isaac, and Jacob, who was later called Israel. God established his covenant with Abraham, when He passed between the two sets of animal carcasses. God promised to make of Abraham's family a nation of God's "chosen people" (see Genesis 15).

Abraham through the Captivity in Egypt (Genesis 12–Exodus 1)

At the end of Genesis 11, we are introduced to the family of Terah. One of his sons was Abraham. Abraham lived from about 2166 to 1991 BC. Abraham was married to Sarah. God called Abraham and his family to be set apart from the rest of the families. Abraham obeyed God and moved from Ur, on the Euphrates River, to Haran. When his father died, Abraham was called by God to go to the Promised Land. You may trace his journey on a map. There were no military or police to provide protection in those days. The journey was difficult, but God promised to protect Abraham and his family. When God saw that Abraham obeyed, God made a covenant to bless Abraham. His family would become God's special people. After years of waiting, Abraham and Sarah had a son named Isaac. Isaac lived about 2066 to 1886 BC.

After Abraham died, God promised to protect Abraham's son, Isaac, if he and his family would worship and serve God. Abraham sent his servant back to Haran to his family to find a wife for Isaac. Rebekah was the daughter of Abraham's nephew from Haran. She agreed to come to the Promised Land and become Isaac's wife. Isaac and his wife Rebekah had two sons, Jacob and Esau. Esau did not follow in the ways of God. But Jacob did follow God. Jacob lived from about 2006 to 1859 BC.

Then God blessed Jacob with a large family of twelve sons. Each of the twelve sons of Jacob later became a father of one of the twelve tribes of Israel.

Jacob's favorite son was Joseph. Joseph was spoiled by his father and given a coat of many colors. His brothers became so jealous that they decided to get rid of Joseph. Some wanted to kill him, but they decided instead to sell him to traders, who were headed for Egypt. Then they took Joseph's coat of many colors, which they had stained with blood, back to their father. Jacob believed that Joseph had been killed by a wild animal.

MAP OF THE JOURNEYS OF ABRAHAM

Meanwhile, upon arriving in Egypt, Joseph was sold into the family of Potiphar. Potiphar was the captain of the Egyptian guard. He made Joseph the steward of his entire household. But Potiphar's wife made trouble for Joseph. Potiphar believed that Joseph had taken Potiphar's wife. Joseph was thrown into prison. He remained in prison for several years. Notice that Joseph did what was right in God's sight. He was not immediately released from prison. It was not until Pharoah could not interpret a dream that one of Pharoah's servants remembered Joseph. Joseph was called to interpret Pharaoh's dream. God then blessed Joseph and gave him both the dream and its interpretation. The dream helped Pharoah understand that a great famine would cover Egypt and the other lands close to Egypt. Pharoah had Joseph released from prison and made him second in command over all Egypt.

Just as Joseph had said, there were seven years of plenty. Then famine came across the land. When the famine became too great, Joseph's brothers came from Palestine to Egypt to buy grain. Now Joseph looked very Egyptian, and his brothers could not tell that Joseph was their brother. A second time they came for grain. Joseph now told his brothers who he was. Joseph called upon his brothers to bring their father and all their family to Egypt. Pharoah gave Joseph and his family the land of Goshen. Jacob, whose name had been changed to Israel, was promised by God that after he died his body would be returned and buried in the Promised Land in Palestine. The sons of Israel were Reuben, Simeon, Levi, Judah, Issachar, Zebulun, Gad, Asher, Dan, Naphtali, Joseph, and Benjamin. Joseph also had two sons, Manasseh and Ephraim. Jacob blessed the sons of Joseph along with his own sons. Joseph lived from about 1915 to 1805 BC.

For the next four hundred years, from about 1876 to 1446 BC, the people of Israel lived in Egypt. During that time the families grew large in numbers. New pharaohs came on the throne in Egypt. They did not have a good attitude toward Joseph or the people of Israel. The new pharaohs enslaved the people of Israel to build their large tombs and monuments from brick and rock. Through these years the people of Israel suffered from the cruel treatment of the Egyptians. God heard the cries of his people Israel and determined that He would bring them out of captivity into the land of promise.

God Delivers His People from Slavery in Egypt (Exodus 1–18)

The cruel Pharoah was trying to kill all of the Hebrew male children. When Moses was born, his mother put him in a watertight basket and placed it in the Nile River. Pharaoh's daughter took pity on the baby. She took him from the river and brought him up as her own son. His real mother was brought to nurse Moses. She taught him about the faith of the people of Israel. Moses learned all that he could of the wisdom and science of Egypt in the palace of Pharoah. When he became an adult, he chose not to be an Egyptian but to be identified with his people Israel. He was forced to leave Egypt and wander in the wilderness of the Sinai Peninsula. He found a home with a priest in Midian. Moses married the priest's daughter, Zipporah. For the next forty years, Moses lived as a shepherd, tending the flocks of his father-in-law.

One day as he was caring for the sheep, he saw a strange sight. There was a bush that was burning. The bush did not burn up and disappear. Moses went to look at the bush. As he drew near the bush, God called to him. God told Moses that He wanted him to lead the people of Israel out of Egypt and out of slavery. For the next several months, Moses and his brother Aaron called on Pharaoh to let the people of Israel go to worship God. Pharoah refused, and each time God would bring a plague upon the people of Egypt. Each plague came upon the Egyptians but did not hurt the people of Israel. These plagues are described in Exodus 7–11 and in the chart on the following page.

Plague	Scripture Reference	Description	Result of the Plague
Blood	Exod. 7:14–24	Nile River turns to blood; fish die; no fresh water	Pharaoh's magicians do the same; Pharaoh refuses to let the people of Israel go
Frogs	Exod. 8:1–15	Frogs come out of the water and the land is covered	Pharaoh's magicians do the same; Pharaoh refuses to let the people of Israel go
Gnats	Exod. 8:16–19	The dust in Egypt becomes stinging gnats; possibly fleas or mosquitoes	Pharaoh's magicians cannot do the same; Magicians believe it is God's hand; Pharaoh refuses to let the people of Israel go
Flies	Exod. 8:20–32	Flies swarm over the land of Egypt	Pharaoh at last promises to let the people go; when the plague is removed, he refuses to let the People of Israel go
Cattle	Exod. 9:1–7	Cattle of the Egyptians die, while Israel's herds are not sick	Pharaoh still refuses to let the People of Israel go
Boils	Exod. 9:8–12	All the Egyptians become very sick with boils	Magicians are also struck with boils, but Pharaoh still refuses to let the People of Israel go
Hail	Exod. 9:13–35	Severe hailstorms strike the land and kill people, animals, and plants	Pharaoh said that he has sinned and begged Moses to stop; Pharaoh still did not let the People of Israel go
Locusts	Exod. 10:1–20	Locusts cover the land and eat everything not destroyed by the hail	Pharaoh's officials advise him to let the People of Israel go, but Pharaoh refuses
Darkness	Exod. 10:21–29	Egypt is plunged into total darkness, but not the Land of Goshen	Pharaoh promises to let the People of Israel go, but after the darkness is removed, Pharaoh refuses
Death of the Firstborn	Exod. 11:1–12:33	The firstborn of people and cattle are killed by the Angel of Death, but not the Israelites	Pharaoh and all of the Egyptians urge the People of Israel to leave; after they are gone Pharaoh wants to chase after them; Pharaoh and the Egyptian army die in the Red Sea

The Egyptians gave gifts to the people of Israel. The date of the Exodus from Egypt was about 1446 and they wandered in the wilderness until 1406. The Israelites left quickly and headed toward the Red Sea. The traditional Exodus led the people south into the Sinai Peninsula. Mount Sinai would have been in the southern region of the peninsula. The most recent research seems to suggest strongly that the people of Israel crossed the Sinai Peninsula and then God opened the sea across the Gulf of Aqaba. That would place Mount Sinai in the desert of what is today the country of Arabia. The route that the Israelites took is not nearly as important as the fact the God protected them by opening the Red Sea for them to cross. When Pharoah and his army came after the Israelites, they were drowned in the Red Sea. God performed another miracle to protect His people on their route to the Promised Land.

The people of Israel never learned their lesson, that God would protect them as He did in the escape from Egypt and the crossing of the Sea. They sinned and did not trust God fully. Even though He had demonstrated his care for them, they continued to sin and disobey. They complained that they did not have bread. God provided manna. They wanted meat to eat. God provided quail, small birds, for their diet. The Amalekites were a people in the land who fought against them. As long as Moses kept his hands stretched toward heaven, God gave the Israelites the victory. It was not what the Israelites did but what God did to save His people. When they were thirsty, God provided water. Moses' father-in-law came from Midian and helped Moses to divide the people into smaller units. Without Jethro's help Moses would have worn himself out. Finally, they encamped below the mountain of God at Mount Sinai.

God Calls the Israelites to Himself (Exodus–Joshua)

While the people were camped around Mount Sinai, Moses went up into the mountain of God and received the Ten Commandments from the Lord. Moses was only gone for forty days, but he was shocked when he returned to the people. They had made a golden calf and were worshipping it. God became very angry. Moses also became angry with the people and broke the tablets of stone. Moses had to return to the mountain of God and receive another set of the Ten Commandments. This was a covenant between God and his people that required their obedience to God's law. Today we still need to obey the Ten Commandments.

TEN COMMANDMENTS

Commandments	Relation-ship to	Scripture References	Meaning
Do not have other gods besides Me	God	Exod. 20:3; Deut. 5:7	Do not put anything else in place of God. He must come first.
Do not make an idol for yourself	God	Exod. 20:4–6; Deut. 5:8–10	Do not make any statues or idols of God. You must worship only the Lord God.
Do not misuse the name of the Lord your God	God	Exod. 20:7; Deut.5:11	Do not misuse God's name by saying false things about Him or using His name as a swear word.
Remember to dedicate the Sabbath day	God	Exod. 20:8–11; Deut. 5:12–15	The Lord's day should be for rest and worship. Encourage each other and remember what Jesus did for you.
Honor your father and your mother	Other People	Exod. 20:12; Deut. 5:16	Love and obey your parents. Listen to their advise and respect them.
Do not murder	Other People	Exod. 20:13; Deut. 5:17	Respect and value life. Treat others as God wants you to act toward them.
Do not commit adultery	Other People	Exod. 20:14; Deut. 5:18	Do not have a love relationship with someone else's husband or wife.
Do not steal	Other People	Exod. 20:15; Deut. 5:19	Do not take things that do not belong to you. Stealing also includes cheating on tests and breaking a promise.
Do not give false testimony	Other People	Exod. 20:16; Deut. 5:20	Do not tell lies about others in court. It also includes gossiping and telling false things about others at any time.
Do not covet	Other People	Exod. 20:17; Deut. 5:21	Do not desire something that is not your own, whether it be money, food, or possessions.

God told the Israelites that they must build a Tabernacle, where God would dwell with His people. This was also the place where the people would worship God. Instructions were also given for the priests, who would lead the worship and sacrifice. The purpose of sacrifice was to substitute the blood of an animal to atone for the sins of the people. The people of Israel were to be a holy people. They were to live moral and godly lives by following God's laws. God promised that when they obeyed him, He would bless them. But if they disobeyed and sinned against Him, He promised to punish them.

God also instructed the people of Israel to celebrate holidays as a remembrance of the care that He provided for them. Passover was the first of these holidays, recalling the way God freed the people from Egypt. Notice that the festivals of

Festival	Bible Reference	Time of Year *(Time varies because of the Lunar Calendar)*	
Passover lasts one day	Lev. 23:5; Exod. 12:2–20	March/April	Recalls God's deliverance for the people of Israel from slavery in Egypt.
Unleavened Bread lasts seven days	Lev. 23:6–8	March/April	Recalls the unleavened bread from the haste to leave in the Exodus from Egypt.
Feast of Weeks (Pentecost) lasts one day	Lev. 23:15–21; Exod. 23:16; 34:22	May/June	Recalls the giving of the Law on Mount Sinai.
Rosh Hashanah (Jewish New Year) lasts one day	Lev. 23:23–25; Num. 29:1–6	September/October	Beginning of the new civil year. Blowing the trumpets begins the new year.
Yom Kippur (Day of Atonement) lasts one day, holiest day of the Jewish year	Lev. 23:26-33; Exod. 30:10	September/October	During the Temple period, the High Priest placed blood of a sacrifice on the Mercy Seat and a scapegoat carried the sins of the people into the wilderness.
Feast of Tabernacles or Booths lasts seven days	Lev. 23:33–43; Deut. 16:13; Num. 29:12-39	September/October	Recalls forty years of wandering in the wilderness.
Festival of Lights (Hannukkah)	John 10:22	November/December	Recalls the rededication of the Temple after the Maccabeans freed Israel from Syria in 146 BC.
Feast of Purim (Esther)	Ester 9	February/March	Recalls the protection of the people of Israel from the wicked Haman in Persia.

Hannukah and Purim were added to the calendar later in the history of the people of Israel.

ATONEMENT
Atonement means "to bring two parties back together again." God provided atonement for His people to bring them back to relationship with Himself through animal sacrifice. The animal's death was a substitute for the penalty of sin for the person who brought the sacrifice.

Unfortunately, when they left Mount Sinai, the people continued to disobey God and were punished. For the next forty years, they wandered in the wilderness. God led them with a cloud by day and a pillar of fire by night. One day Moses, himself, became angry and sinned against God. As a result, Moses was not allowed to enter the Promised Land. Before Moses died, God took him to a high mountain where he could look and see the Promised Land. In his place God provided Joshua to lead his people into the land. The Book of Joshua describes the way in which the people of

Israel conquered the land. The dates conquering the land were about 1406 to 1380. When the fighting was over, the people settled in the land of Israel. Each of the families of the sons of Jacob became a tribe. They settled the land by tribes.

TRIBES
Tribes are social and political groups that came from the twelve sons of Israel (Jacob). The tribe of Simeon was scattered throughout the land given to Judah. The tribe of Levi were priests and placed among each of the tribes. That left ten tribes to settle the land. The two sons of Joseph, Manasseh and Ephraim, made up the additional two tribes. During their four hundred years in captivity in Egypt, each of the families grew in size. By the time they were ready to leave Egypt, each tribe was a large unit that was made up of many families. It may well have been that the tribal jealousies and their traditions contributed to the partition of the land into the Northern and Southern Kingdoms in 922 BC.

Each tribe was given a portion of the land. There were twelve tribes who divided the inheritance.

Life during the Period of the Judges (Judges)

For the next three hundred years, from about 1380 to 1050, the people of Israel lived under the rule of the judges. The twelve tribes were not very close during this period. Each person and each tribe did "what seemed right in its own eyes." Often they got into trouble and sinned against God. God would provide a judge, who would help them out of their difficulty. But when the judge died, they would need a new judge to direct and help in a new situation. It was not the best period in the life of Israel. In the midst of this difficult time, the beautiful story of Ruth and Boaz stands out as a family living according to God's desire. Ruth and Boaz were the great grandparents of King David. Among the judges these are the most important.

Samuel was born in answer to his mother's prayer for a son. His mother, Hannah, promised him to the Lord. After his birth he was given to the high priest, Eli, to guide his life in the Lord's service. Samuel was

BOAZ AND RUTH

called by God to replace Eli, whose sons sinned against God. Samuel judged Israel and called Israel to repent. He also served as a prophet. Since Samuel's sons also sinned and did not walk in the way of their father either, the people called for a king. God directed Samuel to anoint Saul to

MAJOR JUDGES OF ISRAEL

Judge	Reference	Years of Judging	What the Judge Did and Why He is Remembered
Othniel	Judg. 1:12–13; 3:7–11	40	He conquered a Canaanite city.
Ehud	Judg. 3:12–30	80	He killed Eglon, King of Moab, and defeated the Moabites.
Shamgar	Judg. 3:31	Not recorded	He killed six hundred Philistines with an ax goad.
Deborah and Barak	Judg. 4–5	40	Deborah encouraged Barak to defeat the Canaanite King, Sisera. Together they sang a victory song.
Gideon	Judg. 6–8	40	He led three hundred soldiers to defeat 135,000 Midianites.
Jepthah	Judg. 11:1–12:7	6	He made a careless vow to God. He defeated the Ammorites. Later he had to battle his own people, the Ephraimites.
Samson	Judg. 13–16	20	He was a Nazarite and very strong. He killed many Philistines. He was deceived by Delilah. But in the end, he killed thousands of Philistines in their temple. He also died, when he destroyed their temple.
Samuel	1 Sam. 1–7	?	He was the last of the judges. He was the first of the prophets. During his work as a judge, he anointed the first two kings of Israel, Saul and David.

become king. When Saul later refused to obey God, Saul's family was rejected by God from continuing to rule Israel. Samuel anointed another king, David. Samuel died before David took the throne.

THE UNITED MONARCHY OVER ISRAEL

Saul, the First King of Israel (1 Samuel 8–15)

Saul was called by God to become the first king over Israel. He reigned from about 1020 to 1000 BC. He started well. He even prophesied. But later in his reign, Saul disobeyed God and sinned by not following God's instructions about sacrifice. He also did other things that God had forbidden. Samuel carried the bad news to Saul that the Lord had rejected him and his family from ruling over Israel. The Spirit of the Lord left Saul, and an evil spirit came upon him. In his later years he had fits of anger. When David killed the giant, Goliath, Saul wanted David to serve in his court. At times he was good to David and even gave his daughter in marriage to David. But Saul also tried to kill David. At last Saul died in a battle with the Philistines.

David's Reign over Israel (1 Samuel 16– 1 Kings 2; 1 Chronicles 11–29)

David was the greatest king of Israel. He reigned from about 1000 to 962 BC. He had many successes. But he also had some failures. One of his weaknesses was his desire for several wives. Unfortunately, he passed this weakness on to his son, King Solomon. The chart below provides a brief description of the events of his rise to power and his reign as king.

David reigned over Israel for almost forty years, from 1000 to 961 BC. He was very effective as a king. His love for God was an essential part of both David's life and his reign as king. When he sinned, he turned to God for forgiveness. God established

EVENTS IN THE LIFE OF DAVID

Event	Scripture	Successes/Failures
Anointed by Samuel to be king	1 Sam. 16	Success
Killing Goliath	1 Sam. 17	Success
Flight from King Saul	1 Sam. 18–31	Failure
King Saul died	1 Sam. 31	Failure
Crowned King of Judah	2 Sam. 2	Success
Crowned King over Israel	2 Sam. 5	Success
Conquered Jerusalem and made it the capital	2 Sam. 5	Success
God's covenant with David	2 Sam. 7	Success
Military victories	2 Sam. 8	Success
Committed adultery with Bathsheba	2 Sam. 11	Failure
Had Bathsheba's husband killed in war	2 Sam. 11	Failure
Confronted by Nathan the Prophet	2 Sam. 12	Failure
Birth of Solomon	2 Sam. 12	Success
Absalom rebelled	2 Sam. 15–18	Failure
David restored as king	2 Sam. 19	Success
Sinned in taking a census	2 Sam. 24	Failure
Planned and prepared for the building of the Temple	1 Chron. 22	Success
David named Solomon as his successor	1 Kings 1	Success
David died	1 Kings 2	Failure

the throne of David forever. Throughout his life David expressed his thoughts to God in the Psalms. While there were other writers of the Psalms, David was the primary author. Along with the music that he developed for worship of God, perhaps the psalms were David's greatest success. We will study some of David's psalms in the next section.

Solomon as King over Israel (1 Kings 1–11; 2 Chronicles 1–9)

The description in Scripture of Solomon's reign is somewhat brief. He reigned over Israel for about thirty years, from about 962 to 931 BC. In many ways Solomon's reign represented the high point in Israel's history. He enjoyed the blessing of God for part of his reign. When God promised to give him whatever he asked, Solomon asked for wisdom.

God also gave him wealth and honor. Solomon built the great Temple to the Lord.

His weakness for many wives led him to sin against God. Solomon married the daughter of Pharaoh. She brought her many gods with her. His other wives also brought false gods to Israel. These were now allowed to be practiced in Israel, along with the worship of the Lord Jehovah. Solomon also laid heavy burdens of taxation upon the people to keep himself and his wives in luxury. Some of his mines have been located in modern Israel and again are providing support for Israel today.

Like his father David, Solomon was a very good writer. The writer of 1 Kings 4:32 tells us that Solomon wrote three thousand proverbs and 1,005 songs. One of his early writings was the love poem from the Song of Solomon. We will look at parts of this poem in a later section. He wrote a large part of the Book of Proverbs. We will examine some of these proverbs in a later section. Toward the end of his life, Solomon wrote the Book of Ecclesiastes. This is a sad commentary on Solomon's life. He tried everything, but nothing mattered except his relationship with God.

THE DIVIDED MONARCHY OF ISRAEL AND JUDAH

After the death of Solomon in 931 BC, God divided the kingdoms into the Northern Kingdom of Israel and the Southern Kingdom of Judah. Rheoboam, Solomon's son, succeeded his father. His promise of higher taxes caused the people of the Northern Kingdom to revolt and to choose Jeroboam I as their king. Jeroboam I did not want his people to go to Jerusalem any longer to worship God in the Temple. He set up golden calves

MAP OF THE KINGDOM OF DAVID AND SOLOMON

King	Reign	Reference	Character	What He Did
Jereboam I	931–910	1 Kings 11:26–14:34; 2 Chron. 10:12–13:20	Evil	Capital at Shechem; Worship of the Golden Calf
Nadab	910–909	1 Kings 15:25–28	Evil	
Baasha	909–886	1 Kings 15:27–16:7; 2 Chron. 16:1–6	Evil	Led people to Idol worship
Elah	886–885	1 Kings 16:6–14	Evil	Idol worship
Zimri	885	1 Kings 16:9–20	Evil	
Omri	885–874	1 Kings 16:16–28	Evil	Moved capital to Samaria; Military power; Idolatry
Ahab	874–853	1 Kings 16:28–22:40; 2 Chron. 18:1-34	Very Evil	Married Jezebel (non-Jew); Worshipped Baal; Very disobedient to God; Suffered famine
Ahaziah	853–852	1 Kings 22:40–2 Kings 1:18; 2 Chron. 20:35–37	Evil	Worked on a joint trade agreement with Judah
Jehoram	852–841	2 Kings 3:1–8:25; 2 Chron. 22:5–7	Evil	Famine and war during most of his reign
Jehu	841–814	2 Kings 9:1–10:36; 2 Chron. 22:7–12	Evil	Killed Jehoram of Israel, Ahaziah of Judah; but did not follow God
Jehoahaz	814–798	2 Kings 13:1–9	Evil	Worshipped the Asherah
Jehoash	798–782	2 Kings 13:10–14:16; 2 Chron. 25:17–24	Evil	He was evil, but allowed the authority of one of the prophets
Jereboam II	793–753	2 Kings 14:16–29	Very Evil	Enjoyed peace; powerful king; very evil
Zechariah	753–752	2 Kings 14:29–15:11	Evil	Encouraged idol worship
Shallum	752	2 Kings 15:10–15	Evil	
Menahem	752–742	2 Kings 15:14–22	Evil	Heavy taxes
Pekahiah	742–740	2 Kings 15:22–26	Evil	Idol worship
Pekah	752–732	2 Kings 15:25–31; 2 Chron. 28:5–8	Evil	Many people of Israel taken captive to Assyria
Hoshea	732–722	2 Kings 15:30; 17:1–6	Evil	Heavily taxed by Assyria and led to captivity; People resettled
	722			End of the Kingdom of Israel; Shalmanesar, King of Assyria, took people captive

in several places for the people to worship in the north. He also established his capital in the city of Shechem.

The Northern Kingdom was prosperous, but the kings all sinned and did evil in God's sight. The Southern Kingdom continued the line of David, and there were both good and bad kings in Judah. For the next ninety years, the two kingdoms competed with each other. This competition wasted the resources of both nations. The fighting finally came to an end when a link was established between the royal houses of the two kingdoms. Other countries that surrounded both the Northern and Southern Kingdoms took advantage of this. They would take territories from each of the kingdoms and force them to pay tribute money.

The Northern Kingdom of Israel

Above is a chart of the kings of the Northern Kingdom of Israel. Note that some of the dates overlap since they sometimes reigned jointly.

The Northern Kingdom lasted from 931 to 722 BC. Notice that there was not one godly king during the entire 209 years Israel remained.

Two kings were named as very evil. The first was Ahab. He married Jezebel, daughter of Ethbaal, the king of the Sidon. Jezebel brought with her the god Baal and the goddess Asherah. These led the people of Israel into idolatry worship and immoral living. God raised up the great prophet Elijah to denounce Ahab and Jezebel. Elijah held a contest between the idols of Baal and the God of Abraham, Isaac, and Jacob. Baal could not listen to their request to burn the sacrifices to him. He was just a wooden idol. On the other hand, God showed His power by burning the sacrifices, the water, and even some of the stones. But still Israel resisted God and sinned by continuing to break the Ten Commandments. Elisha was the prophet who followed Elijah. He also called the people to repentance. But his message fell on deaf ears, just as Elijah's message had before him.

The second very evil king was Jeroboam II. He ruled for forty-one years. During his reign there was great cruelty among the people. Idolatry increased. Evil increased throughout the kingdom. The prophet Jonah preached in Ninevah and brought the Assyrians to repentance. As a result the Assyrians did not come against the people of Israel to destroy the land. God raised Amos, a herdsman from the country town of Tekoa. He preached about the injustices in Israel. Neither the king nor the people changed their ways. They continued to sin.

During the succeeding years God sent another prophet, Hosea, to the people of Israel. God required Hosea to suffer personal tragedy in his life

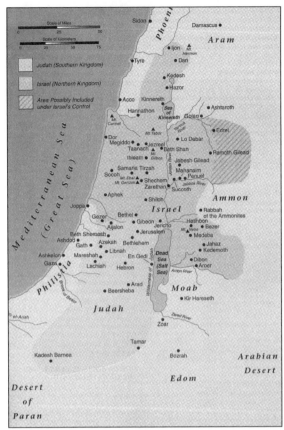

MAP OF THE DIVIDED MONARCHIES

to illustrate how much God loved His people. It did no good. The people continued to sin. They continued to worship the idols and hurt one another. God sent no more prophets to the people of Israel. The downfall of Israel came in waves. Assyria was still the major world power. Assyrian troops were cruel. They came to Israel and took captives from the Northern Kingdom. Finally, in 722 BC they

PROPHETS TO ISRAEL

Prophet	Dates of Prophet	Scripture Reference	Key Verse	Basic Teaching
Elijah	875–850	1 Kings 17:1–2 Kings 2:18	1 Kings 18:21	Jehovah is the Lord, not Baal
Elisha	855–800	1 Kings 19:15–21	2 Kings 5:15	God's power is supreme
Jonah	775	2 Kings 2–9; 13: 2 Kings 14:25; Jonah	Jonah 4:11	God is concerned about not only the Hebrews. He cares about all people, including the Assyrians
Amos	765	Amos	Amos 5:24	God demands justice and righteousness
Hosea	750	Hosea	Hosea 11:8–9	God's love never stops

KING	REIGN	REFERENCE	CHARACTER	WHAT HE DID
Rehoboam	931–913	1 Kings 11:43–14:31; 2 Chron. 9:31–12:16	Evil	Followed God for three years, then idols; fortified cities and economy
Abijam	913–911	1 Kings 14:31–15:8; 2 Chron. 13:1–14:1	Evil	Wicked, but called on God for help against Israel
Asa	911–870	1 Kings 15:8–24; 2 Chron. 14:1–16:14	Good	Destroyed altars to other gods; Worshipped God; Loved by the people
Jehoshaphat	872–848	1 Kings 15:24; 22:41–50; 2 Chron. 17:1–21:1	Good	Destroyed altars to other gods; Worshipped God; Established education; Appointed judges
Jehoram	853–841	2 Kings 8:16–24; 2 Chron 21:1–20	Evil	Married a wicked daughter of Ahab; Led people to idol worship
Ahaziah	841	2 Kin. 8:24–9:29; 2 Chron 22:1–10	Evil	He was a friend of King Jehoram of Israel
Queen Athaliah	841–835	2 Kings 16:16–28; 2 Chron. 22:10–23:21	Evil	Killed all of her grandchildren, except Joash (protected by his nurse); took Temple furnishings for Baal worship
Joash	835–796	2 Kings 12:2–12:21; 2 Chron. 22:11–24:27	Good	Crowned at the age of seven; Led Judah to peace and prosperity; Repaired the Temple; but later left God
Amaziah	796–767	1 Kings 14:1–20; 2 Chron 25:1–28	Good	Good king, but did not get rid of all idol worship; Strengthened army
Azariah (Uzziah)	792–740	2 Kings 15:1–17; 2 Chron. 26:1–23	Good	Good king, Strengthened the country of Judah; Violated the Laws for Priesthood; Punished with leprosy
Jotham	750–734	2 Kings 1532–38; 2 Chron 27:1–9	Good	Rebuilt the gate of the Temple, but allowed idol worship
Ahaz	734–716	2 Kings 16:1–20; 2 Chron 28:1–27	Evil	Allowed child sacrifice to idols; Made an alliance with Assyria in opposition to the counsel of the prophets
Hezekiah	716–687	2 Kings 16:20, 18:1–20:21; 2 Chron. 29:1–32:33	Good	He restored the worship of God in the Temple; Added an orchestra for worship; Destroyed idols; Large construction projects; Foolishly showed his wealth; Allowed another fifteen years of life by God
Manasseh	697–643	2 Kings 21:1–18 2 Chron. 33:1–20	Very Evil	Rebuilt the altars for idol worship; sacrificed one of his own sons; Murdered many of his people; Repented during Assyrian captivity
Amon	643–641	2 Kings 21:18–26; 2 Chron 33:20–25	Evil	
Josiah	641–609	2 Kings 21:26–23:30; 2 Chron. 33:25–25:27	Good	Good king; Loved God and his people; Oversaw destruction of altars to idols; Found the Law and followed it; Brought back the Priests of God
Jehoahaz	609	2 Kings 23:30–34; 2 Chron 36:1–4	Evil	Jailed and taken to Egypt; Died in Egypt
Jehoiakim	609–598	2 Kings 23:34–24:6 2 Chron. 36:5–8	Evil	Burned part of the Scripture; Puppet king for Egypt and later Babylon; First captives taken to Babylon
Jehoiachin	598–597	2 Kings 24:6–15; 25:27–30 2 Chron. 36:8–10	Evil	Many more people of Israel taken captive to Babylon
Zedekiah	597–586	2 Kings 24:17–25:21; 2 Chron. 36:10–21	Evil	Temple burned; Jerusalem destroyed; Captives taken to Babylon; Zedekiah tortured
	586			End of the Kingdom of Judah; Nebuchadnezzar, King of Babylon, took people captive

came and laid siege to the capital city of Samaria. They took over twenty-seven thousand captives from Israel into Exile in Assyria. This brought an end to the Northern Kingdom of Israel.

The chart on the previous page shows the prophets to Israel.

The Southern Kingdom of Judah

Unlike the Northern Kingdom, Judah enjoyed a 450-year period of reign by kings from the line of David. The reigns of the kings were not without their problems, however. Nor was there a line of all good kings. Some of the rulers, including the one queen, Athaliah, were evil and led the people to sin and away from God's purpose for His people. Judah had a more stable government than Israel. Jerusalem and the temple provided the worship center for the people of Judah. It also helped to unify the people.

The chart on the previous page shows the kings of Judah and what they each accomplished.

Several kings of Judah deserve special comment. The first two kings of Judah were evil. They were followed by good kings, Asa and Jehoshaphat, who

both tore down altars to idols and restored worship of Jehovah. Jehoram married an evil daughter of King Ahab from the Northern Kingdom. He restored idol worship, just as his father-in-law had done in Israel. Evil continued through the very evil Queen Athaliah. She tried to destroy her grandchildren but did not succeed in killing Joash. When she was murdered, Joash became king at the age of seven. He restored worship of Jehovah in the Temple. He was followed by two good kings Amaziah and Azariah (Uzziah). At the end of Azariah's reign, perhaps the greatest of the writing prophets ministered in Judah. His prophecies clearly described the doom that would come to Judah because of their continued idolatry.

Jotham came to the throne. He was a good king but failed to rid the land of idol worship. As a result, his son, Ahaz, allowed human sacrifice. He took vessels from the temple and used them in idolatrous worship. He made an alliance with Assyria against the counsel of the prophets. Ahaz's son was Hezekiah. Hezekiah began his reign at age twenty-five. He was a good king. He destroyed the altars to the idols. He restored worship of Jehovah

PROPHETS TO JUDAH

PROPHET	DATES OF PROPHET	SCRIPTURE REFERENCE	KEY VERSE	BASIC TEACHING
Micah	735–710	Jer. 26:18; Mic.	Mic. 6:8	God desires justice, mercy, and righteousness
Isaiah	740–698	2 Kings 19–20; Isa.	Isa. 1:18; 53:4–6	Hope comes through repentance and may require suffering; Judah will suffer captivity for continuing idol worship
Nahum	625	Nah.	Nah. 1:2–3	God is jealous for His people; God will judge the Assyrians
Zephaniah	630	Zeph.	Zeph. 2:3	Humility and righteousness are necessary to please God
Habakkuk	625	Hab.	Hab. 2:4	The righteous will live by faith
Jeremiah	626–584	2 Chron. 36:12; Jer.	Jer. 31:33–34	A new covenant will come and God's Law will be written on the heart, instead of tables of stone; Judah will suffer for her continuing sinful idolatry and injustice
Joel	588	Joel	Joel 2:28–29	Repent and God will give His Spirit
Obadiah	580	Obad.	Obad. 21	Israel will be blessed again

and added orchestral music in Temple worship. During his reign there were additions to the Book of Psalms and their use in worship.

Hezekiah was succeeded by his evil son, Manasseh. His was the longest reign of any of the kings of Judah, fifty-five years. The ultimate destruction of Jerusalem and the captivity are blamed on Manasseh (see 2 Kings 21:10–16). He restored idolatry and murdered many of his own people. He allied with the Assyrians or was controlled by them. His son was Amon, who reigned only two years before he was murdered.

Amon's son Josiah came to the throne at the age of eight. He was the last of the good kings of Judah. Josiah got rid of many of the idolatrous worship centers. During the repair of the Temple, a Book of the Law was discovered in the temple. Josiah had it read and then tore his clothes at the sinful behavior of the people of Judah. Josiah brought the most far-reaching religious changes in Judah. He restored the Passover celebration. He died early, at the age of thirty-nine. But his reign was perhaps the greatest of any of the kings of Judah. During his reign Nahum prophesied the destruction of Ninevah and the Assyrians. This happened in 612 BC.

The last four kings of Judah were evil. Destruction of Ninevah by the joint forces of the Medes, Scythians, and Babylonians brought the rise of power in the Babylonians. The prophet Jeremiah began his ministry in the thirteenth year of King Josiah's reign. He proclaimed the destruction of Jerusalem and Judah by the Babylonians. The remaining evil kings of Judah opposed the message of Jeremiah and had him punished. But Jeremiah continued to preach and urge the people to repent. He urged Zedekiah to submit to the rule of Babylon. Zedekiah refused. Jerusalem was destroyed by King Nebuchadnezzar in 586 BC. Jeremiah was treated kindly by the Babylonians and allowed to continue living in Jerusalem.

See the previous page for a listing of the prophets of Judah.

THE EXILE AND BEYOND

The Babylonian Exile (586–539 BC)

During this time Jeremiah wrote the Book of Lamentations. This was a difficult time for both the exiles and for those who stayed behind. Lamentations states, "Judah has gone into exile following affliction and harsh slavery; she lives among the nations but finds no place to rest." We will briefly examine Lamentations in the books of poetry and wisdom. Later Jeremiah was forced against his will to go to Egypt with some of the residents of Jerusalem. His prophecies ended there.

Meanwhile the people were taken into captivity in Babylon, they became known as Jews. That title has continued with them even today. Daniel and his friends Shadrach, Meschach, and Abednego were carried off to Babylon as young men. They distinguished themselves by not eating at the table of Nebuchadnezzar but ate only the food allowed

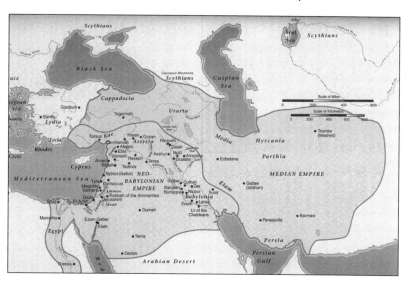

MAP OF THE MEDO-BABYLONIAN EMPIRE

by the Old Testament Law. Daniel was a man who served God all the days of his life, no matter what it cost.

Like Joseph before him, Daniel interpreted a dream of Nebuchadnezzar. It consisted of a metal image and set forth the coming kingdoms. The head of gold foretold the Babylonian kingdom, which lasted less than one hundred years, from 612 to 539 BC. The next part of the image was the chest and arms of silver, telling about the kingdom of the Persians, from 539 to 331 BC. The Persians were defeated by the Greeks under Alexander the Great. The Greeks lasted three hundred years, from 331 to 31 BC. The next part of the image was composed of legs of iron. These represented the Romans, who defeated the Greeks at the Battle of Actium. This serves as a good introduction to the period after the Exile. The Romans conquered Palestine in 31 BC. They continued in control of the Western world until AD 476.

Daniel also led Nebuchadnezzar to worship Daniel's God after Nebuchanezzar recovered from his mental illness, where he ate grass like a cow. Daniel served three Babylonian kings. When he was older, he was called to interpret the handwriting on the wall of the last king Belshazzar, Nebuchadnezzar's grandson. Belshazzar had sinned against God and made fun of using the vessels from the temple to party. God warned him that his kingdom would be taken from him. That night the Babylonians were defeated, and the Persians became the new rulers. Daniel continued to serve the Persian kings and to worship the God of Israel. Some of the Persian princes became jealous of Daniel and had the king sign an order for all subjects to bow down to him. Daniel refused and was thrown to the hungry lions. But God rescued Daniel, and the lions did not harm him. His accusers were thrown to the lions instead.

Ezekiel ministered to the Jewish exiles in Babylon by the river Chebar. This is a canal that

RETURN FROM EXILE

Phase	Date	Scripture Reference	Jewish Leader	Persian Ruler	Return	Events of the Return
First	538	Ezra 1–6	Zerubbabel Jeshua	Cyrus	(1) Anyone could return (2) The Temple was to be rebuilt (3) Money would come from the Royal Treasury (4) Gold and silver taken by Nebuchadnezzar would be returned to the Temple	(1) Burnt offerings were made (2) Feast of Tabernacles was celebrated (3) Work on the Temple started (4) Persian ruler stopped rebuilding of the Temple (5) Darius ordered rebuilding to begin again in 520 (6) Temple completed and dedicated in 516
Second	458	Ezra 7–10	Ezra	Artaxerxes Longimanus	(1) Anyone could return (2) Money would come from the Royal Treasury (3) Jewish civil judges were allowed	The men of Israel intermarried with foreign women
Third	444	Neh. 1–13	Nehemiah	Artaxerxes Longimanus	Rebuilding Jerusalem was allowed	(1) Neighbor rulers opposed building walls of Jerusalem (2) Rebuilding the walls completed in 52 days (3) Walls were dedicated (4) Ezra read the Book of the Law (5) Nehemiah began new rules

PROPHET	DATES OF PROPHET	SCRIPTURE REFERENCE	KEY VERSE	BASIC TEACHING
Daniel	605–534	Dan.	Daniel 4:17	God alone reigns supreme over all the earth; Faithfulness to God is all that counts in life
Ezekiel	593–571	Ezek.	Ezek. 37:12–13	There is a future hope for a new community of worship
Zechariah	520–514	Ezra 5:1; 6:14; Zech.	Zech. 14:9	God one day will rule over all the earth
Haggai	520	Ezra 5:1; 6:14; Hag.	Hag. 2:8–9	You must rebuild the Temple
Malachi	433	Mal.	Mal. 4:2	There is a future hope for a new day will dawn when the Son of Righteousness comes

connects the Tigris and Euphrates Rivers. His wife had been killed back in Israel, but he could take no time to mourn. His message was filled with many symbols. The purpose of his message was to remind the people to stay true to their Jewish faith. God would one day bring them out of captivity.

Some of the exiles made a new life and home in Exile. Among these persons was Esther. The story of Esther and the celebration of the Feast of Purim took place during the captivity in Persia. Esther was chosen by the Persian king, Xerxes, to become his wife. When the wicked Haman wanted to kill all of the Jews, Esther bravely helped the king understand what was happening. As a result the Jews were saved from destruction. This happened about 474 BC.

THE RETURN FROM CAPTIVITY 538–444 BC

There were three groups of exiles that returned to Palestine. The first group came back under the Persian King Cyrus. Zerubbabel and Jeshua led them. The next group returned to Jerusalem in 458, and they were led by Ezra. The final group came in 444, and they were led by Nehemiah. See the descriptions on the previous page.

The prophets after the Exile were Zechariah, Haggai, and Malachi. They looked forward to a new day when God would establish His new kingdom. Haggai preached that the people must rebuild the

Temple. The Temple was rebuilt, but it did not have the beauty or the size of Solomon's Temple. Malachi's prophecy brought an end to the Scriptures from the Old Testament. The prophets of the Exile and postexile are described in the chart above.

PERIOD BETWEEN THE OLD AND NEW TESTAMENTS 433–4 BC (DATES APPROXIMATE)

Jews who were scattered throughout Babylonia, Persia, and Egypt could no longer go to the Temple for sacrifice and festivals. The synagogue now became the local place for Jewish study and worship. The rabbi was the worship leader. Jewish persons would go to the synagogue on the Sabbath day and on the feast days. They still worship in the synagogue today.

Alexander the Great Conquers the World (331–31 BC)

Alexander the Great came from Macedonia or northern Greece. He conquered the world from Greece to Egypt and as far as the Indus River in India. Alexander left no heirs. His conquered territory was divided among his generals. Cassander took Macedonia and Greece. Lysimachus took Thrace and Asia Minor. Seleucius took Syria and the East. Ptolomy took Palestine and Egypt. This Empire lasted from 331 to 63 BC. Greek became the common language. The Jews in Egypt recognized the need for the Scriptures to be translated into Greek. Seventy-two Jewish scholars translated the Scripture into Greek in seventy-two days as requested by Ptolemy II (285 to 247 BC). Ptolemy wanted a Greek translation for his library in Alexandria. Probably the translation included only the first five Books of Moses. By about 100 BC the entire Old Testament was in Greek translation.

The Maccabean Revolt (168–63 BC)

The Seleucid king, Antiochus IV, was an evil man. He ruled from 175 to 163 BC. He wanted all of the conquered peoples to worship the same gods. With the help of a false priest in 168 BC, he persuaded many Jews to worship the Greek god, Zeus. They left worship of the Lord Jehovah. The temple was dedicated to Zeus, and they sacrificed a pig upon the high altar. Some of the Seleucid soldiers partied in the temple. Circumcision and worship on the Sabbath were forbidden. This was a process known as Hellenization.

HELLENIZATION

Hellenization comes from the part of Greece known as Hellas. The spread of the Greek language and culture throughout the world conquered by Alexander the Great was called Hellenization. It resulted in the Koine Greek or common language. Koine Greek was used for the New Testament writings. It produced the Septuagint or Greek version of the Old Testament. The Hellenization of Palestine was not good for the Jews. It took away their Jewish faith.

If the Exile had taught the Jews anything, it was that God would not allow them to worship other gods. They were sick at the terrible things that were done in the Temple. An old Jewish priest, Mattathias, and his five sons began to fight back against the Seleucids. They would raid the camps and destroy the pagan altars. They were only a small but zealous band of several hundred fighting men. They became known as the Maccabeans. With God's help, after only three years of fighting this way, they regained the Temple and cleared it of all the evil pagan altars. The date was December 15, 165 BC. They cleansed the Temple and celebrated for eight days. The oil for the Temple lamps ran low. There was only a supply for one day, but it never ran out. As a result the celebration has become known as the Festival of Lights or Hanukkah. From 142 to 63 BC the Jews enjoyed a brief time of independence.

Judah now became known by its Greek name, Judea. Simon, one of the Maccabeans, exercised leadership both as priest and king in Judea. Recall that Hezekiah got leprosy for exercising the role of priest. Simon's line continued to rule both the temple and the government for the next eighty years.

Three important Jewish groups arose during this period. The first of these was the *Hasidim* or "The Pious Ones." They arose to support keeping Jewish religious rites and study of the Law. They joined forces with the Maccabeans to free Judea from the Seleucids. The *Hasidim* later became the *Pharisees*. They considered themselves the successors to Ezra and to Moses. They believed in the resurrection and supported the Oral Law given to Moses on Mount Sinai. They became a powerful religious group in Judaism.

A second group was the *Sadducees*. These were the wealthy persons who had positions of authority. They were the ruling group. They had a great deal of power. They did not believe in the resurrection from the dead. They believed in using only the Written Law. They favored at least some Hellenization. They were important to the Temple and the Sanhedrin or supreme Jewish council. There was strong rivalry between the Pharisees and the Sadducees.

A third group was the *Essenes*. These people lived in communities, like persons in a monastery. They shared all of their possessions. They devoted their time to study the Torah. They had a long period of one to three years before they were accepted into full membership in the community. Their final acceptance came through baptism. They considered the worship in the Temple to be false and worshipped in communities, away from the rest of Jewish life. One of their main communities was located in caves along the shore of the Dead Sea.

The Romans Control Judea (63 BC–AD 70)

Aristobulus II and Hyrcanus II were in a fight over who would control Judea. They both went to the Roman general Pompey. Pompey brought his Roman troops to Jerusalem and laid siege for three months. Finally, Pompey entered the city and the Temple. Pompey's troops did not destroy Jerusalem. Aristobulus was taken captive, and Hyrcanus was given control of the Temple as high priest. From that point on, the Romans appointed a governor to rule over Judea.

Antipator, a ruler of Idumea, became governor of Judea by authority of Julius Caesar. (Idumea was previously Edom.) Romans had their own civil war, when Julius Caesar was murdered. Antipator's son, Herod promised to regain control of Judea. He was given the title "king of the Jews." Herod continued to control Judea until his death in 4 BC. Herod tried to make the Jews happy by rebuilding the Temple. But the people of Judea hated Herod. Many withdrew to communities like the Essenes. Others became part of the dagger carriers, who would strike down the Romans at any opportunity. The rule of the Romans was so harsh that the Jews finally revolted. The Roman general Titus laid siege on Jerusalem and destroyed the Temple in AD 70. The Temple has not been rebuilt; only the wall stands today. Many Jews go to the wall, known as the Wailing Wall, to pray even today.

THE WAILING WALL

CONCLUSION

The story of the Old Testament is a sad commentary on humanity. There were some persons who lived for God, but most people rebelled against Him. That is not so different from the world today. Even among those who followed God, most fell into sin at some point in their lives. Consider David as an example. There had to be a more complete way of atoning for sin than animal sacrifice. Once each year the High Priest would take the sin offering into the Holy of Holies of the Temple. He would then send the scapegoat with the scarlet cord around his horns into the wilderness to carry away the sins of the people. Each year this practice would have to be renewed.

Something more was needed. The prophets told us that God so loved the people whom He created, that He was not willing to let any perish in sin. *What could God do that would change this situation forever and bring blessing and hope to fallen humanity?* Let's hold that question until we get to the New Testament. In the meantime let's look into the poetry and wisdom from the Old Testament. They have a lot to say that can help us live godly lives today.

Old Testament Poetry: Psalms, Song of Solomon

Nearly one-third of the Old Testament is Hebrew poetry. Most of the books of the Old Testament contain at least one or more lines of poetry. In the Old Testament only the books of Nehemiah, Esther, Haggai, and Malachi do not contain any poetry. We will study two books of poetry, Psalms and Song of Solomon. Let me encourage you to work through the introduction and not just to pass over it. There is a lot of material that will help you understand the Psalms better.

The Psalms—Introduction

The term *psalms* means "praises" or "songs of praises." It came from the Greek translation of the Hebrew Old Testament. The Book of Psalms is the hymnbook of the Bible. There are psalms for every occasion in life. Psalms can lift our spirits when we are sad and lonely and give us comfort. Psalms help us express our joy and praise. When we are overwhelmed with the goodness of God and want to express it, the psalms help. Psalms provide us with ways to express our worship for God when we are worshipping alone or when we are with other believers. Psalms help us express our feelings today even though they were written over three thousand years ago in ancient Israel. A short introduction will help us gain more meaning from the Psalms for our lives today.

There is no other book in the Bible that is quite like Psalms. It is the longest book in the Bible. There are 150 psalms. The shortest psalm is 117, while the longest is 119. If we consider chapters in the Bible, Psalm 117 is the middle of the 1,189 chapters in the Bible. Of the 31,173 verses in the Bible, Psalm 118:8 is the middle verse in the Bible.

Of the Old Testament books, the Book of Psalms is the most quoted in the New Testament.

The psalms were written by many authors over a period of about nine hundred years. Psalm 90 was written by Moses around 1410 BC. The most recent Psalm was 126, which was written around 430 BC. While King David wrote many of the psalms, there were many other authors as well. Among them were Asaph, a priest in ancient Israel; Solomon, David's son; Ezra, the scribe; Ethan, Heman, the sons of Korah, and many other unnamed writers. Korah was the choir director appointed by King David to lead worship in the house of God.

MOSES, THE AUTHOR OF THE 90TH PSALM

Types of Psalms

There are psalms that are *hymns* of praise and thanksgiving. They help us tell God how grateful we are for the good things He provides for us, such as Psalms 37 and 100. *Wisdom* psalms teach us how to lead godly lives in this present world. Psalms 1 and 119 give us advice on living for God. *Teaching* psalms are closely related to the *wisdom* psalms. They teach us the kind of life that should be followed by a believer. Psalm 78 is a *teaching* psalm. It teaches us not to make the mistakes of the past. Another *teaching* psalm that is also a psalm of *repentance* is Psalm 32. Psalms of *repentance* are personal expressions of asking for God's forgiveness for sin. Psalms 32 and 51 are excellent examples of David's sorrow for his sin and helps us express our sorrow for our sin today.

Psalms of *worship* were used by worshippers going up to the Temple in Jerusalem at the Jewish festivals. Psalm 98 is an example of this type of Psalm. *Pilgrimage* psalms were used by the worshippers as they went to Jerusalem to worship God. Psalm 134 is an example of this type of Psalm. *Royal* psalms tell of the coming day when Christ will rule. Psalm 110 is a good example of the eternal reign of the Christ. Songs of *lament* are psalms that express the writer's longing for God's deliverance from trouble. Psalm 3 is an example of this type of psalm. Psalms of *comfort* guide us through difficult times, like Psalm 23. *Majestic* psalms tell of the greatness of God. Psalms 96 and 97 are expressions of worship for the majesty of God and His creation.

One other type of psalm is the *judgment* psalm. This kind of psalm asks God to protect the psalmist from evildoers, such as is told in Psalm 59. Because the ancient world was violent, some of these psalms call down God's judgment upon evil persons. We will not look at any examples of this type of psalm.

Books of Psalms

The Book of Psalms originally ended at Psalm 72. Other psalms must have been added at different times. Later Jewish scholars must have brought the remaining psalms together and created the present Book of Psalms. Psalm 90 was written by Moses and would have existed long before the psalms of David. The scholars later brought all of the psalms together into the Book of Psalms that we have today.

The psalms are divided into five distinct books. At the end of each book, there is a doxology or praise to God as the book ends. Book one includes Psalms 1–41 and ends with this doxology in verse 13, "May the LORD, the God of Israel, be praised from everlasting to everlasting. Amen and amen" (Psalms 41:13). Book two begins with Psalm 42 and ends with a doxology at the end of Psalm 72. The last verse of this psalm tells us that "The prayers of David son of Jesse are concluded" (Psalms 72:20). While David and Solomon wrote most of these psalms, book two was probably added by the men who served the good King Hezekiah. Book three begins with Psalm 73 and continues through 89. These were added by either Hezekiah or later by King Josiah. Book four includes Psalms 90 through 106. Recall that Moses wrote the first psalm in this collection. This collection of psalms was probably added after the Jewish people returned from captivity under Ezra or Nehemiah. This happened between two and three hundred years after the first three books. The fifth book includes Psalms 107–150. Most of these would have come from the days after the Exile. These psalms tell of the greatness of God and His Word.

The psalms roughly trace the history of Israel. The earliest of the psalms is Psalm 90, which was a prayer to God, written by Moses. This would have come from the period of the Exodus from Egypt. The period of the judges did not add much to the psalms. Remember that this was a low period spiritually for the people of Israel. During the period of the kings, however, the majority of psalms were written. The majority of the psalms were written by King David. Some psalms were written during the religious revival at the time of King Hezekiah. Hezekiah's men also gathered more of the psalms of David and added them to the first Book of Psalms. Recall that they were recorded in book two and added to book one. The period of the prophets did not produce a lot of psalms since the people were bent toward idol worship and sin against God. But the period after the return from Exile to Babylon produced a wealth of psalms that we find mainly in books four and five. As you read the psalms, try to identify the period from which the psalm came.

Hebrew Poetry

Hebrew poetry is different from poetry in our language. In our poetry one can usually tell the difference between poetry and prose writing. One way that we help to show the difference between poetry and prose is with the use of rhyming words. In the old New England hornbook, from which children learned their letters of the alphabet, the letter A began with this idea from the Bible,

> In Adam's fall,
> we sinned all.

Notice that *fall* and *all* rhyme. There is no doubt that these lines are poetry. But in Hebrew poetry there are no words that rhyme. Hebrew poetry is closer to our poetry; that is, in the form of blank verse. The differences between poetry and prose in blank verse and in Hebrew poetry are much smaller.

Hebrew poetry has three characteristics. First, Hebrew poetry has *meter*, which is the pattern of stressed and nonstressed syllables. But meter applies to the Hebrew words and does not help us understand the poetic value of the psalms very much. Second, Hebrew poetry has *parallelisms*. When two things are parallel, they are similar. For example, two identical straight lines are parallel when they are side-by-side and run in the same direction. For poetry in its simplest form, this means that two lines of poetry use different words, but the lines mean the same thing. This is the most important feature of Hebrew poetry. Third, Hebrew poetry may have stanzas. These are groups of lines that make larger units of the poem,

and we call these larger units *stanzas*. We will look at some examples of *stanzas* when we examine some of the Psalms. Psalms 42 and 43 make up a single poem. The stanzas have different words, but there is a common conclusion to each *stanza*. These words end each of the three *stanzas*, "Why am I so depressed? Why this turmoil within me? Put your hope in God, for I will still praise Him, my Savior and my God" (Psalms 43:5). The refrain appears at 42:5 and 11 and again at 43:5.

Since the most important feature of Hebrew poetry is *parallelism*, we need to explore the meaning of *parallelisms* and some examples from several psalms. The three most common types of *parallelism* are *synonymous parallelism, antithetic parallelism*, and *synthetic parallelism*.

Synonymous parallelism means that two or more lines have almost the same meaning even though they are said differently. The second line is stated for emphasis. David's cry to God in Psalm 3:1 is a good example. "LORD, how my foes increase! There are many who attack me."

Antithetic parallelism means that two lines have the opposite meaning. The second line is a dramatic contrast to the first. In Psalm 1:6 the psalmist makes sure that we understand the difference between the way of the righteous person and the way of the evil person. He says, "For the LORD watches over the way of the righteous, but the way of the wicked leads to ruin."

Synthetic parallelism means that the second line develops the idea of the first line. This kind of parallelism is more difficult to see in Hebrew poetry, but looking for it is worth the effort. Notice how the first line of Psalm 104:1b gives added meaning when you read the second line. The psalmist is speaking of God and he says, "You are very great; You are clothed with majesty and splendor."

One other way the psalmist helped children and even adults learn the psalms was with the use of an alphabetical acrostic. Just as we learn our ABCs, the Hebrew poet used the first letters of the Hebrew alphabet to help Israelite children remember the instruction from the Lord in the poem. Recall the use of our ABCs from the New England hornbook for New England school-children. In the same way the Hebrew writer began the verse or stanza with the letters from the Hebrew alphabet. Psalms 25 and 34 use all of the twenty-two letters of the Hebrew alphabet to build an acrostic. Psalm 119 has twenty-two stanzas, each of which begins with a letter from the Hebrew alphabet.

One other interesting term that appears seventy-one times in the Psalms is *Selah*. We do not know the exact meaning of the word. It seems to have meant "to raise up." It may have been included as an instruction to the musical instruments to become louder at specific times. Other ancient Jewish writings suggest that it meant "forever." As a result, it may have been an instruction to the people to shout "forever." An example is taken from Psalm 3:4, "I cry aloud to the LORD, and He answers me from His holy mountain. *Selah*."

SELECTED PSALMS

Let's look at several psalms that will help us apply some of the things that we have learned from the introduction. We will explore psalms of each type, like *wisdom* or *worship and thanksgiving*. Psalms will be selected from each of the five books of psalms. Parallelisms, stanzas, and acrostics will also be included.

READ PSALM 1

Many believe that since Psalm 1 does not have any description of the person who wrote the psalm, it was likely added later as an introduction to the entire Book of Psalms. Psalm 1 introduces the great themes of the Book of Psalms very well. The main idea of this psalm has two parts. Both parts relate to the way to find happiness in this life. First, the person who would be happy will not allow himself to become caught up with the evil of this world. Second, this person who would be happy will learn God's Word and make it part of his daily life in everything he does. This psalm is very much like the Proverbs and other *wisdom* psalms and may be found in book one of the psalms. It provides us guidance in what will make us truly happy in life. If we heed its warnings, we will truly have an amazing and happy life in this world and in the world to come. This psalm is closely tied to the idea that God has given us the means for happiness in His teaching, and we need to learn it and live by it.

True Happiness of the Godly Person (Psalm 1:–3)

The psalmist tells us that if you want to live a truly happy life there are at least two things you must do. He starts with a negative idea. You will not be truly happy if you spend most of your time learning or doing things with friends who do not love God. This is the meaning of *not following the advice of the wicked*. This would include teasing, fighting, and bullying other children. It means not watching television programs and listening to music that will make you love this world and the possessions of this world. Repeating bad language that you hear on the playground or repeating bad words from television are not pleasing to God. These will all pass away and do not please God.

Second, the one who wants to follow God will *not take the path of sinners*. The person who would please God will not do things that will lead to evil activities. Drinking, taking drugs, gambling, and partying are not pleasing to God. Neither is watching movies or television shows that are filled with violence, sex, and bad language pleasing to God. Magazines that encourage sinful ways are not helpful either. This kind of living may seem good for a while because your friends are doing them. But remember that God is watching and is very displeased with the one who does these things.

Third, the person who would please God does *not join a group of mockers*. One way is being caught up in the idea of evolution that pokes fun of the idea that God created the world. Another way is by sitting with friends who do not follow God and who make fun of people who do love God and follow Him. Perhaps the worst way this happens is making fun of God directly and using God's name carelessly or as swear words. This is very displeasing to God. Remember that God hears everything you say and watches everything you do. He will hold you responsible one day for the way you lived your life in this world.

If you want to please God, you will learn to enjoy the teaching of God from His Word, the Bible. Law or teaching means the way of God and the entire will of God that I will use to guide my life. To meditate means to apply your mind to thinking about God and His Word so that you will increase in your love for God and that you will live a holy life. It carries the idea of a full-time concern with the teaching of God that is carried on continuously.

The person who lives in this way will be like a palm tree. The palm tree, unlike the oak, will bend in the wind and storm. But the palm tree will not break. When the sun shines again, the palm tree will return to its upright position. The palm will deliver its fruit at the appropriate time. Like the palm, the follower of Jesus will be consistent. God plants the tree where its roots can draw streams of water from the irrigation ditches. As a result the leaves will not shrink or dry out when a drought comes. The person who lives like this will prosper. This does not mean that he will get rich but that his character will be pleasing to God. It is important for this life and life in all eternity.

In the End Sinners will not Stand (Psalm 1:4–6)

Wicked persons will be judged by God for their sin and evil deeds. God's anger against sin will be revealed. The wicked will be judged. In ancient Israel the farmer would empty his grain on the threshing floor. With pitchforks the farmers would take the grain and throw it up into the air. The *chaff* or husks that cover the grain would be blown away by the wind, while the heavier grain would return to the grain pile on the threshing floor and be kept for food.

When the wicked are judged, they will not be able to stand. Like the useless husks that cover the good grain, evil persons will be blown away by the judgment of God. They will not be allowed to stand in the judgment. They will not stand along with the righteous persons. The righteous persons are the ones that were described above. They are the ones who live as they should. They please God. We should live as they live.

In the final verse the righteous are contrasted with the evil ones. God watches over the righteous. God is not only aware of them, but He has a personal relationship with the righteous. But the ungodly will come to a violent, sudden, and terrible end.

This psalm makes it clear that the way of wisdom is to follow God. Each of us must ask himself, "What path am I taking?" "Has my love for God increased?" "Is the direction of my life toward a godly life or am I more concerned about being in the world and being popular with my friends?"

READ PSALM 3

Psalm 3 is taken from book one of Psalms. It is a psalm of *lament*. Remember that *lament* means

---

LAW

The Law or the Hebrew word is Torah, *which means God's will for humankind. The first meaning of the Law is that it was given to Moses on Mt. Sinai. But it has a much wider meaning than that. It was God's will for His people Israel. In the Psalms it means the ways of God, the activities of God, and the teaching of God through His Word. We do not need to obey the ritual laws of sacrifice and Temple worship from the Old Testament. But the moral laws of God are timeless and further explained by Jesus in the New Testament. They must be obeyed by us, even today.*

that the psalmist is crying to God to help him out of a terrible situation. Can you find at least one *parallelism* in this psalm? It contains several *parallelisms*. Look at verses 1 and 3. What do you see? Notice that the word *Selah* appears three times in this psalm. Do you remember what *Selah* means? Notice that we are told at the very beginning about the *historical circumstances* from which this psalm came. It was a time when David was almost forced to leave his throne by his son Absalom. The story is told in 2 Samuel 15–18.

David in Distress (Psalm 3:1–2)

Absalom, David's son, had stolen the hearts of the people away from their king. David had to flee for his life. To add to his pain, Ahithophel, David's trusted advisor, had sided with Absalom. Shimei from Saul's house came out to make fun of David. He said that David was receiving what he had done in stealing the kingship from Saul. David only had a few loyal friends who were with him as they fled from Jerusalem. Night was coming, and they had to camp in the wilderness. David was scared!

David's Hope (Psalm 3:3–6)

But David did not allow himself to stay in fear. He called on God to help him. He prayed. God gave him strength. David said that God acted as a shield to protect him from those who would harm him. Help was available for David from God. Help is available for us today in God also. We just need to turn to Him and pray to Him when things seem to be going wrong. He wants to help, but we must pray.

David was feeling very alone. His head was down. But God even lifted up his head. God restored David's dignity. God answered David from Jerusalem where the Ark of the Covenant was located. It is not Absalom who has received the blessing of God. It is David to whom God speaks comfort and protection.

David says that because he knew God was with him, he could now lie down and sleep. When we are

lonely and afraid, it is hard to sleep. At the very time we need to sleep, we cannot. With the promise of God's protection, David tells us that he was able to sleep. He awoke the next day refreshed.

David was no longer fearful. He could now face any number of soldiers that Absalom might bring against him. God was right there with David. He must have remembered when he fought against the giant, Goliath. David was alone at that time also. But God was with him, and he defeated Goliath. David was sure that God would do the same for him in this situation also.

David's Request (Psalm 3:7–8)

David was God's anointed king over Israel. The threat of Absalom was no less real! But David now had his confidence returned. God was there, and he called on God to protect him from Absalom, who would have stolen the throne. David remembered when he was a shepherd boy. He protected his sheep from the lions and bears. God helped him break the jaw of the lion who would have attacked David's sheep. God would do the same against Absalom and his army.

God saves! Salvation is God's. Now that David was confident in God, he turned to pray for God's people, Israel. If God could protect him, David knew that God could protect His people Israel. God alone could bless them. David prayed for them as well. God will do the same for us if we pray.

Read Psalm 23

Psalm 23 is probably the best loved and most quoted chapter in the Bible. It is found in book one and is a psalm of David. It is a psalm of *comfort*. Persons whose family members have died are still comforted by this psalm. Persons in prisons have found comfort with this psalm. It is a good psalm to memorize. This psalm must certainly have come from David's experience as a shepherd (see 1 Samuel 16:11, 19; 17:15). Did you discover any *parallelisms* in this psalm?

The Good Shepherd (Psalm 23:1–4)

"The LORD is my shepherd" shows how personal David saw his relationship with God. In the Holy Land, the shepherd's life was not a glamorous occupation. The shepherd was responsible for his sheep twenty-four hours a day and seven days a week. He had to protect his sheep. The sheep were helpless without their shepherd to guide and care for them. God does that for His people.

Sheep are easily frightened. They found rest in a grassy meadow when the shepherd was there with calm assurance. The shepherd often had to stop the flowing water of the stream by placing rocks in the riverbed. The sheep can drink from the calm waters but not from water that is noisy and flowing rapidly. When the sheep wandered from the shepherd, the good shepherd would bring the sheep back to safety. The shepherd would guide the sheep on the right path. God did that for David and does the same for all who follow Him, even today.

When the shepherd guided the sheep from one place for grazing to another, the sheep often had to travel on a narrow and dangerous path. They could be endangered by wild animals or snakes. Thorns could also hurt the sheep. The shepherd often had to lead his sheep through places that might pose a death trap. But the protective care of the shepherd would guide them safely through. The child of God receives the same protection from a loving heavenly Father today.

Finally, David showed how the rod of the shepherd provided protection and comfort for the sheep. The rod was a club that was used to drive off wild animals that came after the sheep. The staff had a crook at the end and was used to rescue the sheep from a dangerous spot on the path. The staff might also be used to push away branches that might be in the way of the sheep as he passed along the path. Both the rod and staff were comforting to the sheep. God's Word and His hand of guidance do the same for those who love Him. God alone can lead a person even through the pain of death.

The Lord's Goodness (Psalm 23:5–6)

In the last stanza, verses 5 and 6, the picture changes. God is shown as the gracious host. He cares for His guests, those who follow Him. In an ancient oriental banquet, the king would provide everything that a person could desire at his feast. David said that God supplied all that is needed for the person who loves and follows Him. The host would also pour oil on the head of the honored guest. God does the same for His followers. God provides the constant supply of drink for the guests at His table. In other words God gives us grace to sustain us in the most difficult situations.

God's goodness and love follow all those who trust in Him. Whatever happens in life, God is there for His followers. He loves them with an everlasting love. That love will carry right on to the end of life. I know that I will live in the house of the Lord forever. I will continue to live in a close relationship with God even through eternity.

READ PSALM 32

In which book is this Psalm located? Psalm 32 is one of the psalms of *repentance*. We learn from the first two lines that it is a psalm of David. At a low point in David's life, he should have gone to war. Instead, David stayed home. He was attracted to Bathsheba, the wife of one of his soldiers. David disobeyed God and sinned. Later the prophet Nathan confronted David with his sin against God. David confessed his sin to God and was forgiven. Notice at the beginning of this psalm that it is described as a *Maskil*. We are not positive what the term *Maskil* means. But it may mean that Psalm 32 is a *teaching* psalm. We will find this term again applied to Psalm 78. From Psalm 32 we can learn how to find God's forgiveness for our sin.

The Joy of Forgiveness (Psalm 32:1–2)

David describes the joy and happiness that comes to the person who has willfully sinned against God but whom God has forgiven. Transgression means to defiantly sin against God.

It is that I want my way even if it means I must disobey God. We can know the difference between right and wrong. God has given us the Ten Commandments. In the New Testament Jesus and later the apostle Paul tell us what God does not approve. To go against what the Scripture teaches us means that we sin. Even though the sin may be against other persons, it is *always* against God. Only God can forgive sin. But there are times when we have wronged or hurt other persons. We need to ask their forgiveness as well as the forgiveness of God. David says that when I know the forgiveness of God for my sin, I can be truly happy. I cannot continue to deceive myself or try to deceive God that I am without sin. God will accept only truthfulness and honesty about my sin before Him. This honesty is essential to God's forgiveness.

REPENTANCE AND FORGIVENESS
Repentance means to feel sorry for disobeying and sinning against God. It also involves expressing sorrow for your sin to God in prayer of confession.
Forgiveness means to receive God's pardon for your sin and feel the joy of being restored to fellowship with God. God knows what you say but also what you feel, and He knows if you are sincere.

David's Experience (Psalm 32:3–5)

David went back in time in this psalm to tell about his experience. David had stubbornly refused to confess his sin. As a result he carried a lot of guilt. He may even have become very sick. He felt the punishment of God upon his life. He complained about his situation, but God did not respond to him. David had not yet been honest with God about what he had done. He suffered from the burning fever that went along with his guilt. *Selah* emphasized the importance for David to change his way.

The way to David's forgiveness is described in verse 5. This is the most important verse in this psalm. David tells us that the first thing was to acknowledge or confess his sin to God. Then David no longer hid his sin, nor did he try to cover it up. Rather, he told God that he had sinned and showed the sin for what it was. David told God that he had disobeyed Him. As a result, David received God's forgiveness. The heavy guilt that he was feeling was lifted. Again, *Selah* emphasized the importance of the change that came to David.

David's Hope in God (Psalm 32:6–7)

All who are faithful to God need to pray and confess their sin. When the storms of life come against them, they will find their strength in God. Then David turned directly to God in verse 7. He tells God that he can only find strength in Him. God will guard him from trouble. Glad shouts of joy will come from the deliverance that God provides. This joy is emphasized again with the use of the word *Selah*!

David's Teaching about Sin (Psalm 32:8–11)

There is a better way than to suffer from sin. Be sensitive to God's guidance. Keep up your relationship with God every day. and allow Him to teach you direction. Do not allow sin to break that relationship.

David had learned the hard way about sin and its results. He tells the reader not to be as the horse or mule. Those animals have no understanding. We can avoid being disciplined if we obey God. Horses must be controlled by a bit and bridle. Animals cannot be trusted. But we who live for God can avoid punishment.

David shows the difference between the evil person and the one who follows God. The evil person will have trouble. But the one who follows and obeys God may also have trouble, but that person will be surrounded by God's love. In the end the righteous one can experience the happiness that comes from being forgiven by God. Do you see the parallelism in verse 11?

READ PSALM 47

Psalm 47 is a *royal* psalm from book two. Remember that *royal* psalms were written to tell of the coming reign of Jesus, the Messiah. It is often called one of the *messianic* psalms. The message of the psalm is that God is the great king over all the earth and the heavens. God alone rules all of the nations of the earth. This psalm was written by the sons of Korah. That means that it was written for the worship of God by the descendents of Korah. Korah, you will remember, was the choir director. He was appointed by King David to lead worship in the house of God.

Notice that the first stanza ends with *Selah*. Do you remember what *Selah* means?

God Is Awesome (Psalm 47:1–4)

In the first stanza of this psalm, the writer leads the worshippers in celebration of God. God is awesome! We adore Him. There is no one who is like our God. He is the great King over all the earth. The rulers of the earth have limited authority. But God alone has absolute and universal authority. He defeats the nations of the earth. He protects His people, Israel, and provides them with their inheritance in the land of Palestine. He does this because He loves His people.

Celebrate God's Rule (Psalm 47:5–7)

In the second stanza God is to be praised. The phrases used in verse 5 are the same as those in 2 Samuel 6:15. There David brought the Ark up to Jerusalem, the city of God. The shouts of celebration were the same. Notice the parallelism in verse 6. Wisdom and understanding should come from seeing that God alone is all powerful and King over all the earth.

Sing for Joy because God Reigns (Psalm 47:8–9)

God alone is sovereign! God reigns over all the earth. He is seated on His throne and carries out His sovereign rule. The nobles of the earth will humbly bow before their sovereign Lord. They will do this as the people of Israel did at the time this psalm was written. All people will live under God's rule. For us as Christians, this means that Jesus will one day be worshipped in His rightful place as the Lord of the universe. All mankind will recognize Him as Lord and King.

MASKIL

The word Maskil *is found in seventeen psalms. Some include: 32, 44, 45, 52, 53, 54, 55, 74, 78, 88, 89, and 142. It is also found in some other Psalms in the text. The word comes from a Hebrew word* skl, *which means "to instruct or make wise, or to teach." In most cases, but not all, it suggests teaching.*

READ PSALM 78

Psalm 78 is a *teaching* psalm. Recall from Psalm 32 that *Maskil* may likely have meant teaching. *Maskil* appears at the beginning of this psalm. Psalm 78 comes from book three of the Book of Psalms. Since this psalm contains seventy-two verses, we have selected only the first sixteen verses for our study of Psalm 78. The author is identified as Asaph. Asaph wrote twelve psalms, 50 and 73-83. He was apparently a Levite and a worship leader in ancient Israel. He led one of the worship choirs. Look for the *parallelisms* in these verses.

This psalm guides the hearer to recall the wonderful works that God performed on behalf of Israel to protect them. But the people of Israel did not trust God completely. As soon as the Lord responded to a problem, they began to complain about another problem. The psalmist wants the hearer to pay attention and learn from the mistakes of their fathers. The writer does not want the hearer to rebel against God as their fathers did. He wants the parents to teach their children about the sins of their fathers. The purpose is to guide the children not to repeat the sins of their fathers. Notice that the subtitle for this psalm is "Lessons from the Past." This psalm is one of the best examples of a *teaching* psalm.

Today we can also learn from the past sins of Israel. We need to obey God just as the people of Israel did in their day. We cannot willfully sin against God and expect that He will ignore our sin either. God will punish us for our sin, just as He punished the people of Israel for their sin.

A Warning from the Past (Psalm 78:1–8)

In verses 1 to 3 the psalmist speaks of the hidden truth that comes from the past. If we pay attention to the lessons of history, we will be obedient to God. We will not suffer the evils that fell on our fathers because they failed to learn from their mistakes. The lessons need to be taught to each following generation. The psalmist continues through this entire psalm to give one example after another. We forget so easily. The Gospel writer, Matthew, tells us that verse 2 of Psalm 78 is a prophecy of the way in which Jesus would teach. Instead of lessons from history, Jesus would teach hidden truths in lessons from nature and everyday experiences through parables.

In verse 4 the writer tells us that the things that happened in the past were not just for the people of that generation. The "wonderful works" or miracles were revealed by God for the future generations to see and understand. When the future generations understand, they will praise the Lord for the great things that He did for the people of Israel. Today we study the Scripture to understand the great things God did for us through the life and ministry of Jesus, His death on the cross, and His resurrection that gave us salvation. We need to pass this on to the succeeding generations. We need to learn from the gospel story and praise God for His great works for us as well.

In verse 5, the psalmist tells us that God established a "testimony in Jacob." He is telling about the tables of stone that contained the Ten Commandments and were placed in the Ark of the Covenant. The law of God was to be followed by the people of Israel both in the time that it was given but also for the future generations. The greatest teaching about passing the truth from parent to child is found in Deuteronomy 6:6–9. The psalmist tells us that the miracles of God's redeeming power are to be told from generation to generation. The law or teaching of God through the commandments and other teachings are also to be passed on from generation to generation.

Notice in verse 7 the three activities that must come from the teaching that will be given to the children. First, they must know so that they will "put their confidence in God." Second, they must "not forget" what God has done. These miracles were done by God, not by any person. They must be humble because it would not have happened without God. Third, they must keep His commandments and be obedient to "keep His commandments." If the parents fail to teach the next generation, they will become just as sinful as their fathers (see verse 8). They will also be punished. But punishment can be avoided!

Israel's Disobedience (Psalm 78:9–16)

The next stanza of this psalm describes more disobedience of the people of Israel. The first reference is to the tribe of the Ephraimites. Their archers or bowmen turned back in battle. They did not show courage but fled in the heat of battle. They are a symbol of all Israel. The Ephraimites were probably singled out because they committed other sin found further in this psalm in verse 67. Even though the Ephraimites were an important tribe, their failure to obey God caused Judah to be chosen instead of Ephraim.

In verse 10 and following, the people of Israel are in view for the rest of the stanza. They did not place their confidence in God. They did not keep God's covenant or His law. They forgot the miracles that God had done for them.

What were those miracles? "In the region of Zoan" tells of the area of the Nile delta region where the miracles of the plagues were performed (see verse 12). In verse 13, they forgot that when the Egyptians were coming against them, God performed another miracle. The sea parted, and the people of Israel were able to pass through the midst of the sea on dry land. When the Egyptians followed the Israelites into the sea, the sea came back together, and they were destroyed. Then God led the people of Israel through the wilderness. God provided a cloud by day and a pillar of fire by night. Not only did He lead the way, but when they needed water, God allowed Moses to strike the rock, and fresh water came out.

The Result (Psalm 78:17)

Verse 17 completes the thought, even though it begins a new stanza. The people continued to complain and disobey God. They doubted that He was good to them. They told Moses that God had brought them out into the wilderness to die. They wanted God to show them another miracle of His power. They doubted His love. This stanza and the remaining stanzas recount time after time when the Israelites failed to obey God. They sinned and failed to be confident in His love. They failed to remember the miracles He had done for them.

Read Psalm 98

Psalm 98 is a glorious *praise* psalm. It is found in book four of the Book of Psalms. There are three stanzas of three verses each. Psalm 98 is identified simply as *a psalm*. This is the only psalm that is identified in this way. Recall that the word *psalm* means a song or hymn and carries the idea of praise.

The historical occasion for which this psalm was written was after the return from the Babylonian captivity. God had raised up Persia to defeat Babylon. Cyrus, the Persian king, had sent the people of Israel back to their homeland. God had restored the people of Israel to their land and to the Holy City of Jerusalem. This was a glorious day and one for rejoicing and praising God.

God's Victory (Psalm 98:1–3)

Each of the first three verses contains the word *victory*. God had won a great victory for Israel. The victory called for a new song. The old song was probably the one that the people sang as they rejoiced on the banks of the Red Sea. They saw Pharaoh's army swallowed up by the waters as they destroyed Pharaoh. Now there is cause for new rejoicing as Persia defeated Babylon and allowed the people of Israel to return to the Holy City. It was the Lord who won the great victory over Babylon.

The Last New Song

Psalm 98 is not the last new song to be sung. The day is coming, wrote John the apostle, when God will reveal His salvation in the Lamb of God. Jesus is the Lamb of God. Revelation 5:9–10 tells it this way:

And they sang a new song:
You are worthy to take the scroll
and to open its seals;
because You were slaughtered,
and You redeemed people for God by Your blood
from every tribe and language and people and nation.
You made them a kingdom and priests to our God,
and they will reign on the earth.

That will be a great and glorious day! It will far surpass the victories over the Egyptians and the Babylonians. By trusting in Jesus, we will see that day and be on the victory side.

The victory is not just a victory for the people of Israel over the Babylonians. God displayed His righteousness. He showed the rest of the nations that He cared for His people Israel. The Gentiles, all those peoples of the world who are not Jews, would also see the hand of God in the life of His people Israel. God had shown that with His victory over Pharaoh at the Red Sea. He now shows it again with the return of the Israelites to Palestine from Babylon. God made right what was wrong. God showed the world His love for His people Israel. This is cause for great rejoicing and praise to the mighty arm of the Lord.

Shout to the Victorious King, Jehovah (Psalm 98:4–6)

The King has triumphed! He has gone up to His throne. All the earth is to shout, sing praise, and rejoice at the victory of the Lord. Along with the human voices, the lyre or stringed instrument are to be played. The wind instruments as the cornet and the trumpet are to be played. In 1 Chronicles 16:4–6, the writer tells how David brought the Ark of the Lord up to Jerusalem. It was done with great celebration and rejoicing. Asaph was the leader of the company. They played the cymbals, harps, lyres, and sounded the trumpets. The celebration described in this psalm is no different. But notice also that the ram's horn was sounded. The ram's horn or shophar was sounded in war and in peace. The sounding of the shophar showed how important this victory celebration was to the people of Israel.

> ### THE MAGNIFICAT
> When the angel of the Lord appeared to Mary in Nazareth, he told her that she would be the mother of the Messiah. She could not discuss the situation with Joseph at that time. So she went to the home of her cousin Elizabeth. On the way she must have been meditating on Psalm 98. When she arrived, Mary gave this wonderful treasure, the Magnificat. Compare Mary's psalm of praise by reading Luke 1:46–55 in your Bible with Psalm 98.

Let All of Nature Rejoice (Psalm 98:7–9)

God is not only Lord of the Jews. He is King of kings and Lord of lords over all the Gentiles as well as the Jews. Even nature honors the Lord. He is the Creator. The whole earth is filled with God's glory. Even nature was affected by the Fall of Man in the Garden of Eden. One day all creation will be restored. We could glimpse at the control of God over nature, when Jesus calmed the Sea of Galilee. The Lord Himself will judge the world with righteousness. He knows the hearts of all mankind. He knows our thoughts, and He alone can judge the world fairly.

READ PSALM 100

Psalm 100 is a *hymn* of thanksgiving and praise. Along with Psalm 23 it is one of the best known psalms in the entire book. It is found in book four of the Book of Psalms. We do not know the author of this psalm. This psalm was written as hymn of praise at the dedication of the Second Temple. The first Temple was built by Solomon. The Babylonians destroyed the first Temple in 586 BC. After the return from Babylon under Ezra, the Temple was rebuilt. This was known as the Second Temple. Worship of God was renewed in the Second Temple about 515 BC. This psalm was used with a thanksgiving offering, which was given to God for His special mercies to His people. The offering is described in Leviticus 7:11–34. Psalm 100 was one of several psalms that were used on the occasion of the dedication of the Second Temple.

Praise the Lord (Psalm 100)

Similar to Psalm 98, the psalmist calls upon all the earth to "shout triumphantly to the LORD." The Lord is King of kings and Lord of lords. This is a glad expression of joy in verse 1. Closely connected to praise is service to the Lord in verse 2. In both the Old Testament and the New Testament, there can be no dividing service from worship. The two are linked together. When we worship the Lord, we must also work for Him. The person who worships the Lord does so because he truly is free. God has given us freedom in Him.

Learn from the victories of Jehovah that He is the only true God. See verse 3. In spite of their sin, God preserved and protected His people Israel. He is the One who created us. We are His possession.

Enter the Temple gates and courts with thanksgiving. Find this in verse 4. We must express thanks for loving kindness that God showers upon us. To those who worshipped in the Temple, they are to bring a thank offering and praise in their worship. The thank offering is an expression of thanks for the gracious mercies of the Lord. One day in the future, we will enter freely through the gates and courts of the Temple into the very Holy of Holies, where we will meet with God Himself. This is beautifully described in Revelation 21:22–27.

Finally, the psalm ends in verse 5 with this phrase, "For the LORD is good, and His love is eternal; His faithfulness endures through all generations." This expression was used in many of the services in the Temple after the Babylonian Exile had ended. It was a declaration of the goodness of God.

READ PSALM 119:1–16

Psalm 119 is a *wisdom* psalm. It is located in book five of the Book of Psalms. It is the longest chapter in the Bible, with 176 verses. Psalm 119 is in the form of an *acrostic*. It consists of twenty-two stanzas of eight verses each. The stanzas are organized around the letters of the Hebrew alphabet in order. It is similar to an ABC book for a child to learn the letters of the alphabet. Apparently, the purpose of using the *acrostic* was to assist the learner to memorize this psalm. The author of this psalm is not named. But he must have been a person who had a deep love for the Lord. He was also a person who suffered for his faith in God.

The most important theme of this psalm is love for the Word of God. At least eight words are used to describe God's Word. The most prominent is the word *law*. It comes from a Hebrew word that means "to teach." Often the word is applied to the first five books of Moses. But as it is used in this psalm, it had to do with the teaching that comes from all of God's Word. *Law* can be found in verse 1.

A second word is *commandments*. These are specific commands that were given by God. The *Ten Commandments* are very specific. In Hebrew each of the *Ten Commandments* is given in only one word. *Commandments* are to be obeyed. The word *commandment* appears first in verse 127.

The third word is *testimonies* or *decrees*. This is a declaration of God's will for His people. They are specific instructions in moral and religious duties to be carried out. They are given to avoid the human error of not following them exactly. The psalmist said that he found delight in the *testimonies* of the Lord. This word first appears in verse 2.

A fourth word used for Scripture is *precepts*. This word comes from the idea that an officer is put in charge and must see that every order is carried out in detail. The actions taken must follow exactly as they were given. The psalmist observes to follow the instructions carefully. This word is found first in verse 4.

The fifth term used for God's Word is *statutes*. This word speaks of the time in which the Word of God is in effect. The *statutes* of the Lord are permanent. They last forever. This is found first in verse 5.

A sixth word is *judgments*. This word has several meanings. It relates to the judicial decisions of the Lord that are rules for us to follow. It also means specific acts of Jehovah in judging the sin of wicked persons. These acts reveal and affirm God's law. This is found first in verse 7.

A seventh term that is used is *word*. This is the most general term that is used to apply to all of God's communication to mankind. This is God's truth in whatever form it is given to humanity. This is found in verse 1.

An eighth word is *ordinances*. This term appears in verse 30. It means the Scripture as applied in relations among persons. Scripture is the standard by which God has determined that we should relate in human situations.

The psalmist also uses several other terms that mean something similar. In verse 3 he describes those who follow God's *ways*. In verse 90 the psalmist talks about God's *faithfulness*. Finally, in verse 55 he refers to God's *name*. All of these terms talk about God's way of revealing Himself to us. We come to know the God who created the universe and who loves us through the study of His Word. We do not worship Scripture, but we worship the God who is behind the Scripture. As we come to know the Word of God, we come to know the God who gave us the Scripture.

It would be difficult for us to examine all 176 verses of this psalm. We will look at the first two stanzas, verses 1 through 16. The psalmist enjoyed studying God's Word. Through the Word he came to know the Lord. This is the God who created the vast universe in which we live. He is the God who created us. Because He created us, he knows us through and through. His Word provides light and life. His Word brings stability to our lives in a world that is anything but secure and stable. It is evident from reading this psalm that the writer had a deep love for God's Word. Hopefully, you too will develop your own love for this great treasure from the Lord. You will want to study some of the later stanzas on your own. They provide good insight into the Word of God.

True Happiness—Aleph (Psalm 119:1–8)

Obedience to the Law of the Lord as the path to true happiness is the theme of this stanza. Integrity of life comes from not sinning because the follower of the God is keeping all of the commandments of the Lord. As a child we learn to walk physically by crawling, then struggling to hold on to furniture, until we can stand and finally walk. So as a believer, we must gain knowledge of the Word of God. In so doing, we learn to walk according to God's precepts and follow His will. As we come to know the Word of God, we come to know the author of the Word of God. Learning to follow God is a continuing process.

The psalmist is aware of his failure to live up to all that God desires, but he keeps trying and asking God to help him keep His commandments.

Love the Law of God—Bet (Psalm 119:9–16)

The only way to keep pure from sin is to keep true to the Word of God. First, it is essential to study the Word and know God's commands. Second, we must take heed to the Word of God. We must act on what we understand from the Word of God. This stanza is a prayer to God for help. The psalmist tells the Lord that his intention is to follow God completely. He is afraid that his knowledge of the Word of God is not perfect. His strength to carry out God's will is weak. He does not trust himself and must lean upon God to guide him and keep him from sin.

The psalmist's praise for God in verse 12 is appropriate to his request for further instruction. Notice the verbs in verse 12 and in the succeeding verses. The psalmist asks God to "teach" him. Then the psalmist will "proclaim" God's judgments. Then he will "rejoice" in the Lord's decrees and find them better than riches. Next he will "meditate" upon the precepts of God. This means that he will think about them throughout the day and into the night hours. Finally, he will "delight" or find great pleasure in the statutes of the Lord. We must do as the psalmist to know, understand, and obey God's Word!

READ PSALM 134

Psalm 134 contains only three verses. It is found in book five of the Book of Psalms. Psalm 134 comes at the end of the Songs of *Pilgrimage*. It is called one of the Psalms of *Ascents*. The Psalms of *Ascents* begin with Psalm 120 and continue to 134. The worshippers sang these psalms as they traveled the roads up to Jerusalem and to the Temple. (You may want to look at the material on the Temple that is found in a later section.) These psalms begin, "In my distress I called to the LORD" and end this section with "Now praise the LORD, all you servants of the LORD." The psalm of *ascents* resulted in joyous songs of praise to the Lord Jehovah.

The Call to the Servants of the Lord (Psalm 134:1–2)

This psalm was a song that called upon the Levite singers who served in the Temple day and night. Their work is described in 1 Chronicles 9:23–27. The pilgrims ascended the Temple steps and called for songs of praise to the Lord from these Levitical singers. The Law of Moses also described the work of the Levites in Deuteronomy 10:8. Their work included carrying "the ark of the LORD's covenant, to stand before the LORD to serve Him, and to bless in His name." Thus, the pilgrims were calling upon the Levites to bless the Lord.

The pilgrims called upon these Levites to lift their hands in the holy place. The idea is that the Levites were to raise their hands in prayer. What was the meaning of this? In David's Psalm 24 he wrote, "Who may ascend the mountain of the LORD? Who may stand in His holy place? The one who has clean hands and a pure heart." So the clean hands are a symbol of the pure heart. The hands were consecrated to the service of the Lord.

The Response of the Levites (Psalm 134:3)

In the first two stanzas of this psalm, the worshippers had blessed the Lord. Now the Levites answered the cry of the worshippers on God's behalf. They gave the blessing of the Lord from Numbers 6:24. They added to the blessing that it came "from Zion." They also said that the blessing came from the Lord, who was the "Maker of heaven and earth." In other words, God has the power to bless the worshippers who call upon Him.

READ PSALM 136:1–3

This psalm was known in the writings of the rabbis as the "Great Hallel" or "The Great Psalm of Praise." Along with Psalm 135, it tells of the wonder of God. They were sung at the three important festivals: Passover, Pentecost, and Tabernacles. This psalm was probably written after the Second Temple was built. Such singing about the Second Temple is recorded in Ezra 3:11. Similar singing was done at

the foundation of the first or Solomon's Temple as well (see 2 Chronicles 7:3). The priests and Levites probably sang parts of this great psalm. One group would sing the first line, and the other group would answer with the second line or *refrain*. This repeated second line throughout the psalm forms a *litany*. The psalm tells how God has loved and protected His people down through their history. There are six sets of three verses each and describe great events in the life of Israel. Toward the end of this Psalm, there are two sets of four verses each.

> ### LITANY
> *A litany is in the form of a prayer. In the case of Psalm 136, it is sung as praise to God. Often it is a prayer for forgiveness. The leader voices the prayer to God. The response of the congregation is the same. In Psalm 136, it is "His love is eternal."*

The response of the second line told of God's infinite love. He established His covenant with Abraham and later with the people of Israel at Mount Sinai. Even though the people of Israel were in captivity in Babylon, God protected and preserved them. He brought them back to the Promised Land of Palestine. They rejoiced and sang praises to the great God of the universe for His steadfast love to them. He promised to protect them and love them with an everlasting love. He could be counted on to keep His word, which He has done. This was cause for great rejoicing and praise.

God will do the same for us if we are faithful to Him. He has given us His only Son, Jesus. He promises to be with us and to love us with an everlasting love. He promises to protect, care for, and guide us. But we must follow Him and obey Him to have His blessing.

Psalms—Conclusion

The psalms show us the importance of relating everything in life to God. God provides the strength for us to face the problems that come to us in life. We can find His strength to face these problems through prayer. The psalms are a series of prayers and praise. From the psalms we can learn how to pray and how to receive God's guidance throughout life.

The Song of Solomon— Introduction

The Song of Solomon is a book of eight chapters. It is actually a group of songs that tell about the beauty of love and marriage between a man and a woman. God intended for a man and woman to marry and commit themselves to each other as early as the beginning of creation (see Genesis 2:24). Some have tried to interpret the Song of Solomon as a description of God's love for Israel of the Old Testament or the love of Christ for His church in the New Testament. But the true meaning of the book is the mutual love of a man and a woman. The early part of the book talks about the courtship of a man and woman. Then they marry. The rest of the book describes the growth of love for each other as the years pass by. The poems use word pictures from nature to express the feelings of the two people. The author is identified as King Solomon, and the woman is a Jewish maiden whom Solomon married.

Some have suggested that the Song of Solomon was intended to be sung at the wedding celebration of a couple. In Jewish life the wedding celebration might last as long as a week. The poem would be read as part of that festival. Even today in our churches, a wedding is a service of praise and promise. The man and woman and the wedding guests worship God for the beauty and gift of love that He has given us. The marriage relationship involves all of one's being—physical, emotional, mental, and spiritual union. The man and woman promise to love and honor each other exclusively throughout the rest of their lives. Only then does marriage lead to a life of joy and fulfillment for both the man and woman. Only then does marriage fulfill what God intended to be the most personal and intimate and special relationship on earth.

The beginning of love is described in chapter 2. The marriage of the two lovers takes place in chapter 3 to 5:1. The growth of love in marriage begins in 5:2 and continues through the end of chapter 8.

SELECTED PASSAGES FROM THE SONG OF SOLOMON

READ SONG OF SOLOMON 2:9–10

This is the early stage of love. The woman is describing her love to the daughters of Jerusalem. She compares her beloved to a gazelle. The gazelle is a beautiful animal, known for its beauty, grace, and gentleness. It is from the antelope family. She sees her love looking out through a window. Notice the parallelism in the last two lines of verse 9. There is a silent call for her to go to her love.

READ SONG OF SOLOMON 3:1–2

Apparently the couple is married now. Her husband has gone out, probably on business, and his bride is lonely and looking for him. He is in the town. She goes out to find him and bring him home. Sadly she did not find him and had to return home alone.

READ SONG OF SOLOMON 8:7

This is the key verse in the Song of Solomon. It tells of the beauty of love. The mighty rushing waters of a flooded river cannot stop love. It is very powerful. A man cannot give all of his wealth to find love. Love between a man and a woman is very beautiful and very special. It is as God intended.

Song of Solomon—Conclusion

The Song of Solomon teaches us that God gave us love. God intended that this love is to be exclusively between a man and a woman. God intended for us to enjoy this romantic love exclusively in marriage between a husband and a wife.

Old Testament Wisdom Literature: Proverbs, Ecclesiastes, Job

Wisdom literature is usually written in the form of Hebrew poetry. Life is sometimes very difficult. The wisdom literature was written to help explain how we should live in this world. Wisdom literature guides us to know what is right and how we can treat other persons fairly. Wisdom literature was written by men who were known as *sages*. The *sage* was a wise man. The *sage* served the king and the people along with the prophet and priest. The *sage* would give godly advice. The three books of Proverbs, Ecclesiastes, and Job are this type of wisdom literature. They are the books we will study.

We can learn a lot from these ancient writings. First, they are part of God's Word to us. Second, the advice that they give is still advice that you and I need to live our lives in today's world. The time we spend in studying these books will be well repaid in a godly understanding for our lives today. They will teach us to avoid some of the pitfalls that can hurt us. They will give us guidance to discover things that can help us. Be sure to read the introduction to Proverbs carefully so that you will better understand the Proverbs that follow.

Proverbs—Introduction

Our world is filled today with phrases that will remind us of products that advertisers want us to remember. You will find many of these phrases in television and magazine ads. These phrases are not designed to help you live a better life. They are written to convince you to buy this product. The advertisers want you to believe that this product will make you happy.

Proverbs are ancient sayings that give us truth. They are written to convince you that your life will be better if you obey them. If you follow them, they will lead you through situations where you

SOLOMON

might otherwise stumble. But most important is that they provide us with God's wisdom for living. The Proverbs on the surface seem simply to be wise sayings. But the writer tells us throughout that God is behind the best way to live. He gives us His wisdom in the Proverbs about everyday life. Solomon seems to be telling us that God is not just a God to be worshiped on Sunday. He is just as concerned about what we do each day of the week. The wise person will have to pay attention and follow this godly wisdom. The foolish person will ignore godly wisdom and pay the consequences. The word *proverb* carries the idea that we are comparing something. Proverbs are constructed around an idea, and each is stated in a form that we can all readily see and easily remember.

Recall that Solomon was one of the wisest men who ever lived. When he became king, he prayed to God for wisdom. God answered his prayer.

Solomon gathered more wisdom than all of the sages of his day. We are told in 1 Kings 4:29–34 that he wrote three thousand proverbs and 1,005 songs. Solomon was the primary author of the Book of Proverbs. He wrote the proverbs in chapter 1 through 22:16. He also wrote the proverbs in chapters 25 through 29. But they were added much later by scribes from the court of King Hezekiah.

In addition there were several other authors. Apparently there were a number of other sages who also wrote proverbs. They are identified as "the wise," in 22:17 and 24:23. In addition, Agur wrote some proverbs (see 30:1–33). King Lemuel wrote several proverbs (see 31:1–9). We do not know much about Agur or Lemuel although it is possible that they may have come from Arabia. The remainder of chapter 31, verses 10–31, praises the virtuous wife and seems to have been written by King Lemuel's mother.

What Is a Proverb?

In Colonial America, Benjamin Franklin wrote and published *Poor Richard's Almanac*. For example, Franklin wrote: "Haste makes waste." "A penny saved is a penny earned." "Early to bed and early to rise, makes a man healthy, wealthy, and wise." These sayings have become part of America's heritage. They have become a part of the way we think. The proverb, "God helps them that help themselves," was also taken from *Poor Richard's Almanac*. Many people, even church people, today think wrongly that this proverb was taken from the Bible. In fact, it does not even carry an idea that is biblical. God helps us when we *cannot* help ourselves.

Proverbs in the Bible are remembered because they express an idea that makes sense. They are short and many times witty. They tell of situations that are common to many people. They give us wise advice in responding to situations that confront us each day.

There is some difficulty in interpreting the meaning of some of the proverbs since they do come from the ancient world of the Middle East. In the world of the twenty-first century, some of the ancient ways expressed in the proverbs may seem far removed from our lives. But we will try to overcome this problem as we interpret selected proverbs. Some of the themes in the Book of Proverbs carry throughout the entire book. We will explore these themes and try to make sense of them.

Types of Proverbs

There are three types of proverbs: completing, comparing, and contrasting.

The first type is used in completing a thought. The word *and* connects the first line with the second line. An example is found in Proverbs 1:5a, "A wise man will listen *and* increase his learning."

The second type of proverb is *comparing* two ideas. The word *than* is used to connect the two ideas. An example of this type of proverb may be found in Proverbs 15:17, "Better a meal of vegetables where there is love *than* a fattened calf with hatred."

The third is the *contrasting* proverb. Usually the word *but* contrasts the first thought with the second thought. A good example is found in Proverbs 1:28a, "Then they will call me, *but* I won't answer."

Contents of Proverbs

Proverbs is not divided into books like psalms, but there are some natural divisions in the book. Proverbs 1:1–7 tell the Purpose for the Book of Proverbs. The next section is *A Father's Instruction to his Son*. This section begins in Proverbs 1:8 through chapter 9. Section three is composed of *Brief Sayings*. These may be found in chapter 10 through chapter 29. This is the largest section of the book. Finally, the *Conclusion* of Proverbs may be found in chapters 30 and 31. Chapter 31:10–31 is particularly interesting. There is nothing quite like it elsewhere in Scripture. It describes the characteristics of a good married woman.

Women in Proverbs

The Book of Proverbs was written primarily to boys and young men. Probably the reason for that was that these were persons who would serve in the Israelite monarchy. Such positions were not available for women. The social climate in ancient Israel did not permit women to serve in these positions. Nevertheless, most of the advice, except for counsel directed specifically toward men, would be applicable to girls and young women also. In our study all of the teachings that are included will be applicable to girls and young women also.

In the Book of Proverbs, women are given high respect. The advice that was given to young men came equally from their mothers as well as their fathers. We will study one of these passages (see Proverbs 4:3). Proverbs 1:8 reads, "Listen, my son, to your father's instruction, and don't reject your mother's teaching." Her teaching is equal to that of his father. Proverbs 10:1 tells us that "a wise son brings joy to his father, but a foolish son, heartache to his mother." In addition, chapter 31:10–31 praises a virtuous wife who is a good provider and caregiver for her family. This is one of the best chapters in all of Scripture about the role of a good wife. Although we will not direct our attention to that text in this study, this would be a very important role model for young women to study.

Our culture is quite different from ancient Israel. Good Christian women study in colleges and universities. They serve in the workplace alongside men. They serve in government and most other walks of life. The timeless truths of the Proverbs are just as important for them as they are for young men. As we study the text, do not assume that the advice is directed exclusively toward young men. Apply the insights to girls and young women as well.

Themes of Proverbs

There are several themes to the Book of Proverbs. These themes are scattered throughout the book. Underlying the entire book is the first theme of the *fear of God*. If we fear God, we will live according to God's direction, and life will be much more meaningful and blessed. A second theme has to do with *wisdom and understanding*. What is wisdom, and how do we find it? The writer tells us that finding wisdom relates to the fear of God. The book also describes the foolish person who does not pay attention to wisdom.

A third theme involves *relationships*. These include *parent-child relationships* in the family. A unique section in all of Scripture is the instruction concerning a godly woman. A fourth theme is the *use of words*. Words can either bless or hurt. What we say is important to the way we live. A fifth theme is *life and death*. How we live affects the quality of both. We will explore examples of each theme as we examine this book. There are several other themes, but these are some that are most appropriate for our study.

Selected Themes and Teachings from Proverbs

In the next several pages, we will look at some of the proverbs. We will apply some of the principles set forth in the introduction. Proverbs are mostly written in a Hebrew poetic form. Proverbs have many of the same characteristics of Hebrew poetry that we saw in the Psalms. An example would be the use of *parallelisms*.

THEME: THE FEAR OF THE LORD

READ PROVERBS 1:1–7
Book Title (Proverbs 1:1)

In verse 1 we find the title of the book, Proverbs. The meaning of the title, Proverbs, is that these wise sayings are comparisons. These short messages are intended to make one wise. Even a child can learn from the proverbs. But a person who is older and has more experience can also learn from these wise sayings. Recall that they were written by Solomon, the king of Israel after his father, the godly king David. Verses 1–7 originally formed the introduction to Proverbs, chapters 1–9.

Purposes of the Proverbs (Proverbs 1:2–6)

In these verses Solomon tells us that the purpose of this book is to gain wisdom and be taught. Wisdom is a concrete term with a concrete meaning. Wisdom, along with the teaching, is the means for developing good godly and moral character. Justice, judgment, and equity carry the idea that we must give God all that is due Him in worship, honor, and obedience. It also means to give men the things that are obligations upon us. These would include honesty and sincerity in our lives.

Youth can be impulsive. The writer tells us that the proverbs will help young people develop the wisdom of the ancient sages in their lives today. Only as you listen to wise counsel can you grow in understanding and live as God wants you to live. Shrewdness means cleverness. It is true that shrewdness can be used as a clever trait and lead to sin. The serpent in the Garden of Eden was described as shrewd and caused Eve to sin. But the same trait can be used for good purposes. This entire book is intended to help a young person to be wise rather than foolish.

This book is different from others that we have studied. It appears to leave God out of the instruction. This book says that God is in the midst of everyday life. Decisions in all of life can be affected by my relationship with God. Anyone who listens to this godly instruction will grow in learning and live a better life. He will receive guidance to live aright. By contrast anyone who fails to listen to this godly wisdom is foolish, and his life will show it.

The wisdom of the proverbs will help the wise person to learn the truth. Two types of proverbs are the parable and the riddle. They are useful because they will cause wise person to listen and ponder or think carefully about the truth. Parables have hidden meaning that the hearer must carefully think about in order to discover the meaning. The same is true for the riddle.

Focus of Proverbs (Proverbs 1:7)

"The fear of the LORD is the beginning of knowledge; fools despise wisdom and instruction." This verse is the most important teaching in the Book of Proverbs. This passage carries the first theme of the book, the *fear of God*. The word *fear* does not mean simply "alarm," as it would in common speech. Rather, it means to hold God in *"worshipful awe."* It means *"to obey God out of respect"* for Him. To know God means that we must have a healthy respect for the way God wants us to live. "Fear of the LORD" carries the idea that I respect God so much that I will live according to His commandments and take Him into account in every decision that I make in life. Resolve early in life that you will fear the Lord and follow in God's ways, even when it is not popular to do so. These kinds of fear and reverence are in your best interest, and God will teach you. Your entire life will be better for making such a promise to God now in your youth and keeping that promise throughout life.

READ PROVERBS 2:1–15

In this section Solomon gives the parents' teachings. The teaching is directed to "My son." It was common to address the male young person. But let me repeat that this instruction is just as important for young women as well as young men. The way this instruction is put together follows a common form that was used in the ancient Middle East. This was some of the most important teaching for young people in that day. It is equally important for young people in this day as well.

Quest for Wisdom (Proverbs 2:1–4)

Three "if" clauses are at the beginning of this section. In the first "if" clause of verses 1 and 2, we are told to pay close attention to the teacher. But more than that, we must memorize the instruction given. We need to focus upon the teachings. In the second "if" clause of verse 3, the writer tells his son to desire wisdom as one would plead to God for help in time of trouble. It is as if he said, yearn for this wisdom, strive for it with all your heart, and strongly desire this wisdom. Pray for this wisdom. In the third "if" clause of verse 4, the parent instructs his son to seek after the wisdom that the parent will give as one who lost money and carefully searched for it. Or seek the wisdom as one would hunt for lost treasure.

Understanding from Fear of God (Proverbs 2:5–11)

There are two parts to finding this wisdom. Each part begins with the word *then*. The first part is found in verses 5–8. The writer tells us "then" if you search for this wisdom and desire it more than anything, you will discover it in the "fear of the LORD." Knowing God also results from this diligent search. This is more than just understanding that comes to the mind. It includes our feelings. It comes from a commitment to God. Wisdom is after all a gift from the Lord. See verse 6. God is the great teacher, but His teaching comes to us through the parents' instruction. Right living results in God's protective care. Moral conduct or good character is essential to please God. You will continue through life on the right path.

The second *then* occurs in verse 9 and continues through verse 11. It states that you will understand what is right and live your life that way. You will not live immorally. You will live in a way that pleases God. Pleasing God is really what matters in life. You will treat people with fairness and justice. You will find pleasure in this wisdom. Finally, this wisdom will protect you.

Wisdom Rescues You from Wrong Behavior (Proverbs 2:12–15)

The result of that kind of living will be rescuing you from the way of evil and from evil persons. You will find that you will not be tempted to listen to evil persons who would lead you into sin. You will not be comfortable with their interests or their talk. The image of the path is used again to show that you will not travel down the path of those who would go

down an evil path. You will travel on a path that is pleasing to God and away from doing evil.

READ PROVERBS 6:12–19

The Evil Person (Proverbs 6:12–15)

Watch out for the evil person! He is a troublemaker. He speaks dishonestly. Remember from the Ten Commandments that God charges us not to give false witness. The evil man uses every part of his body to carry out evil—his eyes, feet, hands, and fingers (see verse 13). This was not the purpose for which God gave us these parts of the body. This worthless person tries to corrupt government for his own desires (see verse 14). He deliberately breaks the law and is always trying to stir up trouble. Be sure that God sees what this evil person is doing, and judgment will fall upon this evil person quickly. He will be destroyed!

What God Hates (Proverbs 6:16–19)

Notice how this next set of verses is parallel with the description of the evil person in verses 12–15. They are the seven deadly sins. In the middle ages the church had its own seven deadly sins. They were etched in stone on the frame of the front door of the medieval cathedral. The people could not read, but they could read and understand the sculptures on the cathedral. They were pride, covetousness (wanting another person's possessions), lust (immoral desires), envy (anger) because another person has something you would like), gluttony (overeating), anger, sloth (laziness).

The Hebrew list of the seven deadly sins given here in Proverbs is similar to the list from the medieval church. It begins with "arrogant eyes" or pride. The second sin is dishonesty or not telling the truth. The third sin is anger that leads to harming or killing another person. The fourth is a person who is always trying to bring about evil. He is constantly designing evil. The fifth is one who runs after evil to do things God does not approve. The sixth and seventh sins are more general in describing the character of the evil person. The sixth is one who gives false testimony. Recall the commandment of the Ten Commandments that expressly forbids giving false testimony. The last or seventh sin prohibits one who is a troublemaker.

Both the list of sins from the medieval church and the list in Proverbs 6:16–19 are worth memorizing. You need to learn them to help you not to do them. Both lists represent sins that God hates. Pleasing God is the most important thing in life. Our relationship with Him will continue throughout all eternity. For the young men of Israel, these seven deadly sins were easy to memorize. Each of the first five sins was associated with a part of the body. The last two sins were related to a person's character.

READ PROVERBS 14:26–27

Fear of the Lord (Proverbs 14:26–27)

This pair of verses is not the last time the "fear of the LORD" is mentioned. But these two verses do carry out this theme. Solomon tells us that there is assurance and certainty in the "fear of the LORD." God is a safe shelter for those who love Him. Our attitude needs to be that of one who is ready to learn from the Lord, who is teachable. You can rely on the Lord. He will protect those who trust Him. The Lord turns one from death. The picture in verse 27 is related to an animal that discovers the life-giving water in a fountain to quench the thirst. The opposite is true for the evil person who may easily be caught in the net that will lead to his death. If we are sensitive to God, we can learn from this picture of the animal.

THEME: WISDOM AND UNDERSTANDING

READ PROVERBS 3:1–12

A Parent's Call to His Son (Proverbs 3:1–4)

This set of proverbs begins in verses 1 and 2 with a new call to a son (or daughter, in our day). The call is to listen carefully and follow his parent's instruction. The results will be long life and a good life. This does not mean that the follower will be rich. It does mean that his life will be upright, decent, and wholesome. You will manage your personal life effectively with your physical well-being, your handling of money, and your relationships with others.

The instructions in these verses will lead to good character. They will lead to a life of integrity. Integrity means living an honorable life. Honesty, uprightness, and living a godly life should be among your goals in life. Then your life will be honorable and upright. Similar to Deuteronomy 6:8–9, the writer tells his son to tie these virtues around his neck and write them on his heart. For the Jewish person, the throat held the breath or life, and the heart was the center of his being. Therefore, make good character at the center of the life of the learner. In other words you need to think about this and then live your life in this manner. If you do this, the result will be that you will win favor with God and other persons.

That is sound advice, especially in today's world. The temptations in school, and later in business, are to cheat and be dishonest. The advice of the world is to get all that you can, no matter who it hurts. But that is not God's way. After all is said and done, it is God's evaluation of us that will matter both now and for all eternity.

God Gives Wisdom (Proverbs 3:5–8)

At the root of wisdom is God. Trust in the Lord means to rely completely on God. Rest your entire life on God. The idea is total submission to God. Your support cannot come from your own wisdom. Rely totally upon Him. That means to pray and seek God's counsel in everything you do. If you do that, then God will respond by dircting your path. Remember, we ran across that idea of the path earlier in Proverbs 2. That carries the idea of our way through life.

I am reminded of the painting *The Forest Scene* from the National Gallery of Art in Washington, D.C. by Jacob van Ruisdael. It is located under Dutch painting of the 1600s. It was described in detail in the *Parent/Teacher Handbook, Vol. 2*. You can find it on the Web site of the National Gallery, www.nga.gov/collection. It pictures the tree of life as a healthy tree in the background. The tree of death is pictured as a broken tree in the foreground. To the left is a path with a couple of persons walking into the distance. Overhead the storm clouds are gathering. The picture carries the idea that we walk along the path of life, and the choices we make each day are either choices for life and God or death and evil. Trust in God is the only way to deal with the storms of life that will come into our lives.

This passage does not mean that study in school or research is a waste of time. What it does mean is that all decisions we make need to be submitted to God. It also means that we need to make our decisions about what is right or wrong in relation to God. As verse 7 so clearly states, it is necessary to turn away from evil. This is a personal choice that we must make each day. The results of a life that is not filled with guilt and shame and that looks to God for guidance will be healthy and peaceful (see verse 8).

Honoring the Lord (Proverbs 3:9–12)

We honor God by contributing to the church. We give out of gratitude for His love for us and for His guidance throughout our lives. God has promised to take care of those who honor Him with their possessions (see verses 9–10).

Wisdom expresses itself in verses 11 and 12 by focusing on the teaching and the discipline of the Lord in our lives. We should not make light of either God's instruction or of His discipline in our lives. Discipline does not necessarily mean physical punishment. This discipline concerns God's way of teaching and instructing us in the path we should take. We need to accept this discipline without complaint. It is provided for our good and to the one whom God loves. Sometimes this discipline is hard to accept, but Solomon of the Proverbs tells us that God's instruction and His rebuke are both evidence of His love. God's discipline is similar to the parent's discipline for his son.

Wisdom in this section is not separated from our relationship with the Lord. Wisdom may be passed from one generation to another. God gives us wisdom through our parents as well as through His love and teaching. He also punishes our wrong behavior. Even though the next segment praises wisdom, don't be fooled into thinking that wisdom is something we can gain apart from God. Knowledge is something that can be learned from books, teachers, and other sources. But wisdom is passed on from generation to generation and has its source in God.

READ PROVERBS 3:13–20

A Song to Wisdom (Proverbs 3:13–18)

The song begins with "Happy" and ends in verse 18 with "happy." Wisdom is given the characteristics of a woman. We call this *personification*. Even though this song is in the form of a song, its message teaches us about lady wisdom. The reader is urged to search for wisdom. Along with wisdom, *understanding* carries the idea that wisdom will help you to live a moral and upright life. If you follow this wisdom, it will make you much richer than wealth that comes from having lots of money or precious jewels. There is nothing like this wisdom. It is exceedingly valuable. Nothing that you can think of, like money or precious stones, compares to the value of wisdom (see verses 13–15).

Wisdom promises other blessings as well (see verses 16–18). In her right hand wisdom holds long life for the person who receives this wisdom. In her left hand she holds out riches and honor. Wisdom will make life truly happy, and it leads to fullness of life and to peace. Wisdom leads us to the "tree of life." Recall the painting, *The Forest Scene*, by Jacob van Ruisdael. The "tree of life" symbolizes the wholesome effect, that a man or woman who follows God has in his or her own life and has upon other people.

Wisdom and God's Creation (Proverbs 3:19–20)

Human wisdom has its origin in God's wisdom. God used His wisdom to create the universe. To go against His wisdom is to oppose the very wisdom from which God created the heavens (see verse 19). Nature can be violent, but it can also help us as humans. In verse 20 the writer reminds us of the great destructive power of the rains and floods that destroyed living things at the time of Noah. Solomon also reminds us of the great benefit of the rains that God provided to water our crops. God rules the universe through His wisdom.

READ PROVERBS 8:1–5

The Appeal to Wisdom (Proverbs 8:1–5)

The speaker in this section is probably the parent who tries to show his child that there is a difference between the voice of wisdom and other strange voices. Wisdom is still pictured here as a woman. The parent is telling the child to beware of those others who would call for attention. These others should not be heard (see verse 1). Wisdom alone is worth hearing. Wisdom is not to be found in the temples or in the academic institutions. Wisdom is available in the common places of life. She is not hidden in some secret place but is available to all.

The reference to the "city gate" refers to the place where court judgments were carried out (see verse 3). The elders sat in the "city gate." They gave the benefit of their wisdom in judgments. Wisdom calls out to all who will listen (see verse 4). As verse 5 suggests, wisdom is available to everyone.

READ PROVERBS 15:31–33

Be Teachable (Proverbs 15:31–33)

These three verses are three proverbs on the importance of allowing oneself to be teachable. In verse 31 the writer repeats a topic that we saw earlier. A wise person will listen and respond to correction. By paying heed to the correction, this person is clearly at home among the wise. By contrast in verse 32, anyone who does not listen and respond to the correction does not even care for himself. But the one who listens will develop good common sense.

Verse 33 echoes the focus of the entire Book of Proverbs. Fear of the Lord is the beginning of wisdom (see Proverbs 1:7). The Lord is not only the beginning of wisdom, but He is the path of wisdom. If one is willing to listen to rebukes and correction and exercise humility, then honor will come.

READ PROVERBS 22:1–6

A Good Name (Proverbs 22:1)

This proverb tells us that a good reputation is more important than great wealth (see verse 1). This proverb does not condemn wealth but suggests that the wealth must be gotten honestly. The second line is part of a parallelism. It tells us that silver and gold are not as important as a good report among other persons.

Maintain Wisdom (Proverbs 22:2–5)

God created both rich and poor persons. God does not make anyone rich or poor. Sometimes either condition can come from sinful choices. But God gives His care to both the rich and the poor (see verse 2). In the next verse the careful person looks ahead to predict what results a choice will bring. His careful and thoughtful preparation will result most often in protection. The careless person's approach to life will result in evil consequences. This principle could be applied to salvation. God will bless the person who obeys Him but not the one who carelessly turns aside from following God.

In verse 4, Solomon returns to the major focus of all of the Proverbs. The "fear of the LORD" is the result of having a humble attitude toward God. Not thinking of ourselves more highly than we ought to think and remembering that we have sinned against God are part of humility. The results of that attitude and honor of God are those three things that we want—wealth, honor, and life.

Here in verse 5, the idea of the path comes forward again. As we saw in verse 4, the path of the righteous leads to good results. Now in this proverb the path of the evil ones leads to the undesirable results of thorns and snares. But the righteous one heads down a path that avoids all of these dangers.

Growing Up (Proverbs 22:6)

This proverb counsels the parent to teach the youth aright. The "way" of this verse is related to the "path" that we saw before. The difference between right and wrong should have high priority in teaching the child early in life. When the youth makes his early decisions, those decisions need to be guided by the parent. The parent needs to respect the individuality of the youth but not to allow willful disobedience. The focus is upon the parent's opportunity to make a difference in the life of his child. When he is an adult, he will do what is appropriate. This is especially true for moral decisions of right and wrong.

THEME: RELATIONSHIPS

READ PROVERBS 3:27–35
Wisdom with Other People
(Proverbs 3:27–35)

In this segment Solomon begins by encouraging mercy toward other persons who are in need, from verses 27 and 28. Give comfort, help, instruction, or whatever is needed when the opportunity presents itself. Love is the reason we need to give to others in need. Jesus talked about this in detail. Jesus taught that the Law taught us to love God and to love our neighbor. When one of the teachers of the Law tried to trick Jesus in Luke 10:25–37, he asked Jesus, "Who is my neighbor?" Jesus answered with the parable of the Good Samaritan. The answer states something similar to this verse. Anyone in need is my neighbor.

In verse 29 Solomon turns to the issue of not harming your neighbor. A good example of harming your neighbor is found in the story of Naboth's vineyard (see 1 Kings 21). King Ahab wanted the vineyard of Naboth, which was next to the lands of the king's palace. Naboth refused to sell. Ahab's wife, Jezebel, arranged for Naboth to be falsely accused of cursing God and the king. The false witnesses, whom Jezebel had arranged to have present, had Naboth stoned to death. After his death Ahab and Jezebel

took his property. This is the kind of story that shows what should not be done to one's neighbor.

Verses 31 and 32 tell the reader not to be jealous of the person who gains his wealth by harming other persons. Envy will cause one to desire to follow the ways of the evil person. This is the way that one who opposes God acts. This is not pleasing to God. Recall the importance of what Jesus said, "You shall love your neighbor as yourself." By contrast, God will be the friend or confidential counselor of the one who follows the godly way of love for others.

In verse 33, Solomon tells us that God blesses the home of those who follow Him. He opposes the wicked. It is better to live in a cottage that is blessed by God than to live in a palace which is cursed by God. It is not only the present inhabitant but those who come after that one as well. The righteous are God's friends.

Verse 34 tells us that God opposes those who mock or sneer (see Psalm 1:1). "How happy is the man who does not follow the advice of the wicked, or take the path of sinners, or join a group of mockers!" God does not approve of those who sneer, ridicule, insult, and jeer at things that are godly. This verse is quoted in James 4:6 and 1 Peter 5:5. Jesus stated it a little differently when He said, "Whoever exalts himself will be humbled, and whoever humbles himself will be exalted" (Matthew 23:12).

The last verse in this section provides a fitting conclusion. In the end, things which seem to be wrong will be made right. Those persons who are wise in their life here will be honored. Those who honor fools will be disgraced and dishonored, instead of the honor they desire. God will set things right. It is better to live on God's side and to have His approval than to gain what this world seeks and offers.

READ PROVERBS 11:12–13
The Power of the Tongue (Proverbs 11:12-13)

The person who is mean to his neighbor does not show good common sense (see verse 12). He may attack, fight with, feud with, or abuse his neighbor. Any of those things are wrong. By contrast a person who is wise will keep quiet. We must remember that God is the judge of right and wrong behavior. We are not.

The next proverb almost explains itself. We are not to be talebearers. We are not to tattle on others. Gossip hurts. In school or church there are those other boys and girls that tell tales. They are not people that you want to know any of your secrets because they will tell those secrets to others or say things that will hurt you to others. Telling others about things that should be kept in secret is hurtful. Such a person cannot be trusted.

READ PROVERBS 18:24
False Friends (Proverbs 18:24)

This proverb tells us that making many friends of persons who are not trustworthy will lead to trouble. King Zedekiah (see Jeremiah 38:22) was told by Jeremiah to surrender to the king of Babylon. Instead Zedekiah listened to the false prophets, his counselors, and other false friends. They told him what he wanted to hear, not what he needed to hear. The result was that it turned out just as Jeremiah had said and was a disaster for Zedekiah. In the New Testament Jesus is described as the true friend who sticks closer than a brother. You can have that friend, even today, if you trust in Jesus. He is a friend that sticks closer than a brother.

Good Relations with Others, Especially Employers (Proverbs 27:17–18)

It is good to interact with other persons. They make us sharp. When one wants to sharpen a steel knife, he takes a steel rod and sharpens the knife on the steel on the rod. This is very effective. What is true for steel sharpening steel is also true for people interacting with other persons (see verse 17).

The second proverb in verse 18 tells us that one who tends the fig tree will be able to eat figs. In the same way, one who takes care of and is faithful to his employer will be honored. This is not just intended for the slave and his master but for any employee in relation to his employer. Together with the proverb in verse 17, these proverbs suggest that it is profitable to engage your employer in discussion and care for him. The employee benefits from such behavior.

THEME: PARENT AND CHILD RELATIONSHIPS

READ PROVERBS 4:1–9
A Father's Wisdom (Proverbs 4:1–4)

Solomon tells his sons to listen to their father, who will give them wisdom. When Solomon was a young man, his father David gave him wisdom also. A teacher, government official, or pastor cannot give wisdom like a parent can to his son. The parent has love for his son that makes his responsibility much greater. Love for one's son is at the root for giving this wisdom. This wisdom becomes a heritage of the family, which is passed on from one generation to the next generation. The wisdom must be accepted and acted upon by the son of the next generation to continue as part of this heritage. This wisdom has value now but also for all eternity.

Wisdom and Understanding (Proverbs 4:5–7)

Remember that wisdom was described in a proverb that we studied earlier as better than gold or silver. You must desire this wisdom. It is a gift of God. You must pray to receive it. Then you must live by it. It may have been that the words from his father were from the *Maskil* psalms. You will recall that we discussed them as psalms of instruction or teaching. David taught Solomon in this way. Now Solomon was teaching his sons in the same way. Wisdom is still pictured as a woman of great value. This wisdom cannot be taken away from you. If you love wealth and honor, they may be taken from you. But wisdom will stay with you and help you when you most need it.

Esteem for Wisdom (Proverbs 4:8–9)

In the conclusion to this section, wisdom is honored as a thing to be sought after and retained. If you do this, you will be honored. Wisdom will be a crown of glory. She is worth the effort to retain.

READ PROVERBS 13:24
A Father Who Loves His Son (Proverbs 13:24)

Neither a father nor his son finds discipline an enjoyable experience. But Solomon states here that the father who loves his son will discipline his son effectively. A father who hates his son will leave the son to do as he pleases. The important point of this proverb is that if the parent does not discipline his son through loving correction, then the son has reason to wonder if his parent really loves him. The form of the punishment does not have to be spanking. Other forms of punishment may be equally or even more effective. In the same way God disciplines His children through loving correction because He loves them.

THEME: THE USE OF WORDS

READ PROVERBS 10:18–21
Use Words Carefully (Proverbs 10:18–21)

These proverbs describe right speaking. In verse 18 there are two opposites. Hiding hatred with flattering words is dishonest. This is the person who is angry inside but does not let it show. The other person shows his hatred by telling lies about the person whom he hates.

There are many times when it is better to use few words, verse 19. The more we say, the more we are likely to say something that we will regret later. When people become angry, they tend to talk more. As someone has said, words are like sheep. The more you have, the more likely there will be some that will go astray!

In verse 20 the writer tells us that the use of words betrays the intentions of the heart. A person says what is in his heart. If you are righteous, you will speak in a right way. If you are evil, you will say nothing of real value.

Finally, verse 21 summarizes these proverbs. The righteous will receive enough to help others also. The evil person will not even get enough nourishment for himself. The foolish will say things that come from his evil heart and lead to his own downfall.

READ PROVERBS 12:17–19
Use Words Rightly (Proverbs 12:17–19)

Recall that the ninth commandment prohibits false testimony. The counsel here in verse 17 is to tell the truth. It is clear from the commandment that God takes our honesty very seriously. This verse also implies that our testimony comes from our character. Good character is important. Verse 18 tells us that one who blurts things out without thinking about the words he speaks can hurt another person. It is like the thrust of a sword that strikes and wounds the other person. But the wise person uses his tongue to bring healing, not hurt, to the listener. Verse 19 reminds us that truth is lasting, while lying can undo and lying lasts only a fleeting moment.

READ PROVERBS 16:20–24
Careful Speech (Proverbs 16:20–24)

Verse 20 introduces this set of proverbs on speaking and careful speech. It tells us two things. First, we need to think carefully about our words if we want to be successful. Second, our happiness depends on our complete trust in God. That is related to our careful consideration and use of words.

The proverb in verse 21 reminds us of the connection between the heart and the lips. Out of the heart comes our speech. If the heart is right, the speech will follow. The other half of the proverb describes the effect the speech has on the listeners. They will find it helpful and increase their learning.

Another contrast occurs between the wise and the foolish person. The person with a wise heart is able to give wise counsel to others (see verse 22). The foolish person speaks a lot but does not have much that is worth saying. His instruction is useless. This idea of the wise heart is repeated in verse 23.

Verse 24 picks up the theme of honey or sweetness of words that come from the wise person. These pleasant words are a source of satisfaction and will lead to greater wisdom.

READ PROVERBS 18:20–21

How We Talk to One Another (Proverbs 18:20–21)

These two proverbs go together. In the first one there is a warning against too many words. One is satisfied by expressing himself well. Too many words may lead one astray. The quality of what was said depends upon its appropriateness.

In the second proverb we are reminded that we can give help or hurt by our words. We do have an impact on other people by the words that we speak. Also, we are reminded that one day we will be held accountable for the words that we have spoken.

THEME: THE TWO WAYS

READ PROVERBS 4:10–19

There are two ways in life. The one leads on a path of righteousness to life and happiness. The other leads on a path of sinful pleasure and results in pain and unhappiness. If a son takes the wrong path, he brings shame on himself but also upon his parents. We make choices in life. Our choices will lead us either down a good path or down an evil path.

The Path of Wisdom (Proverbs 4:10–13)

The father again instructs his son to walk on the path of righteousness. Verse 10 picks up the idea from Proverbs 3:2. The promise of long life for following the right path is repeated here. If the son listens to his father, he will stumble neither when he walks nor when he runs. He must not walk on the path of the wicked. That will be hurtful to him. In verse 13 Solomon changes from traveling down the path to holding on to a sacred treasure. He tells the young man to hold on to this treasure and guard it because it is life.

The Path of Evil (Proverbs 4:14–17)

Notice the verbs in verses 14–15. They pick up the pace of this passage. Solomon says, "Don't!" several times. He also says, "Avoid," and "Turn aside" from the way of the evil ones. In verse 16 he tells how these evil people live for committing their crimes. They can't sleep unless they have done wrong. They are excited when they have done something that hurts another person. Wickedness is as much fun for them as the bread they eat. They like to commit violence against persons and enjoy it as they would enjoy their wine.

Contrasting the Two Ways (Proverbs 3:18–19)

For the righteous or those who follow God and His path, the light is faint at first. But it grows brighter as they travel along the path of righteousness. By contrast the way of evil ones is dark. The darkness is heavy around them. It increases and they cannot see, causing them to stumble along their way. We make a conscious choice every day to follow the path of righteousness and light or evil and darkness. Each choice has its consequences—either life or death.

Proverbs—Conclusion

Proverbs provide wisdom for living. The book is composed of many individual proverbs. Some proverbs are grouped together around a theme. They differ from proverbs that we find in *Poor Richard's Almanac* or other books of wise sayings. Solomon makes it clear that wisdom comes from living as God wants us to live. "The fear of the LORD is the beginning of wisdom."

Ecclesiastes—Introduction

Ecclesiastes is another book that was written by Solomon. He identifies himself as a teacher and the son of David, who was king in Jerusalem (1:1). It was written when Solomon was in his later years of life. The author is a person who has lived life to the fullest extent. He has had wealth, pleasure, power, and wisdom. But not one of these things can satisfy him. He tells us that there has to be more to life than what possessions and having fun can provide. His advice was true for the people of his day, but it is just as true for us today. As a young person just starting out on the journey of life, you may want to pay particular attention to the advice of Solomon. You can avoid a lot of frustration and problems in life by listening to the wisdom of his instruction.

Ecclesiastes shares common ideas with the other books of wisdom writings. It is a collection of teachings from the writer. These teachings were probably organized by topics in the later years of his life. The book is not like Proverbs, which contains sayings to help the reader live a better life. This book is more like the Book of Job (see the section on Job). Ecclesiastes forces the reader to think about the big issues of life. What is the reason we are here on earth anyway?

Ecclesiastes is different from any other book in the Bible. It is written from the point of view of a person who only knows the world. The conclusion of the writer is that nothing about life makes any sense by itself. Ecclesiastes is not a story, like Job, about how to find meaning in life. Ecclesiastes uses different types of literary forms to carry its message. There are instructions, poetry, proverbs, and even short meditations. The book tries to answer the question, What is the meaning of life on earth or 'under the sun'? That phrase "under the sun" appears twenty-seven times in the book. The wisdom presented in Ecclesiastes is just as meaningful and true today as it was in the time of its author. The wisdom presented in this book is timeless. Jews read the Book of Ecclesiastes during the celebration of the Feast of Tabernacles. The purpose is to remind us that we do not find security in possessions. Our security and shelter are in God and Him alone.

When you first read the Book of Ecclesiastes, it appears to be gloomy about life. But that is a false impression. Solomon tells us to enjoy life. But when we do, we must remember to balance that enjoyment with the fact that God will judge us one day (see Ecclesiastes 2:24–26). Recall that Solomon was known for his wisdom. Unfortunately, Solomon did not always follow his own wisdom. Solomon enjoyed all that life could offer. Sometimes Solomon did not please God. He allowed his wives to bring their foreign gods into Israel. Many of the people of Israel began to worship these foreign gods, and this brought God's judgment upon Israel. The people of Israel did not do all that God had commanded. So it is not surprising that Solomon in his later years would come to the conclusion that when we enjoy life, we must also balance that pleasure against God's judgment. Only when we are sensitive to God's judgment in our lives can we avoid His displeasure and judgment.

SELECTED PASSAGES FROM ECCLESIASTES

READ ECCLESIASTES 1:1–2— OPENING THEME OF ECCLESIASTES

In these verses the writer identifies himself as Solomon, son of David. He also tells us that he is "the Teacher." In this case Solomon does not want us to see him as the king. A king makes laws and orders people to do certain things and not to do others. Rather, Solomon wants to teach us wisdom by giving us advice and something to think about.

His opening lines in verse 2 tell us what the book is about. "Everything is meaningless." Nothing has any lasting value. Everything is like a vapor. It is here one moment and gone the next. In later chapters he describes a life lived in pleasure. He describes science. He describes learning. He describes owning lots of possessions. Solomon has done all of this. But none of this has any lasting value. Solomon has learned all this from his own personal experience. At the end of the book, he returns to this same saying but then explains what does have value.

READ ECCLESIASTES 7:1—
PROVERB ON REPUTATION

This is a strange proverb when it is connected with one's death. Solomon seems to be saying that one's reputation is not complete until the day one dies. At that point, in death, one's good name is established. Put another way, every day we live provides an opportunity to ruin one's reputation. Fine perfume may relate to the sweet-smelling spices that are used for burial. There also seems to be a contrast between the happiness of a birthday party and the sadness of a funeral. So we need to face death as part of life. It relates to his opening statement that all is absolute futility!

READ ECCLESIASTES 12:13–14—
THE TEACHER'S CONCLUSION

When all is said and done, only one meaning counts in life: a person must fear God and keep His commandments. Only in worshipful submission to God is there any meaning in life. Pleasure, wealth, security, and even life itself are fleeting, like a vapor. The only thing that lasts is our relationship with God. Recall the early chapters of Genesis. People tried all of these things in opposing God. The Tower of Babel was an example.

It would seem that all that the Teacher has been saying would lead to despair. But for Solomon it leads to true spiritual piety. The Teacher cannot control the future. He can only leave the future to God, who controls everything. Even today we cannot control life. We live in a world that is changing constantly. Only trust in God is meaningful. We need to see ourselves as persons who live in humble obedience to a God who deeply cares about each of us. As the Bible states elsewhere, the just shall live by faith. Life then becomes more than a fleeting vapor. It takes on meaning, when lived in relation to the eternal God. The eternal God wants the best for us, and we can rest assured that our lives will have meaning if we completely trust Him.

Job—Introduction

The Book of Job is another book of wisdom literature. It is different from Proverbs or Ecclesiastes. When the book opens, we discover a man who is very wealthy. He owned seven thousand sheep, three thousand camels, five hundred yoke of oxen, and five hundred donkeys. Job had seven sons and three daughters. Job was a man who loved and worshipped God. His sons and daughters would hold large banquets where they would eat and drink together. It was Job's regular practice in the mornings to sacrifice to God on behalf of his children in case they had sinned against God. The book tells us that he lived in the land of Uz and was one of the most powerful men in the East. Beyond that we know very little about when he lived or even where the land of Uz was located. Since his wealth was measured in how many animals he owned, we can believe that he probably lived during a time that was similar to the time of Abraham.

But Job is the story of a man who lived through terrible suffering. We are told in chapter 1 that very quickly Job lost all of his animals, and his children were killed in a storm. We are told that Job did not know why all of these tragic events happened in his life. We learn from the first two chapters of the book that God was talking with Satan. In that conversation Satan told God that Job only served the Lord because God had provided Job with wealth, a large family, happiness, and many good things. God allowed Satan to take all of these good things away from Job. God told Satan that he could not take the life of Job. Satan did not believe that Job would continue to love and trust God if all these things were removed. We are told that Job suffered the loss of everything. But Job refused to blame God for his situation.

In the second chapter Satan again is talking with God. This time Satan told God that if God would remove the health of his servant Job, he would then turn away from God. Again God gave Satan

JOB

permission to strike Job with sores all over his body. God told Satan again that he was not allowed to take Job's life. Job was now miserable! He lost his fortune. He lost his children. He now lost his health. His wife told Job to curse God and let God kill him. Job answered her by telling her that God had given him the good things and now God had taken them away. That was God's choice. Job refused to sin and listen to his wife. In God's sight, Job was still a good man who loved God and refused to speak evil of the Lord.

At this point three of his friends came to comfort him. They were Eliphaz, Bildad, and Zophar. At first they came and sat with Job for a week in silence. They realized the terrible suffering that he was going through. Finally Job told his friends about all the tragedies that had struck him. From then on, Job's friends told him that he was suffering because he had sinned against God. Their message to him was that suffering comes from sin. If he had not sinned, he would not have received God's anger. Job is now suffering more since they are also accusing him of sinning against God. Throughout the major part of the book, the three friends debate with Job about his sin against God. Job declares his innocence. If that is not enough, a very young man, Elihu, comes to talk with Job. He

also believes that the suffering of Job is a result of Job's sin. He adds to Job's misery. This discussion continues through chapter 37.

Finally, God spoke to Job out of the whirlwind in chapters 38 to 41. God never answered the questions that Job raised about why he was suffering. But neither was God angry with his servant Job. God asked Job a series of questions. God controls the entire universe. God has the right to bring suffering upon a man if He chooses. God condemned Job's three friends for their bad advice and told them to ask Job to pray for their forgiveness. Job prayed for them, and they gave Job silver and gold. In the end God restored to Job twice as much wealth as he had in the beginning. He had seven new sons and three beautiful daughters. As for Job, God allowed him to live on for 140 years and he was able to see his grandchildren and great-grandchildren.

There are some times when sin does cause suffering. Recall that there were times when the people of Israel sinned against God. They suffered for their sins. The wandering in the wilderness for forty years was one of those times. We can experience times when that can be a problem for us, as well. We need to make sure that our actions have not caused us to suffer for doing wrong. If we are at fault, we need to ask for God's forgiveness.

But, in the ancient world and in ours, many people believed that God blessed persons who followed Him. They also believed that God only punished people who displeased Him. That explains why Job's friends were telling him that he had sinned against God. His punishment was deserved. But Job maintained his innocence. Job even questioned whether God was fair to him. In the middle of all of his suffering, God finally spoke to Job and assured him that sin was not the reason for Job's suffering. There are times when we may not understand why God allows us to suffer either. We must take comfort in the fact that God loves us and He has His reasons which are beyond our understanding.

SELECTED PASSAGE FROM JOB

READ JOB 42:5–6—SEEING GOD

After God spoke to Job and revealed Himself to him, Job not only heard God, but he also saw Him. At that point Job had the same reaction that Isaiah had when he saw God in the Temple (see Isaiah 6:5a), "Woe is me, for I am ruined." Job saw his own sinfulness in the face of God Almighty. He repented in dust and ashes. He saw that he was unworthy in the questioning that he directed toward God. There was no comfort from his three friends. In meeting God, Job found that he was changed. Job came to have a deepened understanding of who God was and is. When God chooses to reveal Himself, all the arguments are of no value. A fresh vision of who God is can change our lives as well.

Lamentations—Introduction

To lament is to express grief at death. It may be a low mournful cry. This describes the short book of poetry that follows the Book of Jeremiah. Lamentations is a cry of grief over the death of the great city of Jerusalem when Nebuchadnezzar destroyed the city in 586 BC. The book was probably written by the prophet Jeremiah. Jeremiah was living in the city when it fell. He was feeling the pain of the inhabitants of Jerusalem who were left in the city. The Babylonians took the healthy men and women in chains in Exile to Babylon. Only the weak, unhealthy, and elderly persons were left behind in the city. Children, many of which had become orphans, were left. They were crying out for their parents. All the people of the city were hungry, and there was very little food. It was a terrible scene.

Thus, Lamentations is a sad funeral song about the destruction of the great capital of Judah. Solomon's Temple had been destroyed, and all of the beautiful golden items in the Temple were taken by the Babylonians. The people who were left believed that God had left them. They believed that God no longer cared for them. The first four chapters are acrostic poems. Recall that an acrostic begins each stanza with a letter of the Hebrew alphabet. The fifth chapter is a prayer that God will restore Jerusalem.

The people of Judah had not listened to the prophets. They continued to worship idols. They continued to take advantage of one another. They continued to sin against God. They even killed or imprisoned the true prophets of God while listening to false prophets who said that these terrible things would not happen. But God still loved His people, and His punishment would not last forever. Jeremiah looked forward to a better day when the city would be restored and worship of the Lord Jehovah would again take place in the Temple. In the meantime, the writer of this book felt compassion and sadness for the people and their suffering.

Today in Jerusalem all that is left of the Temple is the Wailing Wall. It stands as a sad monument to the greatness that once was the Temple. For at least the last six hundred years, Jews have gathered on the Friday evenings on the eve of Sabbath. They read the Book of Lamentations and mourn over the greatness that once was the Temple to the Lord Jehovah.

SELECTED PASSAGE FROM LAMENTATIONS

READ LAMENTATIONS 3:22–24— GOD'S PROTECTION

In the midst of the pain and suffering, the prophet looks to God for protection and strength. He remembers that the Lord's mercy never ends and the people will be spared. God's love never fails! Jehovah is the one I adore. He is my treasure. As a result I can place my hope and trust completely in Him. Even though our circumstances may not be quite so desperate, we can put our trust and confidence in God, just as Jeremiah and the people of Jerusalem did in that day.

Review of the New Testament

Four hundred years had passed since the end of the Old Testament. (That is two times the number of years, since George Washington was president of the United States.) The world was an evil place. People practiced sin. God's plan for the peoples of the earth was not carried out. Even among the Jewish nation, God's chosen people, there was not much hope. God had not spoken to His people since the last of His prophets, Malachi. The Romans were cruel to their conquered peoples, like the Jews. Many Jewish people suffered and died at the hands of these cruel conquerors. Some Jewish groups, like the Essenes, hid themselves away from the evils of the world and the Romans in communities in the desert. They prayed and waited in hope for the coming of the Messiah. The situation was very gloomy! Remember from the end of the Review of the Old Testament, we left with a question. The question was, What could God do that would change this situation forever and bring blessing and hope to fallen humanity?

The Coming of the Messiah
—The Gospels—
Matthew, Mark, Luke, John

After the years of silence, John the Baptist was born as the last of the prophets. He came before Jesus to prepare the way for the coming of the kingdom of God. And then it happened in the small town of Bethlehem when Mary gave birth to Jesus that God responded by changing the situation that would bring hope and blessing to fallen humanity. He did not have an earthly father. The Holy Spirit overshadowed Mary. Jesus shared both His heavenly nature from the Holy Spirit and His human nature from Mary. Jesus was born as the Son of God. Jesus' birth forever changed the course of human history. By becoming a man, God could now understand the problems that we

JESUS PREACHING TO THE MULTITUDE

face in life. He could understand what it means to get sick. He faced sorrow and even death of His friends. He felt the struggles that we have with temptation. Unlike Adam and Eve, Jesus did not sin. Throughout all of His life, Jesus remained true to His purpose to obey God. He demonstrated to us how much God loves us. God wants us to live as Jesus lived in obedience to Him.

The Gospel writers, Matthew, Mark, Luke, and John, do not provide us with a complete biography of the life of Jesus. But we can try to reconstruct the life of Jesus from their accounts. His life can be divided into three parts: Childhood, Public Ministry, and His Sacrifice.

JESUS BIRTH AND CHILDHOOD
MATTHEW 1–2; LUKE 1–2;
JOHN 1:1–18

The birth of Jesus was a miracle. Recall the beautiful Christmas story. Mary was visited by the Angel Gabriel. God had called upon her to bear His only Son, Jesus. Mary was engaged to be married to Joseph. Through the Holy Spirit she

Life of Jesus									
Childhood	Jesus' Public Ministry							Sacrifice	
	Unknown		Fame		Conflict				
					Later Galilean Ministry	Judean Ministry	Perean Ministry		
	Early Life	Early Ministry	Galilean Ministry					Triumphal Entry	Resurrection
Birth - 4 B.C.	John baptizes Jesus	Jesus Cleanses Temple	Jesus Returns to Galilee	Jesus calls the 12 Disciples		Jesus conflicts with Pharisees and Sadducees		Death	Ascension
Jesus in the Temple - 12 years old	Temptation of Jesus	Judean Ministry		Jesus teaches the Disciples					
	First Year		Second Year		Third Year				

became the mother of the Messiah. Mary and Joseph had to travel to the place from which Joseph's family of David came. They went down from Nazareth to Bethlehem. Since all persons had to return to their family home, there was no room in the inn. Mary and Joseph had to settle for a stable. So Jesus was born in the stable and placed in the manger.

The angels announced the birth of Jesus to the shepherds in the fields of Bethlehem. The angels told the shepherds, "Glory to God in the highest heaven, and peace on earth to people He favors!" The angels brought good news to a world that was sinful and with little hope. These were probably not ordinary shepherds but Levites who raised sheep for the Temple sacrifices. They understood the importance of the message of the angels. They went to Bethlehem and witnessed the birth of Jesus. They went about telling all the people they met about the miracle in Bethlehem. After eight days Jesus was presented in the Temple. The aged Simeon and Anna blessed Jesus and Mary.

Some time later Magi came from the East. They saw the star and followed it to Jerusalem. There they inquired of Herod where the King of the Jews was to be born. The priests told Herod that He would be born in Bethlehem. Herod instructed the Magi to bring word to him about the King of the Jews back to him.

The Magi went to Bethlehem, and there they gave gifts of gold, frankincense, and myrrh. They were expensive and very precious. The gold represented the royalty of Jesus. Frankincense was used in worship. It reminds us that Jesus became our High Priest. Finally, myrrh came from a rare plant that was used for medicine, perfume, and embalming. It reminds us of the death and burial of Jesus. Being warned by an angel not to return to Herod, they went home another way.

An angel of the Lord appeared to Joseph in a dream and told him to take Mary and Jesus to Egypt for protection. Joseph arose and took his family to Egypt. Meanwhile, Herod was furious that the Magi did not return to him. He ordered his soldiers to kill all of the male babies in Bethlehem who were two years and under. Mary, Joseph, and Jesus stayed in Egypt until after Herod was dead. Then they returned to Nazareth, where Jesus grew up.

There is only one incident recorded about his childhood. At age twelve Jesus went to Jerusalem with His parents for the Passover. There He talked with the teachers in the Temple. They were all astonished at the answers He gave. His parents had to return to Jerusalem to find Jesus and bring Him home. The Gospels do not give us any further details of these years of Jesus' life. Only Luke tells us, "And Jesus increased in wisdom and stature, and in favor with God and with people" (Luke 2:52).

THE MINISTRY OF JOHN THE BAPTIST

John the Baptist was a cousin of Jesus. He came as the one to prepare the way for the coming of Jesus. In his final warning to the people of Israel, Malachi had written four hundred years before: "Look, I am going to send you Elijah the prophet before the great and awesome Day of the LORD comes. And he will turn the hearts of fathers to [their] children and the hearts of children to their fathers" (Malachi 4:5–6).

John came as the one who was like Elijah (see Luke 1:17, 76). His appearance was like that of Elijah. Compare 2 Kings 1:8 with Mark 1:6. John was the first true prophet to come since Malachi. The people of Judea were excited. They came out to hear John preach that they must repent of their sins. They stayed and were baptized in the River Jordan, as a symbol of their repentance. Many hundreds of persons came to John. John recognized that he was only the one who prepared the way for someone greater. John told the people that the One who would follow him would not baptize with water but with the Holy Spirit (see Matthew 3:11).

JESUS' PUBLIC MINISTRY
MATTHEW 3–20; MARK 1–10;
LUKE 3–19:27; JOHN 1–11

Jesus came to John at the River Jordan to be baptized. John recognized Jesus. At first, John did not want to baptize Jesus. But Jesus insisted that this was the right thing for John to do. When Jesus came up out of the water, the Holy Spirit alighted on Him in the form of a dove. A voice from heaven said, "This is My beloved Son. I take delight in Him!" Notice that the first phrase comes from Psalm 2:7. This is a psalm that describes the coming Messiah. The second phrase comes from Isaiah 42:1. This is a passage about the Suffering Servant. To a Jewish person, who knew the Scripture, this would have been very significant.

Immediately, Jesus was driven into the wilderness. There he experienced a period of forty days of fasting. During that time Jesus was tempted by the devil. In the first temptation the devil told Jesus to turn the stones into bread. Jesus answered with a quotation from Deuteronomy 8:3 that man should not live by bread alone. Then the devil took Jesus to the top of the temple mount and told Him to throw Himself off and let the angels protect him. Jesus again quoted from Scripture (see Deuteronomy 8:3) that the devil should not tempt the Lord God. Finally, the devil took Jesus to a high mountain. The devil told Jesus that if He would bow and worship the devil, he would receive all the kingdoms of the earth from the devil. Jesus told the devil to go away, and Jesus quoted Deuteronomy 6:13, that only God was to be worshipped. At that the devil left Jesus for a while.

> ### DEVIL
> *The devil is a created being. The Old Testament tells us that the devil or Satan was once an angel of light. He rebelled against God and along with fallen angels was cast out of heaven. The fallen angels became demons. The devil is very powerful but not more powerful than God. He does everything he can to tempt and hurt believers. Many evil people today allow themselves to be controlled by him. Our best defense against the devil and his demons is prayer to God for protection. Eventually, the devil and his demons will be defeated, and they will go to eternal punishment.*

THE YEARS OF JESUS' MINISTRY

After these events Jesus ministered for about the next three and one half years. We might name the first year the one in which Jesus was unknown. In His second year of ministry, Jesus became very popular. Jesus taught and performed miracles during this year. We will call this year His year of fame. In the third year of Jesus' ministry,

Year in which Jesus was UNKNOWN—c. AD 26
Baptism of Jesus by John in the River Jordan (Mark 1:1–11)
Temptation of Jesus by the devil after forty days of fasting (Matthew 4:1–11)
First miracle at the wedding of Cana, where Jesus turned the water to wine (John 2:1–11)
Jesus cleansed the Temple in Jerusalem of money changers (John 2:13–24)
Jesus witnessed to Nicodemus and the Samaritan woman (John 3:1–4:42)
Jesus returned to Galilee. He was rejected by his hometown people in Nazareth (Luke 4:14–30)
Year of Jesus' FAME—c. AD 27–28
Jesus lived in Capernaum (Matthew 4:13–17)
Calling of the twelve disciples and ordaining them (Matthew 4:18–22 and Luke 3:13–19)
Sermon on the Mount (Matthew 5–7)
Miracles Performed (Matthew 8–9 and Luke 5–7)
Feeding of the five thousand (Matthew 14:13–21)
Final Year of CONFLICT—c. AD 29–30
Ministry in Tyre and Sidon (Matthew 15:21–28)
Jesus goes to Jerusalem and the Jewish Feasts (John 7:2–10:42)
The Raising of Lazarus and the faith of Mary and Martha (John 11:1–46)
The plot of the religious leaders to kill Jesus (John 11:47–57)
The ministry in Perea (across the Jordan from Jerusalem) (Mark 10)
The Final Week—c. AD 30

he lost some of His popularity. The people wanted Him to free Israel from the Romans. When Jesus did not do that, the people did not like Him as much. He also came into conflict with the religious leaders—the Pharisees, the Sadducees, and many members of the Sanhedrin. This may be known as Jesus' year of conflict. Above is a chart of a few selected events from Jesus' ministry during these years of teaching, preaching, and healing.

The places where Jesus visited may be found on the map of His travels. Most of His life was spent in Palestine. To protect Jesus from Herod, Mary and Joseph took Jesus to Egypt. Later in His ministry, Jesus traveled to Caesarea Philippi and to Tyre and Sidon.

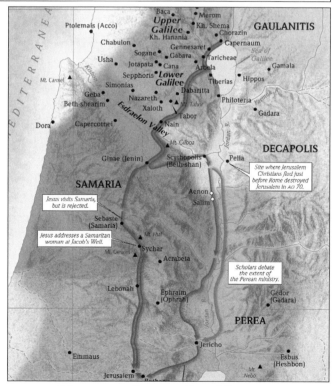

Map of the Land of Jesus' Journeys

Jesus Performed Miracles, Taught about the Kingdom of God, and Chose Twelve to Preach the Gospel

The ministry of Jesus included miracles that He performed, teaching about the kingdom of God and preparing the disciples for His sacrifice on the cross. Jesus taught and demonstrated what God is like. He was gentle, kind, and loving. Jesus had power, but He never used or abused His power for Himself. He used His power for the good of others and to carry out the will of His heavenly Father. Let us look at several miracles Jesus performed. Each of these miracles represents a different part of His power.

In His first miracle, Jesus attended a wedding. When the host ran out of wine for his guests, Jesus turned water into wine. Jesus showed His power over His creation (see John 2:1–11). Jesus had power

MIRACLE

A miracle is an event in human life that shows the power of God. A miracle cannot be explained by natural causes. Jesus performed a number of miracles in His ministry. He demonstrated His power over all of life. Jesus performed miracles to help His followers understand who He was.

over disease. He performed many healings of persons who were sick and diseased. Jesus forgave the sins of the man who was paralyzed, and then He healed him of his paralysis (see Mark 2:1–12). Jesus demonstrated that He had power over the nature. Remember that He fed over five thousand persons with only five loaves and two fishes (see Matthew 14:13–21). In another situation He calmed the storm on the Sea of Galilee, and another time Jesus walked

DISCIPLE	MAJOR EVENTS
Peter	Peter was a fisherman when Jesus called him. He often spoke for the disciples. He was one of the three closest to Jesus. He denied Jesus at the crucifixion. Later he became a leader of the church. He wrote the letters 1 and 2 Peter.
Andrew	Andrew was a fisherman. He followed John the Baptist and accepted what John said about Jesus. He led his brother Peter to Jesus.
James, Son of Zebedee	James was a fisherman, when Jesus called him. His brother was John. He was one of the three closest to Jesus. He was the first of the disciples to be martyred.
John	John was a fisherman. He was the third of the three closest to Jesus. After the resurrection he was a leader in the Jerusalem church. He cared for Mary after Jesus was crucified. He became the bishop of Ephesus. John wrote the Gospel of John; 1, 2, 3 John; and Revelation.
Philip	He told Nathaniel about Jesus. He wondered about the miracle of the feeding of the five thousand. Along with Andrew, he told Jesus the Greeks wanted to see Him.
Nathaniel	At first Nathaniel could not believe that anything good could come from Nazareth, but he accepted Jesus as the Son of God and King of Israel.
Thomas	He encouraged the disciples to go to Bethany with Jesus, even if it meant they would die. Later he had trouble with the resurrection, until Jesus showed Himself to Thomas.
Matthew	He left his profitable work as tax collector to follow Jesus. He invited Jesus to a party with his friends. He wrote the Gospel of Matthew.
James, Son of Alphaeus	Not much is known about this disciple.
Thaddeus or Judas, Son of James	He asked why Jesus would show who He was to His disciples and not to the rest of the world. Not much is known about Thaddeus.
Simon, The Zealot	Simon was one of the Jewish patriots who carried daggers against the Romans. Not much else is known about Simon.
Judas Iscariot	Judas betrayed Jesus.
[Matthias]	He replaced Judas Iscariot after Jesus' resurrection. (Acts 1:26)

on the water (see Matthew 14:22–36). Jesus' most important miracle was raising Lazarus from the dead. Jesus demonstrated His power over death (see John 11:38–44). After this miracle the chief priests wanted to kill Jesus. They also wanted to kill Lazarus along with Jesus (see John 12:9–11).

The kingdom of God was the theme of Jesus' teaching and preaching. Right after the temptation experience, Jesus began to preach about the coming of the kingdom of God (see Mark 1:14–15). The kingdom of God is not so much a place, but a situation in which God is the ruler. The Sermon on the Mount was His greatest proclamation of the qualities needed to be part of the kingdom of God. It is found in Matthew 5–7. In the Lord's Prayer, found in Matthew 6:9–13, Jesus taught His disciples how to pray. Jesus told His followers to ask God to bring His rule to take place in the world. He is the only one who can control this world. Jesus taught that we also ask God to meet the needs of His followers.

This is true because God loves His people and wants to meet their needs. Through His use of parables, Jesus taught about the kingdom of God. The pearl of great price is an example of a parable that shows the extreme value of the kingdom of God (see Matthew 13:45–46).

> ### PARABLE
> *A parable, as told by Jesus, is a simple story that gives insight into life, especially life in the kingdom of God. It is a comparison of something common to the people with a truth about the kingdom.*

Jesus chose twelve men as His disciples (see Matthew 1:2–4 and Mark 3:16–19). He ordained them to His service as apostles (see Luke 6:13–16 and Acts 1:13–14). To replace Judas Iscariot, after he betrayed Jesus, the apostles chose Matthias (see Acts 1:26). Each of the apostles, except John, gave his life for the cause of Christ (see the chart on the previous page).

EVENTS OF HOLY WEEK

DAY	EVENTS
	Triumphal Entry into Jerusalem
Sunday	*Matthew 21:1–11; Mark 11:1–11; Luke 19:29–44; John 12:12–19*
	Entry into Jerusalem on a donkey with the people rejoicing
Monday	*Matthew 21:12–19; Mark 11:12–19; Luke 19:45–48*
	Jesus condemned the fig tree for no fruit; cleansed the Temple; healed in the Temple
Tuesday	*Matthew 21:19–24; Mark 11:20–14:9; Luke 20–21; John12:20–50*
	Fig tree withered; Jesus came into conflict with the Scribes and Pharisees; watched the widow give her mite; discussed the end of time; predicted His death; anointed by Mary with expensive perfumes
Wednesday	No description of events
Thursday	*Matthew 26:17–27:10; Mark 14–15:1; Luke 22:7–71; John 13–18:18*
	Passover meal; upper room teaching; teaching in the Garden of Gethsemene; prayer in the Garden; high priestly prayer; betrayed by Judas; Jewish trials; death of Judas
	Crucifixion
Friday	*Matthew 27:11–60; Mark 15:1–46; Luke 23:1–54; John 18:28–19:42*
	Roman trials before Pilate and Herod; mocking of the soldiers; carrying the cross; crucifixion as "King of the Jews"; burial by Joseph of Arimathea and Nicodemus
Saturday	*Matthew 27:61–66; Mark 15:47; Luke 23:55–56*
	The guard is placed at the tomb
	Resurrection
Sunday	*Matthew 28:1–15; Mark 16:1–14; Luke 24:1–35; John 20:1–25*
	The women visit the tomb and see the angel; Jesus appears to Mary Magdalene; Jesus appears to the other women; guards report to the priests; Jesus appears to the disciples on the road to Emmaus; Jesus appeared to Peter; Jesus appeared to the other apostles

HOLY WEEK—JESUS' CRUCIFIXION AND RESURRECTION
MATTHEW 21–28; MARK 11–16; LUKE 19:28–24; JOHN 12–21

The events of Holy Week are listed on the previous page. This is the week that led to Jesus' crucifixion and resurrection.

Jesus continued to make appearances to His followers until His ascension into Heaven. The disciples gathered forty days after the resurrection at a mountain in Galilee. There Jesus bid the disciples farewell. He promised to send the Holy Spirit to live within them. Then He ascended into the cloud, like the cloud that stood over the Tabernacle in the Wilderness in the Old Testament.

Why Did Jesus Have to Die?

Do you remember our question about what God could do for fallen humanity? God answered that question forever in the life, death, and resurrection of Jesus! God became man in the person of Jesus Christ. He took upon Himself all the sins for the entire world—your sins and mine. The writer to the Hebrews makes clear that "without the shedding of blood there is no forgiveness." Animal sacrifices in the Old Testament were only temporary. But Jesus lived a perfect and sinless life on earth. He was the only one who could be a perfect sacrifice for us. Therefore, to pay the penalty for sin, once and for all time, Jesus had to die. All God asks us to do is to recognize that we cannot please God because we sin. He asks us to accept the free gift of forgiveness that He offers us through Jesus' death on the cross. Jesus became our substitute and died for us. When we accept His sacrifice on the cross, we become part of the kingdom of God and want Him to rule in our lives. We want to please God instead of ourselves.

THE COMING OF THE HOLY SPIRIT AT PENTECOST
ACTS 2–9

The story does not end, even with the resurrection of Jesus. At the Feast of Pentecost, the disciples were gathered in an upper room praying. Suddenly, the Holy Spirit came upon the assembled disciples. Flames of fire stood above their heads. They began to speak in many different languages. People from other countries, who had come to Jerusalem for the Feast, discovered that the disciples spoke in their native languages. Peter addressed the people and more than three thousand persons were added to the church that day alone. Many of the Jewish leaders tried to stop the church from growing by persecuting the disciples. The leaders even killed Stephen for his faith. They stoned him to death.

One of those who stood by and approved of the stoning of Stephen was Saul. He was a devout Pharisee. He wanted to stop the church. Saul was traveling on the road to Damascus to bring Christians back to Jerusalem in chains. On the road Jesus appeared to Saul. Saul, also called Paul, became a Christian believer. Jesus called Paul to be His apostle. From that point on, Paul began to preach about Christ. Paul went into the Arabian desert, and there the Holy Spirit taught him about Christ.

CONVERSION OF SAUL

Meanwhile Peter had an experience that changed his life and the life of the church. Cornelius, a Roman centurion and one who feared God, was directed by the Holy Spirit to send for

Peter to come and preach to him and his household. Cornelius sent two of his men to Joppa, where Peter was staying. At the same time, Peter had a dream about unclean animals. He was told to take them and eat of them. It happened three times. While Peter was still trying to understand what the vision meant, the men arrived from Cornelius. Peter went with them and found that these were people that loved the Lord. He preached to them and they also received the Holy Spirit. Peter had to return to the church in Jerusalem and tell what happened. Gentiles were now coming to Christ and receiving the Holy Spirit also.

THE CHURCH EXTENDS TO THE GENTILES ACTS 10–28

The church now grew rapidly. Many Gentiles accepted Christ and were filled with the Holy Spirit. Persecution arose in Jerusalem. The church was scattered. The church in Antioch now became the center for mission and outreach. Paul had been called by God to become the missionary to the Gentiles. A summary of his life may be found in the chart below.

LIFE OF THE APOSTLE PAUL

EVENTS	DATE
Birth of Paul	The Time of Jesus' Birth
Conversion	AD 33
First Missionary Journey	47–48
Wrote his letter to the Galatians between journeys 1 and 2	48
Council at Jerusalem	49
Second Missionary Journey	49–52
Wrote his letters to the Thessalonians—1 and 2 Thessalonians on second journey	52 52–56
Third Missionary Journey	55
Wrote letters to Corinthians—1 and 2 Corinthians on third journey	56
Wrote letter to the Romans on third journey	56
Arrest in Jerusalem	60–61
Journey to Rome under Guard	61
In prison, awaiting trial in Rome	61
Wrote Colossians, Ephesians, Philemon, and Philippians from prison	62–66
Released from prison, continued ministry	62
Wrote 1 Timothy and Titus after release from prison	66
Arrested and Imprisoned in Rome	66
Wrote 2 Timothy from second imprisonment	67
Executed for his faith in Christ	67

PAUL'S FIRST MISSIONARY JOURNEY (ACTS 13:1–14:28)

DATE	REFERENCE FROM ACTS	LOCATION	EVENTS
AD 47–48	13:1–12	Cyprus	False prophet—Bar Jesus blinded Proconsul Sergius Converted Saul now called Paul
48–49	13:13	Perga (in Pamphilia)	John Mark went home
48–49	13:14–52	Pisidian Antioch	Paul and Barnabas preached in the synagogue; Jews riot
48–49	14:1–5	Iconium	Many Jews and Gentiles believed; Jews caused division in city
48–49	14:6–20	Lystra	Paul and Barnabas called Greek gods; Paul stoned
48–49	14:20–21	Derbe	Many Jews and Gentiles believed
48–49	14:21–23	Lystra	Encouraging disciples; Elders appointed
48–49	14:24–25		Returned and preached
48–49	14:26–28	Antioch (Syria)	Reported on missionary journey

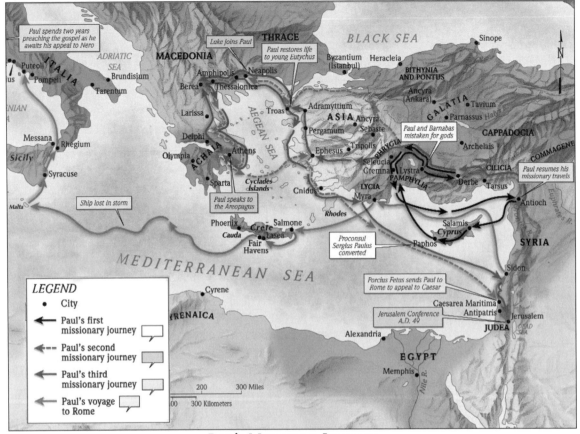

Labels on map:
Paul spends two years preaching the gospel as he awaits his appeal to Nero

Luke joins Paul

Paul restores life to young Eutychus

THRACE · BLACK SEA · Sinope · Heraclea · Byzantium (Istanbul)

ADRIATIC SEA · MACEDONIA · Amphipolis · Neapolis · Berea · Thessalonica

BITHYNIA AND PONTUS · Ancyra (Ankara) · GALATIA · Tavium · Parnassus

Puteoli · Pompeii · Brundisium · Tarentum · ITALIA

Larissa · Troas · Adramyttium · ASIA · Ancyra · Sebaste

CAPPADOCIA · COMMAGENE

Paul and Barnabas mistaken for gods

Delphi · AEGEAN SEA · Pergamum · Tripolis · PHRYGIA · Archelais

Messana · Rhegium · Olympia · ACHAIA · Athens · Ephesus · Seleucia · Cremna · PAMPHYLIA · LYCAONIA · Lystra · Derbe · Tarsus · CILICIA

Paul resumes his missionary travels

Sicily · Syracuse · Sparta · Cyclades Islands · Cnidus · LYCIA · Myra · Antioch · Euphrates R.

Malta · Ship lost in storm · Paul speaks to the Areopagus · Phoenix · Crete · Salmone · Rhodes · Salamis · Cyprus · SYRIA

Cauda · Lasea · Fair Havens · Proconsul Sergius Paulus converted · Paphos · Sidon

MEDITERRANEAN SEA · Cyrene · CYRENAICA

Porcius Festus sends Paul to Rome to appeal to Caesar

Caesarea Maritima · Antipatris · Jerusalem

Jerusalem Conference A.D. 49 · JUDEA · DEAD SEA

Alexandria · EGYPT · Memphis · Nile R.

LEGEND
- City
- ← Paul's first missionary journey
- ←--- Paul's second missionary journey
- ← Paul's third missionary journey
- ← Paul's voyage to Rome

200 · 300 Miles
00 · 300 Kilometers

PAUL'S MISSIONARY JOURNEYS

The Life and Ministry of Paul

THE THREE MISSIONARY JOURNEYS
ACTS 13:1–21:26

Paul took Barnabas and John Mark to Cyprus and then to what is present-day Asia Minor. Notice that Paul and Barnabas returned to the church at Antioch to report on what God was doing. A summary of their trip is given on the next page.

You may follow their trip from Antioch through Cyprus and into Asia Minor on the map above. Notice that the two other missionary journeys are outlined on this map also. The journey to Rome is also shown. You will want to refer to this map for the successive journeys.

To prepare for the second missionary journey, Paul and Barnabas had a dispute over John Mark. Mark had returned home from Perga. So Paul and Barnabas parted ways. Barnabas took Mark, and they went on their own mission. Paul took Silas and went to the churches in Asia Minor. They went on to Greece in Europe through the vision of the call to Macedonia. The events are given on the next page. Notice that they returned to report what God was doing to the church at Antioch.

Paul and Silas went on a third missionary journey. They returned to many of the churches where they had been before. On the way back home, Paul went to Jerusalem. There he took a Jewish vow. This led to the next venture for his faith in Christ.

Paul's Second Missionary Journey (Acts 15:36–18:22)

Date	Acts Reference	Location	Events
AD 49–51	15:36–40	Antioch	Barnabas wanted to take Mark; Paul did not want Mark and took Silas
50–52	15:41	Syria and Cilicia	Strengthened churches
50–52	16:1	Derbe	Timothy joined Paul and Silas
50–52	16:1–7	Lystra; Iconium	Strengthened churches
50–52	16:8–9	Troas	Paul's vision to go to Macedonia
50–52	16:10–40	Philippi	Conversion of Lydia; Paul and Silas in jail; jailer converted
50–52	17:1–9	Thessalonica	Many believed; Jews caused problems and mobbed Jason's house
50–52	17:10–14	Berea	Many believed; Jews from Thessalonica stirred up the people against Paul
50–52	17:15–34	Athens	Paul preached about the "Unknown God"; conversion of Dionysius and Damaris
52	18:1–17	Corinth	Crispus—ruler of the synagogue—converted; many believed; church founded; met Priscilla and Aquila
52	18:18–21	Ephesus	Priscilla and Aquila went with Paul to Ephesus
52	18:22	Antioch	Returned to home church

Paul's Third Missionary Journey (Acts 18:23–21:26)

Date	Acts Reference	Location	Events
AD 52–56	18:23	Antioch to Galatia and Phrygia	Preaching in Galatia; disciples strengthened
	18:24–28	Ephesus	Priscilla and Aquila won Apollos to faith in Jesus
53–56	18:24–19:41	Ephesus	Church founded; Paul taught in the Hall of Tyranus; Paul performed miracles; riot of silversmiths
53–56	20:1–6	Macedonia	Plot to kill Paul on sea voyage
53–56	20:7–12	Troas	Eutychus fell asleep in the window and fell; Paul brought him back to life
53–56	20:13–38	Miletus	Paul encouraged the Ephesian elders and said "good-bye"
53–56	21:1–16	To Jerusalem	The prophet Agabus warned Paul that he would be taken captive in Jerusalem
53–56	21:17–26	Jerusalem	Paul reported to the church at Jerusalem and took a Jewish vow

The Journey to Rome (Acts 21:27–28:31)

Paul took his Jewish vow and went into the Temple. In the inner court of the temple, only Jewish persons were allowed. Signs were posted that a Gentile would be put to death if he went into the inner court of the temple. The Jews believed that Paul brought one of his Greek converts into the temple. They became angry and tried to kill Paul. He was rescued by the Roman guard. This led to the adventure that caused him to appeal to Caesar and go to Rome. The story is summarized in the chart below.

The end of the story of the growth of the church may have come in the Book of Acts in the Bible, but the church continues to live and grow in the world today. We will look at that growth in volume 4 of this series. Before we move on, we will examine some of the letters that Paul and other disciples wrote to the churches that were started on these missionary journeys of Paul.

Paul's Journey to Rome (Acts 21:27–28:31)

Date	Acts Reference	Location	Events
AD 56	21:27–36	Temple in Jerusalem	Paul is accused of taking a Gentile into the Inner Court of the Temple; arrested
56	21:37–22:22	Temple in Jerusalem	Paul makes a defense to the people
56	22:23–23:9	Sanhedrin and Fortress of Antonia	Paul tells the commander that he is a Roman citizen and talks to the Sanhedrin
56	23:12–22	Plot of Jewish men to kill Paul	Commander had Paul taken to Caesarea by night
56–59	23:31–25:12	Caesarea	Paul in jail with some freedom; brought before Felix and Festus; Paul appeals to Caesar
59	27:1–12	Mediterranean Sea	Under guard, Paul sails for Rome; Paul advises crew not to sail
59	27:13–44	Mediterranean Sea	Storm and shipwreck at sea; Paul encourages the people to keep faith in God
59	28:1–10	Malta	Local people are kind to Paul; Paul was not killed by a snake; Paul healed a man
60	28:11–31	Rome	Paul is accompanied by believers at Three Taverns and goes to Rome; Paul is guarded by Caesar's guard; many become Christians

Letters of the New Testament

Following the four Gospels and Acts are twenty-one letters in the New Testament. The last book of the Bible is Revelation. In this volume we will look at each of the letters. The letters of the New Testament were important because they answered many of the problems that arose in the early church. Today they are still important for at least two reasons. First, they guide us to live our lives in ways that are pleasing to God. Second, they also deal with many of the same problems that arise in the church today.

The Missionary Letters of Paul

Thirteen of these letters were written by the apostle Paul. Refer to the chart of Paul's life in the Review of the New Testament to see when he wrote each of the letters. We will examine each of the letters in the order in which they were written.

Paul was a gifted person. He was educated by the great teacher of the Pharisees, Gamaliel. He had a thorough knowledge of the Old Testament and his Jewish faith. As most Jewish boys, he had a trade of tent making that allowed him to make his living. He was educated in Greek education, and he held Roman citizenship. The Holy Spirit was able to use Paul's learning and citizenship and his willingness to be led by the Spirit to make Paul the great missionary to the Gentiles.

GALATIANS

Key Verses: Galatians 2:19b–20

The letter to the Galatians was the first letter written by Paul; probably to the churches of Antioch, Iconium, Derbe, and Lystra (see Acts 13 and 14). Recall that Paul founded churches there on his first missionary journey. He probably wrote the letter around AD 48. Galatians was written between the first and second missionary journeys. The Galatian Christians were being encouraged by the Jewish teachers to go away from the true gospel. These teachers wanted the Christians to practice all of the Jewish laws in addition to practicing their Christian faith. They were also telling the Christians that Paul was not really an apostle.

Condemning the Evil Persons (Gal. 1:1–10)

In his opening remarks, Paul condemned these persons who were trying to lead the Galatian Christians back to slavery to the Jewish law. He expressed surprise that they had left the true gospel.

Defending His Call as an Apostle (Gal. 1:11–2:21)

He told the Galatians that God had called him to preach the gospel. The gospel that Paul preached was approved by the disciples of Jesus in Jerusalem. A person cannot come to Christ and at the same time practice all the Jewish law in order to go to heaven. God's grace is given freely to all who believe in Jesus.

Arguing for the Gospel (Gal. 3:1–4:31)

We are justified by the grace of God, not by any good works that we may do. Then Paul told his readers about Abraham. Abraham believed God by faith and God credited him for righteousness. Paul showed the Galatians that the law could not save us. We became God's children by faith and then we became members of the family of God. The Spirit of God prays for us. We have been made free in Christ.

Teaching on Christian Freedom (Gal. 5–7)

Since the Galatians have been adopted as God's sons, why do they still practice the laws of the Jews? The life of faith means practicing love. Faith is not a reason to sin. We need to practice what the Spirit gives us—love, joy, peace, patience, kindness, goodness, faithfulness, gentleness, and self-control. We need to do good for others.

Read Galatians 5:22–26. *What attitudes do we need to have as believers and how do we get those attitudes?*

THE LETTERS TO THE THESSALONIANS

Thessalonica was the capital city in Macedonia at the time of Paul. It was a "free city" and ruled by its citizens. It is about one hundred miles west of the city of Philippi. It was located on the Via Egnatia, which is the main Roman road and the east to west trade route through Macedonia. It also had a natural harbor sea trade. The governor of the province lived in Thessalonica. The city was very prosperous. There were several pagan temples in the city. There was also an important synagogue in the city.

Paul came to Thessalonica on his second missionary journey. He founded the church there. A great deal of opposition grew toward Paul's ministry in Thessalonica. Paul and Silas had to slip away in the night and went on to Berea, a town that was fifty miles away. Paul was the target of their anger. He was not able to stay in Berea. Silas and

Timothy stayed longer. Paul traveled 250 miles south to Athens. This is described in Acts 17:1–10.

Paul wrote these letters around AD 52 from Corinth on his second missionary journey. Unlike some of the other places Paul visited, the Thessalonians were mainly Gentile Christians. Paul wanted to encourage them. The letter was written in a gentle style. Paul defended himself against those who were accusing him falsely. He wanted the Thessalonians to understand that Christian morality is different from the world's immoral form. He also wanted to correct misunderstanding about the second coming of Jesus.

1 Thessalonians
Key Verse: 1 Thessalonians 3:13

Personal Thoughts about the Church in Thessalonica (I Thess. 1:1–3:13)

After giving the church his personal greeting, Paul expresses his thanks for the church. He explained his personal conduct and described his ministry. He was encouraged by the report about the church that he received from Timothy. He prays for the church.

Teaching on Practical Issues for the Church (1 Thess. 4:1–5:28)

His first instruction to the church at Thessalonica was on the need for holiness. He encouraged the people to live disciplined lives. He then taught about the second coming of Jesus Christ. The day will come when Christ will return to earth, and Christians will go to be with Jesus for eternity. He told them how important it was that they live godly lives. In closing, Paul gave a benediction and his final instructions.

Read 1 Thessalonians 5:12–22. *What can we learn about how to live from this passage?*

2 Thessalonians
Key Verse: 2 Thessalonians 3:5

After a few months had passed, Paul felt the need to write to the Thessalonians again. The young church was still having difficulties. Some people were criticizing their faith. It may have been Jewish teachers, as we saw in other churches. In his first letter Paul had tried to correct the persons who did not believe that Jesus was coming back again. By the time of the second letter, many of the people had become so interested in the second coming that they failed to do their everyday work. Others believed that Christ had already come back, and that Paul was teaching this. Paul wanted to correct both wrong ideas.

Comforting the Church in Time of Suffering (1 Thess. 1:1–12)

After giving his personal greeting, Paul wanted to encourage the Thessalonian believers. He taught about the coming Day of Judgment. Since this day will come, he encouraged them to live a life of godliness.

Teaching about the Future (1 Thess. 2:1–17)

Before the Lord returns, the opposition toward Christ will increase. Those who practice evil will be easily confused. But for Christians it is important to remain true to Christ.

Warnings about Acting Wisely (1 Thess. 3:1–18)

In the final chapter Paul gave the church final instructions about the way in which they should live their lives. They must not become lazy, looking for the return of Christ; some were making other Christians in the church support them. They needed to act wisely.

Read 2 Thessalonians 2:13–17. *How do we receive encouragement and strength?*

THE LETTERS TO THE CORINTHIANS

Corinth was a very important city in Greece. It was located on the isthmus between northern and southern Greece. Corinth was a seaport city. Ships would unload their cargo on the Aegean Sea and carry it across the isthmus and reload it on the Adriatic Sea. For many it was a city of leisure with many sinful pleasures. Corinth was a proud city of art and culture. Corinthians worshipped the Greek goddess, Venus.

Paul visited Corinth on his second missionary journey. Crispus, the ruler of the Jewish synagogue, and many Gentiles became Christians (see Acts 18). Paul remained in Corinth for a year and a half. Apollos taught in Corinth after Paul. The church was growing, but not following God. It was more concerned with sinful values of the city of Corinth. Paul wrote several letters, but only two have survived. They are very helpful because churches today experience many of the same problems. Paul was probably in Ephesus when he received news that the church had problems he needed to address.

1 Corinthians
Key Verse: 1 Corinthians 13:1

In Paul's letter of I Corinthians, he deals with one problem after another. First Corinthians is more difficult to describe than Romans. But in one of the greatest chapters in the entire Bible, 1 Corinthians 13, Paul seems to say that most of the problems come from a lack of love.

Divisions in the Church (1 Cor. 1:10–4:21)

Groups within the Corinthian church were following different leaders. Some were boasting that they had come from Paul. Others had come from Apollos. The ones who claimed to be the most spiritual said they had come from Christ. Each group was proud of the leader it claimed. To this Paul answers that the church is from Jesus Christ. Patience and kindness are needed to stop the divisions in the church. They need to look out for one another, rather than being selfish and self-centered. In 1 Corinthians 13:4, Paul wrote, "Love is patient; love is kind. Love does not envy; is not boastful; is not conceited."

Wrong Behavior in the Church (1 Cor. 5:1–7:40)

In this section of his letter, Paul corrects the Corinthian church for open sin among several members. Another problem is that the members are not settling their problems within the church. They had turned to the government courts. They were dragging all of their bad relationships before the world. The Corinthians had problems with married and unmarried people. Paul had to instruct them. He wrote in 1 Corinthians 13:5–6 that there is a better way, "[Love] does not act improperly; is not selfish; is not provoked . . . ; finds no joy in unrighteousness, but rejoices in the truth."

Looking Out for the Other Person (1 Cor. 8:1–11:1)

In this section Paul teaches us that we should not hurt another Christian believer. Because we love as Christ loved, we need to be sensitive to others. Paul writes about our Christian freedom, "'Everything is permissible' but not everything is helpful . . . not everything builds up" (1 Corinthians 10:23). Paul wrote that there is a better way in 1 Corinthians 13:7, "[Love] bears all things, believes all things, endures all things."

Worshipping in the Church (1 Cor. 11:2–14:40)

Paul expressed his concern for men and women worshiping in the church. He wanted them to act appropriately. He also taught the Corinthians how to conduct the Lord's Supper correctly. They ate a meal together. The rich people brought lots of food. The poor had little or no food. Their practice denied the purpose of the Lord's Supper. Finally, Paul taught the Corinthians about the use of spiritual gifts in the church.

Describing the Resurrection of Jesus Christ (1 Cor. 15:1–58)

Paul wrote one of the great chapters in Scripture about the resurrection of Jesus Christ. Apparently some of the Corinthians did not believe in the resurrection. They denied this major truth. Paul says that if Christ did not rise from the dead, we are still in sin. But Jesus did rise, and we will one day rise with Him.

Giving a Gift for Jerusalem and Personal Greetings (1 Cor. 16:1–24)

In this final chapter, Paul reminded the church about the need for helping the church in Jerusalem. He told the Corinthians about his plans to travel through Macedonia and perhaps to come visit the church at Corinth. He told them, "Be alert, stand firm in the faith, be brave and strong" (1 Corinthians 16:13). Then he closed the letter with personal greetings.

Read 1 Corinthians 13. *What do we learn about love from this passage?*

2 CORINTHIANS
Key Verse: 2 Corinthians 5:20

Paul was concerned about the way his first letter was received by the Corinthians. He sent Titus to Corinth. Titus reported back that most people had received the letter well. They corrected many of the things Paul talked about. But there were some in Corinth who criticized Paul. Others did not even believe that he was an apostle because he was not one of the original twelve. Paul was on his third missionary journey, when he wrote the second letter.

Describing His Ministry (2 Cor. 1:1–7:16)

Paul told the Corinthians why he was not able to come to visit them. Then he described his ministry in detail. He did what God had called him to do. The teachers of the Jewish law were against Paul and tried to turn the Corinthians against Paul as well. Paul told the Corinthians that the true Christian believers are witnesses to the gospel that he brought. Paul was Christ's ambassador to reconcile people to God through Jesus Christ. He asked the Corinthians to open their hearts to him and to be assured of his love for them.

Collecting Money for the Church in Jerusalem (2 Cor. 8:1–9:15)

In Paul's first letter to the Corinthians, he had asked them to give money toward the relief of the church in Jerusalem. In this letter he asks them

again for a gift. He encourages them to give joyfully. He reminded them of God's gift to both the Gentile and Jewish Christians.

> ### RECONCILIATION
> *Reconciliation means that because we sin, we are no longer able to relate to God. But reconciliation or establishing a new relationship with God happens through our relationship with Jesus Christ. His death on the cross and our belief and acceptance of His salvation allow us to be reconciled to God.*

Reminders of His Apostleship and His Concern for Them (2 Cor. 10:1–13:14)

Paul defended himself as an apostle of Jesus Christ. He tried to show them how the false apostles were trying to lead them astray. They were trying to steal the Corinthians from Paul. He tried to show them that he was a true apostle. In his last remarks Paul warns the Corinthians that if they do not believe he was God's apostle, then they had better look at their own salvation. They had better make sure that their salvation is real.

Read 2 Corinthians 5:16–21. *What is reconciliation, and how does it affect us?*

THE LETTER TO THE ROMANS
Key Verses: Romans 1:16–17

Look back at the chart on the life of Paul. You will see that this was the fourth letter Paul wrote. He wrote this letter on his third missionary journey, about the year AD 56. Unlike his other letters to

> ### FAITH
> *Faith is absolutely necessary to become a Christian. It means to trust and to believe that Jesus Christ bought our salvation by His death on the cross and resurrection from the dead. We are no longer our own persons. We belong to God, and we need to obey God.*

churches, this was written to a church Paul had not established. Roman Jews and converts to the Jewish faith were present at Pentecost (see Acts 2:10). Probably some were converted and took their new faith in Jesus back to the city of Rome and started a church there. Paul probably wanted to go to Rome on his way to Spain and strengthen the church. His plans did not work out the way he had hoped. Instead he was arrested in Jerusalem. After several years in prison, he appealed to Caesar to be his final judge. He was sent off to Rome. As a result, Paul went to Rome and built a deeper relationship with the church there.

Rome was the capital and largest city of the Empire. Rome was founded in 753 BC. Rome does not become important to Jews until it conquered Judah under the Roman general, Pompey, in 63 BC. In the New Testament era, Rome was the greatest city in the world at that time.

We Are by Nature Sinful (Rom. 1:1–3:20)

We are all sinners. It does not matter whether we are born into a Jewish family or a Gentile family. We can do nothing to earn God's forgiveness. When we are born into a human family, we are by nature sinners. Adam passed sin on to all people after him. It is like an apple tree. You can gather bright shiny red apples, but the tree will not produce pears or peaches. God pronounces His judgment on all humanity. There is no one who is righteous. We have all sinned.

We Can Become Righteous before God (Rom. 3:21–5:21)

We climbed to the top of Black Mountain in North Carolina. I could no more touch the stars from the bottom of the mountain than I could from the top of the mountain. We are all guilty before God. We cannot please God by our own righteousness any more than I can touch the stars from the top of the mountain. Everyone who comes by faith in Jesus Christ can have God's righteousness without any cost. It is not difficult to find God's forgiveness. By faith in God Abraham was declared righteous before God, even though the rest of the world was evil and sinful. What was true for Abraham is also true for us. God gives us the righteousness of Jesus when we trust in Him. Jesus lived a sinless life of obedience to God. When Jesus died, He took my sin and your sin to the cross. God declares that we have received the righteousness of Jesus when we accept Him as our Savior.

We receive God's forgiveness. I stand condemned, but I can find life in Christ for what He did for me by dying on the cross in my place. All you need to do is confess that you are a sinner before God. Ask Jesus to come into your heart and save you.

> ### JUSTIFICATION
> *Justification is a legal term that means God gives us as sinners a new standing before Him. When we are in our sin, we are condemned by God. But through faith in Jesus Christ, we are no longer condemned. It is just as if we had never sinned. We are declared righteous, just as Jesus was righteous.*

How to Live as a Christian (Rom. 6–8)

Jesus bought our salvation through His death on the cross. Our sinful nature cannot do what is right or good. Our sinful nature opposes God. It is not possible for me to live the Christian life by myself. We become slaves to sin.

But God has provided a way. The same Holy Spirit who raised Jesus from the dead can give you and me the power to live for God. God's Law is good. It was given to Moses on Mt. Sinai. But the law cannot help me live for God. Only the power of God's Holy Spirit can give you and me this power!

All who are in Christ have the power of the Holy Spirit in their lives. The Spirit comes to live within a believer. He gives us the power of God. He prays for us.

Israel's Failure (Rom. 9–11)

What happened to God's chosen people, Israel? They have tried to follow their own righteousness. They failed to listen to the prophets. God chose to turn to the Gentiles. He has not completely rejected Israel, and one day many will turn to Christ as their Messiah. In the meantime, they have been scattered throughout the world. Many have suffered. Be careful! God can reject us if we fail to obey Him also.

Living for God (Rom. 12–16)

After we have been saved by God's grace and have come under the control of God's Holy Spirit, we are fit for service to God. Up to this point we have not had anything to do for God. It has been all God. Now He calls us to live for Him. The old Jewish sacrifices killed an animal and sacrificed it on the altar. Now we are called to be living sacrifices to God. We do not always need to have our way. We do not need to do things that will bring us close to evil or specifically wrong. We need to live as God wants. We need to show our love for God by living for God.

Read Romans 12:9–19. *What does God expect of us?*

THE LETTERS FROM PRISON

When Paul arrived in Rome, he was placed under guard by a Roman soldier from the emperor's household. Paul used these opportunities to witness to his faith in Jesus Christ. Many soldiers and members of Caesar's household became Christians. Paul wrote letters during the time he was in prison. These letters were Colossians, Ephesians, Philemon, and Philippians. They were written to churches that needed Paul's guidance. The letter to Philemon was a personal letter, and it was not written to a church. According to our time line, they would have been written in AD 61.

Paul was in prison for a year and a day, waiting for the trial. Apparently the Jewish priests did not come to Rome to accuse Paul. It is likely that Paul was

released after this time. Many believe that Paul went from Rome to Spain, where he intended to preach the gospel. In AD 66 he was brought back to Rome and again put in prison. It is believed that he was executed during the next year in AD 67.

EPHESIANS

Key Verse: Ephesians 1:3

Ephesus was one of the most important cities in Asia Minor. It was located on the Cayster River. Pasta was one of the most important foods in the diet of Romans. The grain was imported by ship from Alexandria. Because the seas were rough in the winter, the ships would stay for the winter in port at Ephesus. Several years before Paul visited Ephesus, the river had become filled with mud. It was almost impossible for the big grain ships from Alexandria to navigate the river. They were forced to go to other ports.

Ephesus continued to remain as one of the most important cities. It was a cultural and university center. It had a large stadium that seated more than twenty-five thousand people. It was also a religious center. There was a large temple to the goddess Diana. It was one of the seven wonders of the ancient world.

The apostle Paul went to Ephesus on his second missionary journey. He left Priscilla and Aquila there. They probably started the church at Ephesus. When Paul returned on his third missionary journey, he stayed for three years. That was the longest period of time that Paul spent in any one city during his journeys. He taught the people every day about their faith in Jesus Christ. At the end of his stay in Ephesus, the silversmiths rioted. Paul had hurt their business of making idols of Diana. He was told not to go to the stadium and he escaped unharmed (see Acts 18:19–21 and 19:1–20:1). He also visited the Ephesian elders at the nearby city of Miletus (see Acts 20:17–38).

Paul's letter to the Ephesians was written from his prison cell in Rome. Several people from

St. Paul at Ephesus

The purpose for which we have been saved is to grow toward maturity in Christ. Consistency in the Christian life is essential. Paul describes the relationship that should exist between husbands and wives. He compares the relationship between husbands and wives with the relationship between Christ in his church. These topics are covered in chapter 5. Paul continues in the first half of chapter 6 to talk about children obeying their parents and employees doing what is right for their employers. In the last half of chapter 6, Paul tells us about the spiritual enemy we face. Finally, we need to be covered with the whole armor of God, the shield of faith, the power of prayer, and the sword of the Spirit, which is the Word of God.

Read Ephesians 6:1–4. *How does the Bible teach us to behave toward our parents?*

different churches came to visit Paul in Rome. Among them was Tychicus from the Ephesian church. This letter does not address a specific problem as many of his other letters do. Paul did not write personal notes to specific persons, as he had in his other letters. It is believed that Paul intended for this letter to be circulated among other churches in the area. The letter is a wonderful description of the church of Jesus Christ and what life should be like for those who are members of the church.

How Christians Are Blessed (Eph. 1:1–3:21)

In the first chapter of Ephesians Paul tells us that God the Father (see 1:4–6), God the Son (see 1:7–12), and God the Holy Spirit (see 1:13–14), are all involved in our salvation. Paul then prays that the Ephesians will understand the greatness of their salvation. In the second chapter Paul describes the power of God in our salvation. The riches of God's grace are available to us if we will use them. He describes them in chapter 3.

How Christians Should Live (Eph. 4:1–6:20)

In the remaining chapters, Paul tells Christians how they should live. Our attitudes must be right.

PHILIPPIANS

Key Verses: Philippians 4:6–7

The city of Philippi is located in Macedonia. Philippi was a Roman colony. It was one of the most important cities in Macedonia. The Roman road, Via Egnatia, went right through the center of the city. It was an important trade route through Macedonia. It was named for Phillip II, the father of Alexander the Great. Many of the citizens of Philippi were Roman soldiers who had retired and settled there. Having retired Roman soldiers in the city, it helped to preserve the Roman peace. As a result, Philippi was given several honors by Rome, including having the same rights as cities in Italy.

The apostle Paul visited the city on his second missionary journey after entering Macedonia and Europe. Lydia was baptized in the city of Philippi. She was a wealthy citizen of the city. Acts tells us that she was a "seller of purple." This meant that she, as a businesswoman, harvested the purple dye that was used in robes for the emperor's family. The dye came from shellfish. It took many of the fish to produce enough dye for even one robe. After Lydia became a Christian, she invited

Paul and his companions to stay in her home (see Acts 16:11–15).

Trouble arose for Paul and his companions, and they were thrown into prison. God miraculously delivered them through an earthquake. The prison doors flew open. The jailer was about to kill himself when Paul told him that all the prisoners were there and safe. The jailer came to know Christ as a Savior. He and his family were baptized. When the leaders in the town found out that Paul was a Roman citizen, they made public apology for putting them in prison. Paul and his companions left Philippi and went on to preach at the Thessalonica (see Acts 16:16–40). Paul visited Philippi again on his third missionary journey.

The letter to the Philippians was written from Paul's prison cell in Rome about AD 61. The Philippian church had contributed to the needs of the church in Jerusalem. When they discovered that Paul was in prison in Rome, they also contributed to his support. The Philippians sent Epaphroditus to help Paul in his ministry. Unfortunately, Epaphroditus almost died of an illness in Rome. Paul sent the letter back to Philippi with Epaphroditus. Paul had several purposes for writing the letter. He wanted to thank the Philippians for their generous gift. He wanted to explain why Epaphroditus was being returned to them. He did not want them to think that he did not appreciate having Epaphroditus with him. Paul also wanted to tell the Philippians about his situation in Rome and to encourage them. He also wanted to tell them about false teachers. This letter relates the inner joy that comes from being a Christian.

Telling the Philippians about His Situation (Phil. 1:1–30)

Paul tells the Philippians that he is grateful for their kindness to him. It brings him great joy. He tells the Philippian church that he is continuing to uphold them in prayer. He also informs them that the gospel was continuing to be preached, even though he was in prison. He is willing to live or die as long as he could please the Lord Jesus Christ. He wants the Philippians to have the same attitude.

Describing the Example of Christ (Phil. 2:1–30)

There are appropriate attitudes that one should hold as a Christian believer. Christ is our example. He showed the way by living a life in which he submitted to the will of the Father. He did not push himself but looked after the interests of others. He put aside all of his privileges as God and became a man. He died on the cross in obedience to God the Father. He will one day reign as Lord of the universe. Both Timothy and Epaphroditus are good examples of the faith.

Warning the Philippians about the False Teachers (Phil. 3:1–21)

In Galatians and Corinthians Paul warned about false teachers who would try to make the Christians return to the laws of the Jewish faith. Paul warns the Philippians about the same problem. There are men who would take away their freedom in Christ. A Christian should depend only on Jesus Christ and not on any righteousness that they would gain from practicing the law. Dependence on Jesus is through faith. The cross of Christ is enough!

Encouraging and Thanking the Philippians (Phil. 4:1–23)

Two of the women, Euodia and Syntyche, were disagreeing with each other. Paul urges them to stop and to follow the example of Jesus. He calls on the Philippians and upon us to rejoice and not fight. He asks that we control our thoughts and keep them in line with Christ. After thanking them for their support, Paul ends the letter with personal words of greeting.

Read Philippians 2:5–11. *What did Christ do for us? How does this affect us?*

COLOSSIANS

Key Verses: Colossians 2:9–10

If you look at the map of Paul's missionary journeys, you will discover that Colossae is a city that lies about one hundred miles southeast of Ephesus. Originally it was on the trade route that went from Laodicea to Ephesus on the coast. By the time of Paul, the city was much smaller. As a place of trade, it was much less important. Paul never visited the city of Colossae. The church there was probably started by Epaphras, who came from Colossae. Since he was with Paul at the time this letter was written, Paul most likely got his information about the church from Epaphras.

The letter to the Colossians was written for the purpose of correcting the errors of false teaching in the church there. This teaching was not the teaching of the Jewish leaders, who wanted the Christians to return to the Jewish law. This was a group who taught that knowledge was everything. It was the way to salvation. Many of these people worshipped other gods, as well as Jesus. Paul wrote to the Colossians about the completeness of salvation in Christ. Any other teaching was false.

Prayer for the Colossian Christians (Col. 1:1–14)

Paul expresses his thanks for the Christians at Colossae. Then he prays that they will be filled with the knowledge of Christ. He wants them to grow toward spiritual maturity and understanding. He talks about the salvation that comes from both the heavenly Father and Jesus Christ the Son.

Describing the Greatness of Christ (Col. 1:15–29)

This is one of the great passages of Scripture, Paul talks about who Christ is. Jesus can be seen, but God cannot. Jesus existed before God created anything. It was Jesus who created the heaven and earth. Jesus is the head of the church. He is the one who rose from death. He is fully God. Because Jesus is God, we must worship Him, learn about Him, and obey Him. Paul said that his task is to minister for Jesus.

Calling for Loyalty to Christ (Col. 2:1–23)

Since we know that Christ is over all, he urges the Colossians Christians not to follow the evil teachers. These teachers will take away the truth of the Gospel of Jesus Christ. The Colossians Christians must not follow the ideas of men, nor those of the Jewish teachers. They must follow Christ.

Teaching about New Life in Christ (Col. 3:1–4:6)

Paul tells them that they must not follow the evil ways of the world. We have been raised with Christ to a new life. It is a life of kindness and love. This life begins at home between husbands and wives, parents and children, and employees and employers. Paul also tells the Colossians to pray, to witness, and to guard what they say.

Remembering His Friends (Col. 4:7–18)

Paul talks about his friends at Colossae and the neighboring cities. He talks about those who are helping him in Rome. He tells them to be sure to read the letter he sent. This may have been the letter to the Ephesians. Then he bids them farewell.

Read Colossians 1:9–14. *What can we learn about prayer from Paul's prayer for spiritual growth?*

PHILEMON

Key Verse: Philemon 6

At the same time that Tychicus brought Paul's letter to the Colossians, he also carried a personal letter to Philemon. Philemon had come to know Christ through the ministry of Paul. The church at Colossae met in Philemon's home. Philemon owned a slave by the name of Onesimus. Onesimus had run away from Philemon's home and stole some of Philemon's property. According to Roman law, a runaway slave would be crucified on a cross. Onesimus had fled to Rome. He thought he could disappear there, but instead he met Paul and became a Christian. Now Paul sent Onesimus back with Tychicus and the letter to Philemon, asking for forgiveness. Onesimus' name meant "useful." Before he became a Christian, Onesimus was not useful, but now as a believer he had become useful to Paul. Paul asked Philemon to send Onesimus back to him in Rome.

Paul's letter to Philemon begins with his greetings to Philemon, his wife Apphia, and Archipus, probably Philemon's son. Then Paul tells Philemon about the conversion of his former slave, Onesimus. He is now a brother in Christ. Paul tells Philemon that he will repay any damages that Philemon has suffered from his runaway slave. Paul concludes with a final greeting.

Read Philemon 1:4–7. *Whom can we pray for and encourage?*

THE PASTORAL LETTERS

In early days of the church, there were no schools for pastors, like seminaries. Older pastors had to provide help for younger men. In the three letters known as the pastoral letters, Paul wrote to Timothy and Titus. The first letter to Timothy was written after Paul had been released from prison. Then he wrote the letter to Titus. The second letter to Timothy was written while Paul was in prison the second time. He was waiting in prison to be executed for his faith.

1 TIMOTHY

Key Verses: 1 Timothy 3:14–15

Paul's purpose in writing this letter was to give Timothy guidance. The false teachers were causing problems in the church at Ephesus. Timothy's help was needed to correct the situation.

Importance of Sound Teaching (1 Tim. 1:1–20)

Paul opened this letter by greeting Timothy. Sound teaching is important if God's people are to be instructed and live as God desires. Next he tells Timothy about his personal experiences. Paul wants Timothy to follow his advice and be strong in the ministry.

Instructions on the Church (1 Tim. 2:1–4:16)

Through the next three chapters, Paul instructs Timothy about worship in the church. The first section deals with the importance of prayer. Next he gives Timothy some instruction about the role of women in the church. Chapter 3 begins with the qualifications for leaders in the church. He gave Timothy an understanding of what a leader should be like. This is useful in the church, even today. Paul adds a section on godliness. Chapter 4 gives a description of false teachers. Paul concludes this chapter by teaching Timothy about godly teachers.

Instructions on the Work of Pastor (1 Tim. 5:1-6:2a)

In this section of the letter, the apostle gives instruction about ministering to the elderly, widows, and church leaders. He teaches slaves to obey. They honor the gospel by being effective servants.

Warnings for the Pastor's Personal Life (1 Tim. 6:2b–21)

The pastor must be careful to avoid false teaching. He must not love money. He needs to have the proper character and motivation for service for God. For persons who are wealthy, they need to be encouraged to do good for others. He concludes by encouraging Timothy to guard what has been entrusted to him.

Read 1 Timothy 2:1–6. *What can we learn about prayer from this passage?*

TITUS

Key Verses: Titus 2:11–13

Paul wrote this letter to Titus at about the same time he wrote 1 Timothy. He instructed Titus that there were some evil persons who were trying to hurt the church on the island of Crete. Paul sent Titus to stop these people from damaging the church further. Paul told Titus to choose elders for the church. They must teach sound doctrine. Titus was also to teach within the church and serve as an example.

Appointing Elders (Titus 1:1–16)

Paul sent Titus to the Island Crete. Titus was to bring an end to the false teaching. Titus was instructed to appoint elders in each town. Paul told Titus how to select men who would be qualified to guard the church against these evil teachers.

Providing Sound Teaching (Titus 2:1–3:11)

Paul told Titus to help the Christians on Crete to live godly lives. He gave instructions for older men and older women. He gave instructions for slaves. He also gave some final instructions for all Christians. The reason we need to live godly lives is to please the one who bought our salvation by dying on the cross, Jesus Christ. The coming of Christ might occur at any moment. We need to be ready.

Importance of Good Works (Titus 3:12–15)

Paul gave final instructions and then sent his blessing to Titus and the church.

Read Titus 2:11–15. *How should we live as Christians?*

2 TIMOTHY

Key Verses: 2 Timothy 4:1–2

The second letter of Timothy was written from Paul's cell. He was awaiting execution in Rome. In this letter Paul is trying to encourage Timothy to carry on the ministry after Paul's death.

Counsel for His Son in the Faith (2 Tim. 1:1–18)

Paul expressed his appreciation for Timothy and his sincere faith. He encouraged Timothy not to be ashamed of the gospel of Christ or of Paul.

He encouraged Timothy to be loyal to sound teaching.

Advice to Be Strong (2 Tim. 2:1–26)

In his chapter Paul compares Timothy's work as a teacher to a soldier, an athlete, a farmer, and a worker. He encourages Timothy to be a clean vessel. God cannot use persons who are engaging in sin. He encourages Timothy to be strong, gentle, and good.

Advice about the Evil of the Last Days and Combatting Evil (2 Tim. 3:1–17)

Paul told Timothy that the day was coming when evil was going to increase. Men would be lovers of pleasure rather than lovers of God. The only way to combat this evil is by staying true to the Word of God. The Word of God has everything we need to live a life of godliness.

Final Instructions to Timothy (2 Tim. 4:1–22)

In his final section Paul charges Timothy to proclaim the message of the truth. The apostle then bids Timothy farewell.

Read 2 Timothy 2:1–7. *What does it mean to be strong in the grace of Christ?*

THE GENERAL LETTERS

The general letters were written by several different authors. The letter to the Hebrews does not follow the same pattern as the other letters. All of the letters, except Hebrews, name the author. Paul's letters named the church to which they were written. These letters were written close to the time of Paul's death or after his death. These letters addressed problems the church faced.

HEBREWS

Key Verses: Hebrews 1:1–2

The letter to the Hebrews is interesting. We believe that it was written to Jewish Christians who were in danger of going back to their Jewish ways. Returning to their Jewish ways would have been a big mistake. Jesus is far superior to any of the Old Testament heroes of the past. Jesus was Prophet, Priest, and King. Jesus was the very Son of God.

Hebrews was probably written sometime before AD 70. You will remember that AD 70 was the date when the Roman army under Titus destroyed the Temple in Jerusalem. It is also likely that the letter was written to Jewish Christians in Rome. It may be that these Christians were Italians, who were writing to Jewish Christians back in Rome (see 13:24).

Jesus Was above the Angels (Heb. 1:1–2:18)

Many Jews came very close to worshipping the angels. For this reason, the writer to the Hebrews shows that Jesus is far superior to the angels. Angels were created by the Lord Christ, just as we were. The angels actually worship Jesus. Jesus is the Creator of the universe and the Savior of all mankind.

Jesus Was above Moses and Joshua (Heb. 3:1–4:13)

The writer tells us that Jesus was superior to Moses. Moses was God's choice servant. He led the people out of captivity in Egypt. He was a great man of God. But Jesus is far superior to Moses and Joshua. God wanted to lead the people into His rest. God did not want the people simply to have a happy life in Palestine. He wanted them to find the rest that comes from the salvation He freely provides. God wants obedience from His people. We cannot hide our attitude from God. He sees and knows all.

Jesus Was above Any Priest (Heb. 4:14–10:18)

Aaron and his descendents were God's choice for priests of Israel. Even though Jesus did not come from the tribe of Levi, He was a far superior priest to Aaron. He understands our weakness, and Heenters the Tabernacle in the heavens on our behalf. Jesus was tempted as we are tempted, but He did not sin. This priesthood, that Jesus represented, is like that of Melchizedek. Abraham gave Melchizedek his worship and honor (see Genesis 14:17–20 and Psalm 110:4).

Jesus is the high priest in heaven for us. Jesus started a new covenant through His blood shed on the cross of Calvary for our sin. The Law of Moses was not able to take away our sin. Each year on the Day of Atonement, a priest had to enter the Holy of Holies and take a sacrifice for the sins of the people. This was no longer necessary after Jesus became our sacrifice once and for all to take away our sin forever.

Jesus Calls Us to Be Faithful and to Endure (Heb. 10:19–13:25)

Since we have received so great a salvation, we need to turn away from sin. We need to look back at the great men and women of faith from the Old Testament. They are good examples for us to follow. As Christ taught us, we must love others. We must keep ourselves from the sin that is in the world. The writer closes with a benediction.

Read Hebrews 10:19–32. *What does it mean? How does it help you live for Christ?*

JAMES

Key Verse: James 1:22

James was the half brother of Jesus (see Mark 6:3). He probably wrote this letter around AD 58, since he was martyred in AD 61. James wrote to Jewish Christians who were outside of Palestine. They were experiencing persecution. He wanted to encourage them in their faith. He drew heavily upon the Sermon on the Mount. He drew upon Jesus' sermon at least fifteen times.

Trials Strengthen Your Faith (James 1:1–18)

Trials and difficulties are not happy experiences. But trials and difficulties can produce joy because they help us to gain endurance. Those who keep at it will receive the crown of life. We should be clear that God never tempts us. God never causes us to do evil. Our own evil desires tempt us.

Hearing and Doing the Word (James 1:19–27)

We need to act on God's Word. It is not enough to say we believe without doing. We must learn to control our tongues. We must care for widows and orphans. These are examples of actions that lead to the practice of true religion.

Love Does Not Show Favoritism (James 2:1–13)

Jesus taught us that we must love others as we love ourselves. If, for example, we show favoritism to persons who are rich and ignore the poor, we are not practicing true religion. We must show mercy if we expect to receive God's mercy to us.

Good Works Are the Proof of Faith (James 2:14–26)

If a person has faith, he will demonstrate that faith by what he does. If we say we believe and do not practice what we believe, do we really have faith? Faith is alive. Look at the lives of Abraham and Rahab.

Control Your Tongue (James 3:1–12)

Teachers must be careful to teach right belief. They will be judged if they do not teach as God desires. Controlling what one says is another evidence of faith. The tongue can do a lot of harm.

Find Wisdom from Heaven (James 3:13–18)

God provides wisdom for us from heaven. God does not want us to practice evil. We need to be peacemakers.

Be Humble and Not Proud (James 4:1–5:6)

God looks for humility, not pride. Submit to God and resist the devil. Boasting is evil. Practice what is good. Beware of riches. Sometimes they can lead us away from God.

Wait on the Lord in Prayer (James 5:7–20)

If you are going through trials, wait on the Lord in prayer. Be patient. Live a godly life.

Read James 1:1–27. What does it tell us about suffering? How do we need to practice our faith?

_____

THE LETTERS OF 1 AND 2 PETER

Peter, as leader of the disciples and one close to Jesus, wrote two letters on behalf of the church. The letters of 1 and 2 Peter were written to Christians who were being persecuted. The apostle Peter wanted to remind them that this world is not their home. Their home is in a far better place, heaven. Life may be difficult until the time they reach their home in heaven. Peter encouraged them to remain faithful to the end. The first letter appears to have been written from Rome. Peter used the code name Babylon to refer to Rome (see 5:13). It appears that the letters were written to Christian churches in what is today northern Asia Minor. The first letter was written during the persecutions of Emperor Nero, around AD 64. The second letter does not have any geographical references or time events, but it may have been written to a similar audience near the same time. The second letter was written while Peter was waiting his own execution, around AD 67.

_____

1 PETER

Key Verse: 1 Peter 4:14
The Christian Salvation (1 Pet. 1:1–2:10)

We are blessed; the salvation that we received came through Christ. Our hope does not rest on some false belief. Rather, it rests on the eyewitness accounts of persons like Peter. It is a living hope because Jesus was raised from the dead. Jesus suffered, and we may be called upon to suffer. If we do suffer, it should be for the sake of Christ, not because we have done something wrong.

A Christian's Holiness (1 Pet. 2:11–3:12)

Since we only live on earth temporarily and our home is really in heaven, we ought to live our lives for God in this evil world. We should live right in relation to our government, our employer, our families, and even if we have to live under unfair circumstances.

A Christian and Suffering (James 3:13–4:19)

If we are called upon to suffer, we should do it graciously. We should remember that Jesus Himself suffered. Do not fear suffering, but know that God cares, and in His mercy and grace, you can experience His joy.

The Christian Church (James 5:1–14)

Peter encouraged the leaders of the church to shepherd the flock. They were to provide good examples. For all Christians, Peter encouraged humility and love. He warned of the dangers of Satan and how Christians must resist him. He concluded the letter with a benediction.

Read 1 Peter 1:13–25. *How does the apostle tell us to live? Why?*

2 PETER

Key Verse: 2 Peter 1:3

Growing as Christians (2 Pet. 1:1–21)

The Divine power of God has given us everything we need to grow in our faith in Jesus Christ. We need to keep growing in order to please God. Peter draws upon his experience with Christ to support his argument. Recall his experience with Christ at the transfiguration.

Judgment Will Come to the False Teachers (2 Pet. 2:1–22)

Many false teachers will come and try to steal away the believers. Peter gives a long description of these teachers and the ways that they will hurt believers. He warns Christians not to be taken in by them.

The Day of the Lord Will Come (2 Pet. 3:1–18)

There are those who will make fun of the fact that Jesus has not yet returned. Do not listen to

THE APOSTLES PREACHING THE GOSPEL

them. The day of the Lord will come, and God's judgment will fall on those who do not live in accordance with God's will. Be on your guard. Grow in God's grace and the knowledge of Christ.

Read 2 Peter 1:3–15. *Try to think about the meaning of each of these words, from faith (verse 5) to love (verse 7). What will happen if you grow in each of these characteristics? Hint: Look at the verses before and after the list.*

THE LETTERS OF 1, 2, AND 3 JOHN

The letters of 1, 2, and 3 John were written by the apostle John. They were probably written toward the end of his life, around AD 90. We believe that they were written while he was the bishop at Ephesus. We are not exactly sure to whom the letters were written. But they were probably written to several churches in Asia Minor, which is present-day Turkey. There are many similarities between the Gospel of John and the letters of John. The Gospel of John was written to convince believers that Jesus was the Christ, the Son of God. The letters of John were written to strengthen the believers, who had already put their trust in Jesus, and to remind them that Jesus was not only God but truly human as well.

1 JOHN

Key Verse: 1 John 1:9
Finding Fellowship with Christ and Other Christians (1 John 1:1–2:14)

John tells his readers how he experienced his relationship with Jesus Christ while Jesus was here on earth. John continues to have a special relationship with Jesus and the heavenly Father. We can also have that relationship. It happens because we are believers in Jesus Christ, and His Spirit helps us to have that relationship. In order to continue that relationship, we must obey Christ.

Avoiding Those Who Deny Our Relationship (1 John 2:15–29)

We cannot love this evil world and have close fellowship with Christ. We must not make our friends among those who oppose Christ. John calls them Antichrists. They deny the Christian faith. They try to lead those who are believers away from Jesus.

Knowing That We Are among the Chosen of God (1 John 3:1–5:21)

There are several identifying marks of a true believer. Leading a pure and holy life is first. Second, loving others who are Christians is important. Third, believing that Jesus has come as God, but also as a true human being, is essential. If we pass these tests, we can be sure that we are members of God's family.

Read 1 John 1:1–10. *What do they tell us about our relationship with Christ and one another?*

2 JOHN

Key Verse: 2 John 7

This short letter continues the idea set forth in the first letter. John wrote that there are two main ideas, love and truth. We must love others and follow the commands of Jesus. We must also believe the truth and oppose all those who deny the truth that Jesus came as God and man. We should not have any relationship with such persons. They are Antichrists.

Read 2 John 1:4–6. *What is the command that we have had since the beginning (from the time of Jesus)?*

3 JOHN

Key Verse: 3 John 11

This letter is written to a particular person, Gaius. He was a person who was helping preachers and one who was walking in the truth. Another man, Diotrephes, was not living for God but for himself. John encouraged Gaius not to follow the evil example of Diotrephes. Rather, Demetrius, who carried the letter to Gaius, was a good example to follow.

Read 3 John 1:1–4. *What is the main idea that John is telling Gaius? What can we learn from it?*

JUDE

Key Verse: Jude 1:3

Like James, Jude was a half brother of Jesus (see Mark 6:3). Jude must have received a copy of 2 Peter. His letter is the last letter in the New Testament. He tells us that he intended to write about our common salvation. But instead the need to write about evil teachers was greater.

Evil people had come into the church. They denied that Jesus Christ had come to save us, and they practiced evil. There are many examples of such people in the Old Testament. They experienced the judgment of God. These people are no different and also are condemned by God. They do not have the Spirit of God. Therefore, true believers need to turn away from such people and practice holy faith. Jude closes his letter with a beautiful benediction.

Read Jude 1:20–25. *How are we to live as Christian believers? What do the words of the benediction tell us?*

The Tabernacle in the Wilderness

The Tabernacle was a movable building that was constructed by the Israelites, where God could meet His people. God Himself told Moses how to construct the Tabernacle. In Exodus 25:8–9, God instructed Moses, "They are to make a sanctuary for Me so that I may dwell among them. You must make [it] according to all that I show you—the design of the Tabernacle as well as the design of all its furnishings." In the Bible there are fifty chapters describing the Tabernacle. Contrast that with only two chapters devoted to the creation of the world in Genesis. From God's perspective, the Tabernacle plays an important part of the relationship between God and man.

The Book of Exodus gives five names for the Tabernacle. It is first called a "sanctuary," which means chapel or holy place (see Exodus 25:8). The second term used is "tabernacle" (see Exodus 25:9). This term means a dwelling place or place of habitation. It carries the idea that God would live among His people in the Tabernacle. The next term used for this structure is a "tent" (see Exodus 26:36). It carries the idea of a home. The fourth term is found in Exodus 29:42, where it is called the "tent of meeting." This carries the idea of an assembly or congregation together between God's people and the Lord. The final term that is used in Exodus is "the tabernacle of the testimony" (see Exodus 38:21). This term carries the idea that the Ten Commandments were located in the Tabernacle. It implies that the people are required to obey the Commandments.

So why is this all so important? The problem of sin by Adam and Eve passed upon all humankind. To please God, the problem of sin had to be dealt with. God cannot have fellowship with persons who disobey His law. God spoke to Abraham and called him from his home in Ur, to Haran, and then to the Promised Land of Palestine. Abraham and his family continued to worship God and to sacrifice to God. But there was no permanent dwelling place for God among His people. After the patriarchs, four hundred years passed while the children of Israel were in captivity in Egypt. The people of Israel worshipped God as best they knew how.

But now as they left Egypt, it was time for a more meaningful worship experience to take place on a regular basis in a place designed for worship. The problem of sin among God's people required sacrifice of the life of an animal to cover this sin of the people. In order to provide both the place of worship and a place for sacrifice, God called Moses into His holy mountain, Mount Sinai, to instruct him on building a house for the Lord. This house would permit sacrifice and cleansing from sin while at the same time providing a place for worship and communion between God and His people. Such a house had to be movable so that the people could wander for the next forty years through the wilderness before they settled in the Promised Land. Actually, the Tabernacle served as a meeting place between God and His people for the next four hundred years.

The Tabernacle in the Wilderness represented God's program for redeeming His people from their sin. We will find it helpful to study the Tabernacle in order to understand the way in which God has provided redemption for us from our sin. For this reason God allowed the large number of chapters in the Bible to be devoted to the Tabernacle. If we come to understand the meaning of the Tabernacle, we can also come to understand the meaning of the redemption that Jesus provided for us through His sacrificial death on the cross. Through Jesus, God dealt permanently with the sin problem for all time. We all sin and will continue to sin throughout this life. But we do not have to sacrifice animals today in order to receive forgiveness for our sins. God has provided a better way. We must accept the forgiveness for our sins that God freely provided for us through Jesus' death on the cross and His resurrection from the dead. In other words Jesus, who never sinned, became sin for us. Jesus became the sacrifice that provides God's forgiveness for us. We will talk about Jesus' role in God's plan further along.

DESIGN OF THE TABERNACLE

The Tabernacle was located at the center of the Hebrew community. The twelve tribes of Israel surrounded the Tabernacle. The tents for the priests and Levites were located directly joining the Tabernacle. Beyond the priests and Levites there were the twelve tribes, with three each located to the north, south, east, and west. Altogether there may have been about three million people among the Israelite tribes. It has been suggested that the total area taken up by the people of Israel would have been about twelve square miles. If, when the people were on the move, they walked about fifty persons across in a line, then the line would have measured about forty miles in length.

The outer court of the Tabernacle measured about 150 feet in length and 75 feet in width. The outer court was protected by an outer curtain that was attached to sixty pillars. The pillars were made of acacia wood covered with bronze. Acacia wood was a hard wood that could withstand the weather. It would last for many years and protected the Tabernacle. A silver bar was attached to the top of each pillar. Each pillar was strung to a stake by rope, which held it in place. Ropes were placed on both the inside and the outside of the curtain. Within the enclosure, separated from the outside, were the altar of sacrifice and the Laver and the Tabernacle.

The Tabernacle was about forty-five feet long, fifteen feet wide, and ten feet high. The walls consisted of polls of acacia wood, covered with gold. These walls could be taken down for transportation, as the people moved from one location to another. Tent ropes supported the Tabernacle,

RECONSTRUCTION OF THE TABERNACLE

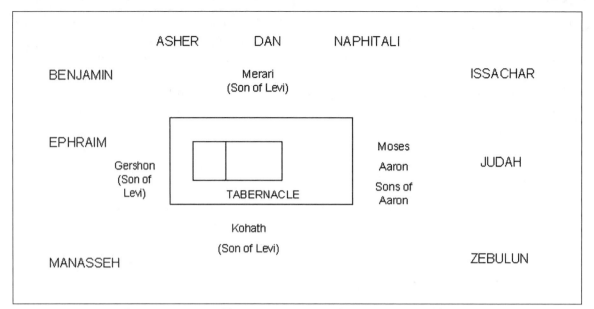

LAYOUT OF THE TABERNACLE WITH SURROUNDING TRIBES

similar to the ones that were used to support the curtains that surrounded the enclosure. There were also a series of coverings that protected the Tabernacle. These were placed across the top along the sides and across the back of the Tabernacle. There were different colored curtains, including a seraph-pattern covering, white covering, red covering, blue covering, and purple covering. These were made of fine linen. Over the top of these coverings were coverings of goat hair. The outer layers were ram and goatskins. The purpose of these coverings was to protect the entire Tabernacle from the weather conditions.

The interior of the Tabernacle consisted of two rooms. The outer room was called the Holy Place. Only the priests were able to enter the Holy Place. It contained several pieces of furniture. It measured about thirty feet by fifteen feet. The inner room was the Most Holy Place. The Most Holy Place was a perfect cube of fifteen feet, by fifteen feet, by fifteen feet. It contained one piece of furniture, the Ark of the Covenant. The Most Holy Place was only entered by the high priest one day out of the year, on the Day of Atonement. The Holy Place was separated from the Most Holy Place by a veil. The veil

was embroidered with cherubim, the sacred guardians of the Most Holy Place. All of the workmanship in the Tabernacle was of the highest quality. The Tabernacle must have been a beautiful sight to the Israelite people as they looked toward the middle of their encampment. It would shine in the sunlight and the beautiful coverings were visible from outside the enclosure.

THE COURT

The court of the Tabernacle is surrounded with a white linen curtain. It stood 7 1/2 feet in height. The curtain was supported by pillars of bronze. This is described in Exodus 27:9–18 and 38:9–20. The purpose of the court was to protect the dwelling place of the Lord among His people from any careless entrance by persons from the camp of the Israelites or from wandering animals. The court contains an area about 150 feet long and 75 feet wide. Recall that enclosed in the court are two pieces of furniture, the altar and the Laver, as well as the Tabernacle itself. The Tabernacle always faced toward the east. The entrance to the Tabernacle was gained through a curtain of linen that differed from the white curtain. It was dyed blue, purple, and scarlet. Israelites could enter the outer court to bring their sacrifices to the priests. But they were not allowed to go any farther into the Tabernacle. Only the priests are allowed to go to the Laver and beyond to the Tabernacle itself.

THE ALTAR

The first piece of furniture one could see upon entering the enclosure was the altar of sacrifice. The altar is described in Exodus 27:1–8 and 38:1–7. The altar was constructed of wood that was covered with bronze. The altar was hollow on the inside. At the bottom it had a grate, which would allow the priests to remove the burned coals. The priests used little shovels, pans, and fire pans for the removal of the coals. There were four horns at each of the corners of the altar. These were used to anchor the sacrifice to the altar. They were also used by the priests to sprinkle the blood of the sacrifice on the horns of the altar. The Old Testament tells us that a criminal could seek protection by clinging to the horns of the altar.

In the New Testament we can see how Jesus became our sacrifice when He died on the cross for our sins (see Romans 3:25–26). As a result, when we trust in Jesus, God declares us to be justified and removes our sin. Jesus' death on the cross purchased salvation for everyone who believes.

The Laver

Standing behind the altar but in front of the Tabernacle was a large bronze basin that was known as the Laver. When the priests completed the blood sacrifices, their hands were covered with blood, and their feet were dirty from the sandy courtyard. They were required to use the Laver to wash their hands and feet before they entered the Tabernacle. The Laver was never used by common Israelites. It was for the exclusive use of the priests. The priests had to wash and make themselves clean before they could enter the Holy Place of the Tabernacle in their service for God.

THE TABERNACLE ITSELF

The Tabernacle is described in Exodus 26:1–37. The Tabernacle was a tent. It was a symbol of God's dwelling among His people. It was constructed so that they could easily be taken apart and transported to a new location. When they arrived at a new location, it could easily be reassembled and again become the center of the encampment of the people of Israel. The Tabernacle represented God to the people. The Tabernacle itself and all of the furnishings served as symbols of God's relationship with His people. The Tabernacle was beautiful and constructed of the best materials. The best craftsmen were employed to create this sanctuary for God.

The Four Coverings

It was covered with four coverings. The first covering was made up of ten linen curtains. These formed the inner side walls and ceiling for the Tabernacle. When the priests would work in the Holy Place or the Most Holy Place, they would see these inner curtains. Each time the priest entered the Tabernacle, he would be in the presence of the God of Abraham, Isaac, and Jacob. These curtains helped the priests to understand the holiness of God. As the priest looked at the ceiling, he would see linen curtains with a background of blue, purple, and scarlet. The blue was a reminder of the God's heavenly nature. Purple called attention to God as king. The scarlet help the priest understand God's love for human persons by allowing them to come to Him through sacrifice. The holiness of God was represented by the cherubim, which were embroidered on each curtain. Surrounded by the beauty and symbols of God's majesty and love, the priest would certainly have been overwhelmed in his personal worship of God.

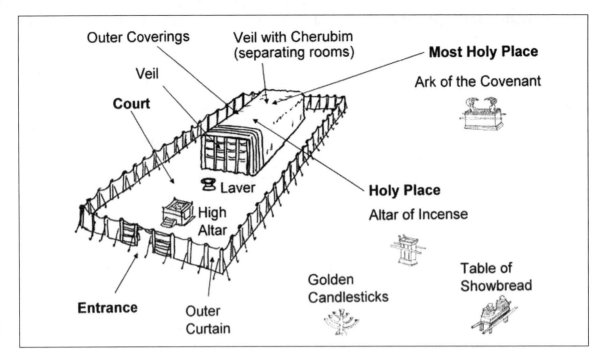

TABERNACLE AND FURNITURE

Over the linen curtains was a second covering of goat hair. This was probably black in color. The texture of this covering was coarse. It was not attractive. While the inner curtains reminded us of the beauty and majesty of God, the goat-hair covering was a reminder of human sin. Sin is never attractive. Sin must always be forgiven before a person can enter the Tabernacle of God.

On top of the goathair was a third covering of ram skins. These skins were dyed red. The red skins remind us of the sacrifice that must take place for us to find fellowship with God. The fourth and final one over the Tabernacle was the leather or sealskin covering. This was a protective covering for the tent or Tabernacle. It was a symbol of the separation of the holiness of God from the world that surrounded the Tabernacle. The weather would have caused harm to the Tabernacle if it had not had a good protective covering. The scorching sun from the heat of the desert, the heavy rains, and the sandstorms would all have damaged the Tabernacle, but the sealskins provided a good shelter.

The Structure of the Building

Recall that the Tabernacle was constructed of the hard wood from the acacia tree. The wooden supports held the weight of the heavy curtains. The supports were boards that were placed upright. Each board was fifteen feet long and two and a half feet wide. The boards could be taken apart for easy movement when the Tabernacle had to be transported. Under each board was a socket of silver, which weighed about 75 pounds. Each Israelite contributed silver as part of the atonement money given to God. Silver represented the redemption of man from his sin. The instructions for building the Tabernacle were complete. God told Moses to build the Tabernacle exactly according to His instructions. The Israelites were not free to change the plans for the Tabernacle in any way.

Passing through the curtain at the entrance to the Tabernacle itself, the priest would enter the Holy Place. This was a room that measured about thirty feet long and fifteen feet wide. It contained three pieces of furniture. The first was the golden menorah or candlesticks. The menorah provided light for the priests to work within the Holy Place. The second was the Table of Showbread. This contained twelve loaves of bread, representing the twelve tribes of Israel. The third piece of furniture was an Altar of Incense. It provided a sweet-smelling fragrance within the Tabernacle. Each of these pieces of furniture had to be tended regularly by the priests. We will look at each of the pieces of furniture in greater detail.

An inner veil separated the Holy Place from the Most Holy Place. This inner curtain separated God, who dwelled in the Most Holy Place, from the place where the priests served. The room was about fifteen feet by fifteen feet. The priests were not permitted to enter the Most Holy Place. Only once a year on the Day of Atonement or Yom Kippur, the High Priest would enter the Most Holy Place and place the blood sacrifice on the Mercy Seat of the Ark of the Covenant. The inner veil protected the presence of God Himself in His majesty and holiness from sinful humankind. Sinful mankind did not have any access to a holy and righteous God, apart from the Mercy Seat. God's mercy provides the only means by which people can come to a holy God. God is the one who invites us to this inner place of meeting to come to Him and receive his mercy. Humans can only approach God through fear, awe, respect, and reverence.

Through Jesus Christ it is now possible to come directly to God. Jesus' death on the cross provided the sacrifice that was necessary for us to find a relationship with God. When a person comes to new life in Christ, he or she receives the Holy Spirit to live within his or her life. As a result, we no longer need to come through a priest. Access to God comes directly through the Lord Jesus Christ. The veil that was necessary in the Tabernacle no longer prevents us from coming directly to God. God loves us so much that he provided His own perfect Son to be the sacrifice that opens the gates of heaven to us.

The outer curtain, which separated the outer courtyard from the Holy Place, was similar to the veil that separated the Holy Place from the Most Holy Place. There was one important difference, however. The outer curtain did not have the cherubim embroidered upon the cloth. It was a symbol of entering the presence of God from the outer courtyard.

The Furniture of the Tabernacle

The Golden Lampstand stood on the left or south side of the Tabernacle. It was the most beautiful piece of furniture in the outer room or Holy Place. It was made of gold and weighed about eighty pounds and was fashioned by skilled craftsmen. The lampstand had a center stem and three branches on each side. There were three almond blossoms on each branch. There were four blossoms on a center stem. The oil that was used in the lamps was pure olive oil. The olives were beaten instead of being ground in a mill. This process gave the purest form of oil for burning in the Tabernacle.

The lamps were kept burning at all times. This was one of the tasks for the priests. Each morning and evening the priest would come and trim the lamps. The flickering flames from the lamps would have added to the awe of the Holy Place. Again God provided strict instructions on how to produce the Golden Lampstand. Since the Holy Place would have been in complete darkness without the lampstand, this was an important piece of furniture in the Tabernacle.

For the Christian today, Jesus is the light of the world (see John 8:12). Jesus is the only way by which we can find light that will lead us to eternity with God. The gold in the lampstand reminds us that Jesus was the Divine Son of God. When He lived as a man here on earth, Jesus did not sin. He was pure.

The Table of Showbread stood on the north side of the Tabernacle. The table was made of acacia wood and covered with gold. Skilled craftsmen constructed the table. The table was about 3 feet long and 1 1/2 feet wide. It had a rim around the table that probably served to keep the bread from slipping from the table. The serving plates were made of pure gold. The term showbread tells of the presence of God. The bread represented a meal offering that was given to God. The showbread consisted of twelve loaves that were changed each week. The bread was made of the finest unleavened flour. In the Bible leaven often represents sin. It is not surprising that the bread on the Table of Showbread would be presented before the Lord without leaven. Each loaf represented one of the twelve tribes of Israel. The priests were able to eat the loaves of bread after they were removed from the table. But they were required to eat the bread within the Tabernacle.

The life of Jesus pictured him as the Bread of Life. Jesus was born in the city of Bethlehem. *Bethlehem* means "the house of bread." In many places Jesus used bread during his ministry. The miracle of the feeding of the five thousand involved the multiplication of loaves of bread. During the Last Supper, Jesus broke the bread for His disciples. He told us to follow His example. He referred to His body as bread of life, broken for us on the cross at Calvary. For a Christian it is important for us to have the bread of God's presence in Jesus and the opportunity to worship Him.

The Golden Altar of Incense was much smaller than the High Altar. It was located at the west end in the center of the Holy Place, in front of the curtain that led to the presence of God. The Golden Altar of Incense was about 3 feet high and 1 1/2 feet square. Like so many other pieces of furniture in the Tabernacle, the Golden Altar of Incense was made of acacia wood and covered with gold. The altar had poles on each side, which were used for carrying the altar when the Tabernacle was moved. The priest would take a censer that was full of burning coals from the altar. He would add incense, which provided a sweet smell as the smoke rose in the Holy Place.

The Lord instructed Moses to use three fragrant spices. They were stacte, a sweet smelling gum from the storax tree; onycha, from the shell of a shellfish that gave off a sweet fragrance; and galbanum, a sweet milky sap that also gave a sweet fragrance. The incense was burned continually. This was a symbol of the prayers that arose on behalf of the people of Israel before God. For the priest this must have been a very beautiful opportunity to have fellowship with God. Since the altar was the closest piece of furniture to the Most Holy Place, it was the closest that a priest could come to the presence of God. God told Moses that no strange incense could be burned on this altar. He also told Moses that no fire could be used on the altar that did not come from the brazen altar. Like the high altar, the Altar of Incense had one horn at each corner. On the Day of Atonement the high priest would take some of the blood that would be sprinkled on the Mercy Seat and would place it on the horns of the Altar of Incense. This would make atonement for the people's sins and make the people holy to God. The altar also served to cleanse the sins of the priests as well as the people of Israel.

In one of his psalms, David referred to the incense rising before God as a symbol of prayer. He wrote }in Psalm 141:2, "May my prayer be set before You as incense, the raising of my hands as the evening offering." Much later John wrote in Revelation 5:8, "When He took the scroll, the four living creatures and the twenty-four elders fell down before the Lamb. Each one had a harp and gold bowls filled with incense, which are the prayers of the saints." The Lamb here refers to Jesus Christ as the Lamb of God, who was sacrificed on the cross for our sins. Jesus still pleads before the heavenly Father for those who have put their trust in Him. The golden altar is also a symbol of the atonement that Jesus provided for us, through His crucifixion. Just as the high priest sprinkled blood on the horns of the altar on the Day of Atonement, so Jesus purchased our atonement on the cross the Calvary.

Beyond the curtain that had the cherubim embroidered on the cloth was the Most Holy Place. It contained only one piece of furniture, the Ark of the Covenant. This was a symbol of the presence and throne of God. God gave very clear instructions to Moses on the construction of the Ark of the Covenant. This was the most important piece of furniture in the entire Tabernacle. The Ark showed the glory and mercy of a holy God.

Like many of the other pieces of furniture in the Tabernacle, it was constructed of acacia wood that was overlaid with pure gold on both the inside and the outside. The Ark was in the shape of a box or chest that measured about 3 1/4 feet long, 2 1/4 feet wide, and 2 1/4 feet high. There were gold rings attached to the side of the Ark. Through those rings, staves of acacia wood covered with gold could be placed for movement of the ark when it had to be transported. Once the staves were in place within the rings, they became a permanent part of the Ark. Only the high priest was permitted to enter the Most Holy Place or Holy of Holies. The high priest placed the blood of the sacrifice on the mercy seat of the Ark. This was only done on the Day of Atonement.

Three items were placed in the Ark. Each of these items was important to the relationship between God and His people. The first item was the Ten Commandments that God had given to Moses on Mount Sinai. God had taken the tables of stone and written the Commandments on them. This event is described in Exodus 20:1–17. Because the law was included, sometimes the Ark was known as the Testimony of God. The law bound the people to God. It provided guidance for the people's everyday life and the rules that govern the community. They were preserved in the very presence of God.

The second item included in the Ark was a pot of manna. You will recall that manna was given by God from heaven to the children of Israel for food, as they wandered for forty years in the wilderness. This is described in Exodus 16:11–36. *Manna* in Hebrew meant, "what is it?" It was also referred to as "angel's food," "bread of heaven," and "light bread."

The third item to be placed in the Ark was the rod that Aaron carried. This rod head budded to show that Moses and Aaron were God's chosen persons to lead His people, Israel.

On the top of the Ark were two cherubim that faced each other. It is believed that the cherubim were in the form of angelic beings bowed in reverence before God. Their wings covered them. Between the two cherubim was the mercy seat where the high priest placed the blood on the Day of Atonement. The mercy seat was important as a symbol of God's forgiveness for sin by the people of Israel. When the blood was shed in the sacrifice and placed on the mercy seat, God forgave the sins of His people. In the midst of the cherubim was the Shekinah glory of God. This was the symbol of God's presence in the Holy of Holies (see Exodus 25:22). Later, the psalmist wrote of the Shekinah in Psalm 80:1, "Listen, Shepherd of Israel, who guides Joseph like a flock; You who sit enthroned [on] the cherubim, rise up."

The Ark provided a special place where God could meet his people. The people could go to the Tabernacle and know that they were entering into the presence of God. They could worship Him and seek His forgiveness for their sins. The Ark was a symbol of God's mercy and love.

The Ark played an important role in the life of Israel. It is mentioned more than two hundred times throughout the history of the people of God. When the people of God failed to obey Him, the Ark was taken into captivity by the Philistines. When news of the capture of the Ark came to Eli, he fell over and died (see 1 Samuel 4:18). The Ark became a curse to the Philistines (see 1 Samuel 5–6). Later, when David secured Jerusalem, he had the Ark brought up to Jerusalem. After Solomon built the Temple, the Ark was placed in the Holy of Holies in the Temple. It is not known today what became of the Ark. It may have been destroyed when the Babylonians took the people of Judah into captivity. It may have survived and still lies buried under the Temple Mount. There are several other explanations for what happened to the Ark. No one knows for sure. It is possible that it may return again at some future time.

The Priests and Levites of the Tabernacle

God set aside priests to serve in His Tabernacle. The priests served in between the people of Israel and God. They had to live by a higher standard than the average person among the people of Israel. Because they served God and ministered to the people, they were certainly responsible to intercede on behalf of the people for God's pardon for sin. A priest was called by God to serve as a priest in God's service. When Aaron was the high priest, he sprinkled the blood of the sacrifice on the horns of the altar in the holy place, and then he came out from the Tabernacle and blessed the people of Israel (see Leviticus 9:22–24).

Only one family was called and allowed to serve as priests. This was the family of the tribe of Aaron. Every member of the priesthood had to prove that he was descended from the family of Aaron. If he had any physical defects, he could not serve as a priest. A priest had to be morally upright and pure. The purpose of these requirements was to keep the priesthood holy. Exodus 28 is devoted to careful instructions about the garments and robes the priests wore. God gave Moses complete instructions about the priest and the priesthood. Each of the garments was important and was a symbol that spoke to the people about God and his holiness.

The first responsibility of the priests was to offer sacrifice to God. They did this on the altar of sacrifice. In most cases they had to kill the animal sacrifice, sprinkle the blood on the altar, and keep the fire on the altar burning. The priests participated in judging the people. This major responsibility was given to them (see Deuteronomy 17:8–13).

The priests were also responsible to teach the Word of God to the people. Along with conducting sacrifice, teaching the people was one of the most important tasks for the priest (see Deuteronomy 33:10). The priest was to give guidance to the people on the laws of purity and impurity. The priest was to teach the Torah. The books of the law were kept by the priests. During the reign of King Hezekiah, the priests rediscovered the law that had been lost for generations. The priests were also expected to be holy to the Lord. They were consecrated at their ordination service. The service lasted for seven days. Even though there were many priests, the priests could not do all of the work that was required to manage the Tabernacle. As a result God gave that responsibility to the family of Levi.

The high priest had special privileges and responsibilities. The high priests that followed Aaron came from the eldest son in his family. The high priest was more important than the regular priests. He wore a miter on his head. This was similar to the crown that a king would wear. He was anointed with oil, similar to the anointing of a king. His garments included the colors of gold and purple, suggesting royalty. If he had any physical disabilities, he was disqualified from becoming the high priest. From his earliest experiences he was designated to become high priest and had to live and act accordingly. He carried important responsibilities in tending to the service in the Holy Place. The consecration of the high priest, as he was installed in his office, was extensive. The most important task that the high priest carried out during the course of a year was to officiate in the Holy of Holies on the Day of Atonement. He was the only priest who could make atonement for the sins of the people, the priests, and his own household. He was responsible for tending the furniture in the holy place. From its origin with Aaron, the position of high priest was always very important.

Jesus was our high priest. But Jesus was not after the order of Aaron. The writer to the Hebrews tells us that Jesus was after the order of Melchizedek (see Hebrews 5:1–14; 6:20). Melchizedek was a priest to the Most High God, by whom Abraham was blessed and to whom Abraham gave a tenth of his possessions (see Genesis 14:17–20). Jesus was the perfect high priest. Since Aaron and his sons had also to seek God's forgiveness for their sins, Jesus could not be from the tribe of Aaron. As the Son of God, Jesus provides forgiveness for us by the sacrifice of His own blood and therefore can bring us into the very presence of God. We are truly blessed to have Jesus as our high priest!

The Levites were set apart for their office by Aaron (see Numbers 1:47–54). They could not carry out the roles designated to the priests unless the number of priests had become so small that they were unable to carry out their responsibilities. The Levites did not receive a parcel of land when the distribution of land took place under Joshua. Rather, they had a number of cities set apart throughout the land of Palestine. The Levites lived in these cities when they were not working in the Tabernacle. There were three groups within the tribe of Levi. Each group had its own responsibilities in caring for the Tabernacle during the time the Tabernacle was moved from place to place. The Kohathites were responsible to carry the Tabernacle furniture. The Gershonites were responsible to care for the coverings of the Tabernacle, the screens and hangings. The Merarites were responsible to carry and to put up the Tabernacle when the people of Israel arrived at a new location.

Recall from the diagram of the placement of the tribes of Israel around the Tabernacle that the three groups of Levites were placed in an area closest to the Tabernacle. In this way they could help to protect the Tabernacle from persons who might intrude wrongly and dishonor the dwelling place of God among His people.

The Sacrifices of the Tabernacle

One of the most important parts of the Tabernacle was the brazen altar. On the altar there were five different types of sacrifices were offered to God. The purpose of the sacrifices was first to atone for the sin of the people. Some animals were sacrificed for the entire community. Other animals were sacrificed by the priest for an individual.

When it was a sin offering, the person who came to bring the offering placed his hand on the head of the animal. In this way he passed the sin that he had committed onto the animal, who died in his place. In the Book of Hebrews, the writer under the guidance of the Holy Spirit made clear that the priest was responsible to shed the blood of an animal for the sins of the people. "In the same way, he sprinkled the tabernacle and all the vessels of worship with blood. According to the law almost everything is purified with blood, and without the shedding of blood there is no forgiveness" (9:21–22).

Second, there were some additional sacrifices that were designed to express gratitude in thanksgiving to God for his goodness to the people. Offerings were divided into sweet and nonsweet sacrifices. The nonsweet sacrifices were offered to atone for sin. The sweet sacrifices were offered to God as a way of expressing gratitude, love, and worship. The sweet offerings were the burnt offering, meal offering, and peace offering. In all, five offerings were sacrificed on the altar to God. Five different animals were used in the sacrificial system. They were the bull, goat, lamb, turtledove, and the pigeon. The sacrifices are described in Leviticus 1–7. Similar to the construction of the Tabernacle, God prescribed every detail that was necessary for the sacrifices. The priests were to follow these prescriptions carefully.

The Burnt Offering

The burnt offering is described in Leviticus 1. The burnt offering was carried out every day in the morning and evening. Its purpose was to atone for the sins of the people. Two lambs that were a year old and without blemish were sacrificed. Recall that when a person brought a sacrifice, he placed his hand on a head of the creature to indicate that he was surrendering to God (see Leviticus 1:4). In this way the worshipper asked that God would accept the offering in his place. The worshipper made atonement for his sin. In this type of sacrifice, the entire animal was consumed by the fire, except the skin. The skin was kept by the priest, but none of the animal was eaten. Whether the worshipper brought a bull, a lamb, a goat, a turtledove, or a pigeon depended upon his financial situation. At the birth of Jesus, Mary and Joseph were poor and had to sacrifice a pair of turtledoves.

The Meal Offering

The meal offering was different from other sacrifices. A description of this offering is provided in Leviticus 2. The Hebrew word for meal carries the idea of the gift. This offering did not require the shedding of blood. There were several types of meal offerings. Leaven was allowed in the peace offering as a thanksgiving to God for His goodness and for the peace He provided. Olive oil was often mixed with the meal offering. Salt is often used with this offering, probably to preserve the meal. No honey was used in these offerings. The meal offering was often a thank offering for providing daily bread. The portion of this offering that went to God was consumed by the fire. The remainder of the meal offering was eaten by the priests either in the court or in the Holy Place. When the meal offering was given by the worshipper for the expression of thanks to God for the crops, the whole harvest was dedicated to the Lord. This was a sweet offering to the Lord. The worshipper also put frankincense on the offering, which gave it have a sweet smelling scent (see Leviticus 2:14).

The Peace Offering

Leviticus 3 describes the peace offering. This is an offering given to God in worship. The Hebrew term used for this offering is *shalom*. It means "peace." It also means an offering of thanksgiving and fellowship with God. The person bringing the offering presented it to Lord as an act of worship. A bull, cow, lamb, or goat might be given as a peace offering. This offering was similar to the burnt offering to this point. But in this offering only the fat and kidneys were burned on the altar to the Lord. The rest was taken by the offerer and eaten by both the priest and the person bringing the offering. In other words, it was a peace offering of communion between God and the worshipper. This offering was also a sweet offering to the Lord.

The Sin Offering

The sin offering is described in Leviticus 4. The sin offering was not a sweet offering to the Lord. It was necessary and the foundation for all other offerings because it was intended to pay for the sin the worshipper had committed. Notice that this is not an offering for sin that one committed by intentionally breaking one of the Commandments or rebelling against God. There is no offering designed to forgive intentional sin. Only God alone can forgive such sin. The blood of the offering was sprinkled in the Holy Place, on the golden altar of incense, and poured out at the brazen altar. There were different types of sin offerings that were prescribed for a whole congregation, for rulers, and for individuals.

The Trespass Offering

The fifth offering was the trespass offering, described in Leviticus 5. The trespass offering was similar to the sin offering, but it emphasized sin against another person. The sin offering provided atonement for the sinner, while this offering emphasized repairing the damage or hurt done to another person. It involved paying money for sins of ignorance where another person might have been cheated. If a person were hunting and accidentally killed an animal belonging to a neighbor, the trespass offering would have been given to repair the damage. The person who committed the wrong would offer the amount of money to the priest and also to the person who was wronged. In the trespass offering the person who had sinned would pay double the amount he had taken. He would add an extra 40 percent (see Leviticus 6:5–6).

The Temple of Solomon

Several hundred years passed from the time of the Exodus under Moses and the founding of the Tabernacle to the time of the kings of Israel (see 2 Samuel 7). The Tabernacle had served well over these years. But when the Philistines, a sea-faring and war-like people from the southern coastal region along the Mediterranean Sea, fought with the Israelites and won, they took the Ark of the Covenant. It had been kept in Shiloh. The defeat of the Israelites by the Philistines allowed the Ark to be captured and taken back to their country. The Lord allowed this to happen because the Israelites were not following God as they had promised. They were worshipping the idols of the peoples around them. But when the Ark caused the Philistines many problems, they finally returned it to the people of Israel.

While there may have been a small temple at Shiloh, it was clearly time for the Israelites to build a Temple to God and a permanent place for the Ark of the Covenant. After David became king, he captured the city and Jerusalem. It was occupied by the people called the Jebusites. David's men entered the city through an old well that went under the wall. They opened the gates, and the Israelite soldiers were able to capture the city. David did not believe that a tent was adequate to house the Ark of the Covenant. He built a palace for himself, and he wanted to build a Temple to God. The prophet Nathan told David that God did not want him to build the Temple. David had been a man of war. God told David that his son Solomon would build the Temple. David made all the preparations necessary by collecting materialist such as gold, silver, wood, and stone that would be used in the temple. Before continuing, you might search for and find Shiloh, Philistia, and Jerusalem on an Old Testament map.

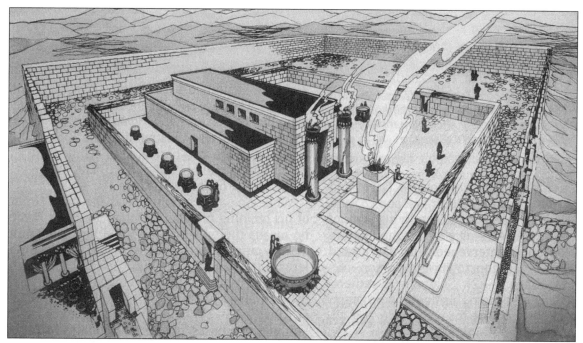

RECONSTRUCTION OF SOLOMON'S TEMPLE

SOLOMON BUILDS A TEMPLE

The Temple that Solomon built was very large. The dimensions of the Temple were ninety feet in length, thirty feet in width, and forty-five feet in height. The outside of the Temple was stone block, while the inside was lined with cedar along the walls and cyprus on the ceiling. The floor was made of fir. The walls of the Temple may have been as much as nine feet thick. The Temple was about two times the size of the Tabernacle. There were three rooms in the Temple, as there had been in the Tabernacle. The inner walls were lined with gold. The first room was a vestibule that opened into the Holy Place. Outside the vestibule were two large bronze pillars. They were named Jachin, which means "He will establish" and Boaz "in the strength of." The names of both pillars had reference to God. A person had to enter the second room through two massive doors. The second room was the Holy Place and contained the Golden Lamp Stand, the Table of Showbread, and the Altar of Incense. The Ark of the Covenant was placed in the third room or Holy of Holies. This chamber was completely dark or as the Scripture describes it, "thick darkness" (see 1 Kings 8:12).

Outside the Temple stood the large bronze altar. It was fifteen feet high and thirty feet square (see 2 Chronicles 4:1). Behind the altar and in front of the doors that entered the Temple stood the Molten Sea. This was an enlargement of the Laver from the Tabernacle. It was 7 1/2 feet high and in the shape of a cup that was 15 feet across. The Molten Sea was set on the twelve bronze oxen in sets of three on each of the four sides. It held ten thousand gallons of water. It is believed that there was some form of siphon system to refresh the water each day. Before the priests could enter the Holy Place, they had to wash in the Laver. It was no different in the Temple.

Alongside the Temple and on either side were ten small lavers. Each of these held two hundred gallons of water for washing the utensils that were used in sacrifice. These Lavers were set on wheels, in order to move them around the courtyard (see 2 Chronicles 4:6).

The Temple stood facing the East, just as the Tabernacle had before it. The site on which the Temple was constructed was on the eastern hill of the two hills on which Jerusalem was built. To construct the Temple there, the builders had to cut off a large section of the hill and build up the section that went into the Valley. Archaeologists have found large supports that were built by Solomon's builders to hold the immense structure of the Temple. This was all done without the use of modern earth-moving equipment or cranes to move large stones.

The hill on which the Temple was placed is known as Mount Moriah (see 2 Chronicles 3:1). You may recall that Mount Moriah was the mountain on which Abraham was called by God to sacrifice his son Isaac. Abraham's obedience on that occasion allowed God to substitute a ram for Abraham's son.

This is important today since the Temple was destroyed almost two thousand years ago, and in its place the Dome of the Rock has been constructed by the people of Islam. The gold Dome can be seen as a dominant structure in Jerusalem today. The only remaining part of the temple in Jerusalem today is the Western Wall. This is still sacred to the Jewish community.

To build the Temple, Solomon had a workforce that included thirty thousand laborers, who worked in Lebanon to bring cedar and cyprus wood for the Temple. He had seventy thousand porters, who transported stone for the Temple. In the quarries he employed eighty thousand men as stonecutters. There were also thirty-three hundred overseers. The building project took seven years to complete (see 1 Kings 5:13–18).

Dedication of Solomon's Temple

The Temple was started in the fourth year of Solomon's reign and completed seven years later (see 1 Kings 6:38). The dedication of the Temple took place at the Feast of Tabernacles (see 1 Kings 8:1–11). After several hundreds of years had passed, the only items in the Ark were the two tables of stone on which God had written the Ten Commandments. The Ark, containing the Ten Commandments was brought by the priests to the Temple. Meanwhile the priests were sacrificing many sheep and cattle. King Solomon blessed the people who had come to celebrate the opening of the Temple. Solomon prayed to bless the Temple and ask God to come from his heavenly throne to this earthly Temple. The presence of God was within the Temple, as the *Shekinah* glory of the Lord appeared in a cloud.

After Solomon had finished his entire building program, the Lord appeared to Solomon for a second time. The first time God appeared to Solomon He promised to grant Solomon whatever he wanted. Solomon prayed for wisdom, and it was given to him along with wealth. God told Solomon that if he and his sons would worship God alone and not the gods of the neighboring peoples, then the Lord God would bless the throne of Solomon. God promised that the Temple would continue to be God's dwelling place among his people. But if Solomon and his sons did not keep the Commandments of the Lord, then God would leave the Temple, and it would be destroyed. The people of Israel would suffer the consequences of being taken into captivity and their land would be destroyed. The temptation to sin was ever present, and unless there is a wholehearted repentance, God will not stay with his people. They were to stay away from idols and mixing the

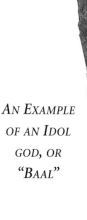

AN EXAMPLE
OF AN IDOL
GOD, OR
"BAAL"

worship of their neighbors with the worship of the Lord Jehovah.

Later History of Solomon's Temple

Solomon failed to follow what God had commanded. He married many wives from other nations. They brought their gods with them. Solomon did not do what his father David had done. Solomon built many altars to the gods of his wives. The Lord became angry with Solomon (see 1 Kings 11:1–10). The Lord only spared Solomon's kingdom for the sake of his father David, who had walked in the way God desired.

Evils of Later Kings

After Solomon's death, the kingdom split in two. Solomon's son Rehoboam promised to tax the people more than his father. The northern ten tribes left Rehoboam and followed Jeroboam. Jeroboam did not want his people to go to Jerusalem to worship God. He set up altars to idols at Bethel and Dan. But the southern two tribes of Benjamin and Judah continued to serve Solomon's son Rehoboam. Rehoboam married Maacah, who was an idol worshipper. When her son Abijam came to the throne, she brought many evil practices into the Temple. (see 1 Kings 15:1–8).

The next king, Asa, took away many of the evil practices, but he took money and silver from the Temple to pay tribute to Ben-Hadad, king of Syria. He wanted the Syrian king to help him fight against the king of Israel. Later, Queen Athaliah brought more evil practices by taking things that were dedicated to the Lord Jehovah from the Temple and used them for her idol gods, the Baals (see 2 Chronicles 24:7).

Good King Uzziah opposed idol worship and restored the Temple worship of the Lord God Jehovah. But he received leprosy when he entered the Holy Place and offered incense. Remember that only the priests could enter the Holy Place. Other kings took gold from the inside of the Temple to pay tribute to foreign kings, who threatened the security of Judah. Perhaps Ahaz was the worst of all the evil kings. He not only took treasures from the Temple but replaced the brazen altar with an altar to the pagan gods. He also removed the oxen from the base of the Molten Sea.

Attempts to Bring Worship Back to God

Hezekiah wanted to bring religion back to the service of God. But to preserve the kingdom, he had to pay tribute to the Assyrian king, Sennacherib. He had stripped the gold and silver from the Temple (see 2 Kings 18:13–16).

When Manasseh led the people into idolatrous worship of the sun god and the Asherah, these evils were brought into the Temple itself. It remained for King Josiah to make repairs in the Temple and to discover the Book of the Law. A new covenant was reestablished with the Lord God. There was a cleansing of the Temple, and the evil places to worship the idols were torn down (see 2 Kings 22). Sadly, the people's hearts were not changed. As soon as Josiah left the throne, the people turned back to the idol gods they had worshipped earlier. Even the prophets of God were not able to change the direction toward worship of idols and evil (see Ezekiel 8:5–18).

The End of the Temple

Jehoiachim was the son of Josiah. He came to the throne in 609 BC, and he was controlled by the Egyptian Pharaoh Neco. When Egypt was defeated by Babylon, he transferred his allegiance to Babylon. After three years he rebelled against the Babylonians. His son, Jehoiachim, came to the throne. Because of Jehoiachim's rebellion, Nebuchadnezzar, King of Babylon, came against Judah and took many of gold vessels from the Temple. He also took the Jehoiachim into captivity.

The next king, Zedekiah, rebelled against Nebuchadnezzar. Nebuchadnezzar brought his army and laid siege to Jerusalem for eighteen months. When the people were starving, Nebuchadnezzar entered the city. The Babylonians destroyed Jerusalem and the Temple. Everything was destroyed and burned. Anything that had value was taken off to Babylon. It may have been that the Ark of the Covenant was destroyed at this time as well. We do not know. But we do know that the destruction and burning of Jerusalem brought a final end to Solomon's Temple.

SERVICE IN SOLOMON'S TEMPLE

The primary service in the Temple was to bring offerings to God. These would be in the form of sacrifices on the high altar. These were discussed among the five different types of sacrifices that were given previously in the description of the Tabernacle. Included were sacrifices for sin and sacrifices that would allow the worshipper to come closer to God. In addition to these, a worshipper could make a vow to God in the Temple. In the Temple the person making the vow would also fulfill that vow.

Pattern of Worship

There is no mention that music was sung in Tabernacle worship. It is particularly interesting that the work of the Levites changed when they no longer had to put up the Tabernacle and move it from place to place. Their new work is described in 1 Chronicles 23:28–30: "But their duty will be to assist the sons of Aaron with the service of the LORD's temple, being responsible for the courts and the chambers, the purification of all the holy things, and the work of the service of God's temple—as well as the rows [of the bread of the Presence], the fine flour for the grain offering, the wafers of unleavened bread, the baking, the mixing, and all measurements of volume and length. They are also to stand every morning to give thanks and praise to the LORD, and likewise in the evening."

Notice that the work of the Levites included purification of the holy things, providing for the grain offerings, and especially giving thanks and praise to the Lord. The Levites became skilled in singing and accompanying with lyres, harps, and cymbals (see 1 Chronicles 25:1 and 2 Chronicles 29:25–26). With the help of the Levites, worship now included singing songs of praise and thanksgiving to the Lord.

Many of the psalms that sing praise to God were written by the Levites, like Asaph. He was a leader in worship music among the Levites during the time of David. There are twelve psalms, (see Psalms 50; 73–83) that he is credited with having written. He was also the founder of a group of musicians who served throughout the history of the Temple as talented musicians to lead worship. Several other important Levites, such as Heman, wrote Psalms. He wrote Psalm 88. Jeduthun was another, and he is credited with Psalms, 39, 62, and 77.

Psalms of thanksgiving often accompanied thanksgiving and free will offerings to God. Recall Psalms 107, 118, and 136. Psalms 113–116 and 135 give praise to God. These were sung before the Lord. Consider the first three verses of Psalm 113: "Hallelujah! Give praise, servants of the LORD; praise the name of the LORD. Let the name of the LORD be praised both now and forever. From the rising of the sun to its setting, let the name of the LORD be praised."

There were also the psalms of ascents. These were sung by the worshippers themselves as they made their way up to the holy mountain. The Temple Mount was also known as Mount Zion. The worshippers sang these hymns of praise to God, such as Psalms 120–134.

The pattern for church worship today originated in worship in the Temple. Prayer and praise were an essential part of worship for groups like the Pilgrims, who came to America in 1620. While they did not have musical instruments in their worship, they did sing psalms. One of their favorite praise psalms was Psalm 100. The Pilgrims also engaged in prayer, similar to that which the Levites rendered to God.

Temple Ministers

Similar to the Tabernacle, the priests were descended from the family of Aaron and served as the primary ministers in the Temple. In addition, the Levites served to care for the treasures of the house of God. The Levites also conducted the musical activities in the Temple.

Many other persons served to support persons in the service in the Temple. These were known together as the Nethinim. One of these groups was the Gibeonites. They had surrendered to Joshua back when Joshua led the Israelites to conquer the land of Palestine. They had acted like a people who came from a far country. Actually, they lived in Palestine. They deceived Joshua, in order not to be killed as the other Canaanites, when Joshua conquered the land (see Joshua 9:22–27). As a result they were assigned the tasks of carrying water and cutting wood, needed in service for the Temple. While they were not allowed to marry among the Jewish people, they were treated kindly in every other way, similar to members of the Jewish nation.

Along with the descendents of the Gibeonites were other groups. Some of the Nethinim had been conquered under David and Solomon. There were also bond servants under David and Solomon. They performed other similar tasks that were required in the Temple.

Even after the captivity in Babylon, the Nethinim returned with the Jewish people and helped to rebuild the walls of Jerusalem. They also continued to carry out their tasks in the Temple. Nehemiah said that the Nethinim all settled near the water gate in Jerusalem (see Nehemiah 3:26).

THE SIGNIFICANCE OF THE TEMPLE

The Presence of God

The Temple was first the place where God's presence was found. The Ark of the Covenant was placed within the Holy of the Holies in the Temple. The Temple was the place preferred by Jewish people to engage in prayer. They experienced the warmth and closeness that comes from a relationship with the true and living God. In spite of the fact that many Jewish people violated the law of God and engaged in worship of idols, there were many more Jewish people who loved and served God. They found the Temple to be a special place where they could worship Him.

Even in captivity in Babylon, the Jewish people would turn toward Jerusalem to engage in prayer. The jealousy of the other leaders against Daniel for his high position in the court of Darius caused them to look for something that would bring Daniel down from his high position. They could find nothing except that he prayed to his God every day. They had Darius make a decree that no one could pray to any other God than the king. Daniel knew of their plot but still turned his face toward Jerusalem in prayer to God three times each day. When he was thrown to the lions, he trusted God and was protected from the lions (see Daniel 6:10).

A National Center

The Temple also became a national center for the Jewish nation. The evil families of King Omri and his son Ahaz tried to destroy worship in the Temple and replace Temple worship with worship of the evil gods of the Canaanites. They created shrines and places of worship to these evil gods. You will also recall that the evil Queen Athaliah wanted to destroy worship of Jehovah and replace it with worship of idols. She also created shrines to these evil local gods.

Both King Hezekiah and King Josiah opposed and destroyed the high places that were set up for the worship of these idolatrous gods. They worked hard to create a national worship center to the Lord Jehovah in the Temple. Even the prophets never spoke evil of the Temple. They were opposed to prayers that were simply memorized words, with no meaning. They were opposed to sacrifices and offerings that did not come from a repentant heart. They were opposed to religious acts that were performed before God while the person lived a godless life (see Isaiah 1:10–15 and Jeremiah 14:10–12).

After the destruction of the Temple by the Babylonians in 586 BC, there was a clear desire to rebuild the Temple and restore its central role in Jewish national life. Ezekiel told of a vision for the future Temple (see Ezekiel 40–48). The prophet Haggai criticized the people who had returned to Jerusalem for their failure to rebuild the Temple. He preached on God's behalf to call the people to this important task (see Haggai 1–2). The prophets Zechariah and Malachi also called the people to purity of Temple worship and renewing the covenant that God had established with His people generations earlier at the time of the Tabernacle (see Zechariah 1:16; 6:12; 8:3 and Malachi 1–3).

Festivals of the Jewish Year

Each Jewish male was required to make a pilgrimage three times a year to the Ark of the Lord (see Exodus 23:14–17; 34:18-23; and Deuteronomy 16:16). After the Temple was built, this requirement continued. The three primary feasts for pilgrimage became Passover, Pentecost, and the Feast of Tabernacles. You will find additional details on all of the major Jewish festivals in the *Parent/Teacher Handbook, Volume 2*, pages 39–51. The worshippers had to come to the Temple on these occasions to fulfill that requirement. In the New Testament the city of Jerusalem was filled with pilgrims at the Passover when Jesus was crucified. It was filled again with pilgrims at the feast of Pentecost when the disciples received the Holy Spirit and Peter preached his sermon. Peter's sermon described what God was doing for His people through Christ. Many of these pilgrims accepted Jesus Christ as Messiah on that day and came to faith in Him.

Feast days were an important part of the celebration in the Temple. They occurred regularly throughout the Jewish year. There were appropriate festivals in the Temple on each of these occasions. Imagine the excitement you would experience as a boy or girl going up to Jerusalem with your family and along with many other families. You would sing the psalms and participate in expressions of love for God. The festival atmosphere would be contagious. You would enjoy carrying the palm branches and carrying out the other activities that were part of the festival celebration. On the way to Jerusalem, you would stop at specially prepared places where pilgrims could spend the night. By staying at these places, they would not become unclean and not be disqualified from participating in the Temple worship. Imagine also the wonder of seeing the magnificent Temple on Mount Zion You would watch the priests as they carried out their tasks. You would hear the Levite choirs as they sang their magnificent anthems. You would engage in sacrifice and prayer to the Lord God Jehovah. This would truly be a wonderful, unique, and unforgettable experience!

THE TEMPLE OF ZERUBBABEL

The Persians defeated the Babylonians in 538 BC. Cyrus of Persia made a decree the following year to allow the Jewish refugees to return to Palestine. Cyrus also helped the people rebuild the Temple. He provided money, silver, gold, and many other things that would be necessary for the rebuilding to take place. Cyrus allowed the return of the sacred vessels that had been taken by the Babylonians from the Temple to be restored. He taxed some of the peoples in the eastern provinces to pay for the rebuilding of the Temple.

Rebuilding the Temple

Unfortunately, many of the people who had been taken into captivity by the Babylonians had made a new life in Babylon and other places. They did not want to return to Jerusalem. Only forty thousand Exiles decided to return. They were led by Sheshbazzar, a prince of Judah (see Ezra 1). Sheshbazzar began the work to rebuild the Temple, but he was unable to do more than start the foundation (see Ezra 5:16–17). Opposition from the persons who remained in Palestine during the time of the captivity forced the project to stop. Many believe that Sheshbazzar was the uncle of Zerubbabel, who took over and continued the rebuilding of the Temple. Zerubbabel was also the grandson of Jehoiachin, who had been king when the Jews were taken into captivity by Nebuchadnezzar.

Zerubbabel, with permission from the new Persian emperor Darius, continued the rebuilding of the Temple. Zerubbabel disappeared. We do not know what happened to him, but the prophets Haggai and Zechariah urged the builders to continue. By 516 BC the Temple was finished (see Ezra 5–6). We know from documents found in Persia the emperor wanted this project to be completed. We do not know much about the size of the new Temple or how it was situated. Apparently the size was similar to Solomon's Temple, but it was not nearly as glorious and majestic. Some even cried when they saw it as they remembered the beauty of the Temple of Solomon.

Zerubbabel's Temple did become the symbol of God's presence among his people. It became the center of Jewish worship again. The priests carried out their responsibilities in sacrifices and worship. The people had a center to which they could go on the feast days and throughout the year to give their offerings and worship to God.

The Maccabean Revolt

The Old Testament came to an end with the prophecies of the prophet Malachi. We can learn from the books of the Maccabees and the writings of the Jewish historian Josephus about the fortunes of the Second Temple. One of the most important events that occurred during the four hundred years between the end of the Old Testament and the beginning of the New Testament was the Maccabean revolt. You can read about Alexander the Great in the geography section which follows.

Since Alexander had no heirs, his kingdom was divided among his generals. Ptolomy took Egypt and Palestine and ruled from Alexandria. The Jews were allowed to worship God and were protected in Alexandria.

Seleucus took Syria and the East. Seleucus founded the city of Antioch. A bitter rivalry developed between the Ptolemies and the Seleucids. As the kingship passed from one generation to the next, significant changes occurred. Antiochus III sent his army against the Ptolemies of Egypt. Antiochus III gained control over Palestine. Antiochus III was a friend to the Jews and the Temple. He provided oil, frankincense, wine, flour, and salt for the Temple. He encouraged the priests and others who served in the Temple by not requiring the payment of taxes.

Antiochus III was followed by Seleucus IV. He carried out a similar policy as his predecessor toward the Jews and the Temple. There was one exception. He did not hesitate to take money from the Temple treasury when he was in debt financially.

Seleucus IV was followed by Antiochus IV Epiphanes. He was king from 175 to 163 BC. Antiochus IV Epiphanes was an evil king. He believed that the best way to keep the kingdom together was to have all people serve the same god. This god for Antiochus was the Greek god Zeus. Antiochus marched toward Egypt, and reports came back that he had been killed there. He had not been killed. Realizing the joy that news of his death brought to the people of Israel, Antiochus marched back to Jerusalem determined to punish the people of Judah. He took control of the Temple. No longer was the Temple dedicated to

Jehovah God. Antiochus dedicated the Temple to Zeus. In place of the normal sacrifices on the altar, Antiochus had sacrifices of pigs placed on the altar every day. The people of Israel were no longer able to carry out their Jewish practices.

Before the captivity the people of Israel easily followed other gods. But captivity changed God's people. They were now zealous for the Lord God Jehovah. A godly old priest named Mattathias and his five sons organized a revolt against the Seleucids. They raided the Seleucid military camps. They tore down the altars to the foreign gods. Even though their forces were no match for the military might of the Seleucids, they inflicted so many problems upon the Seleucids that the Seleucids sued for peace. Three years after the Seleucids had entered the Temple and disgraced it, the Maccabeans freed Palestine on December 15, 165 BC.

The Temple was cleansed from the foreign gods of the Seleucids. All of the remains of their idolatrous worship were taken from the Temple and Israel. The Jews had eight days of celebration in which they rejoiced over the defeat of their enemy from the north. There was only enough oil to keep the lamps lit in the Temple for one day. But God miraculously supplied oil for the eight days of celebration. The oil never ran out. This celebration became known as Hanukkah. *Hanukkah* means the "Festival of Lights" or "Festival of Dedication." This holiday continues to be celebrated by Jews all over the world even today, as an important event in the life of Israel.

HEROD'S TEMPLE

Years passed. Rome became the ruler over Palestine. You will find additional information on this subject in a geography section on Rome. Herod the Great became the new ruler of Israel in 37 BC. He came from Idumea. The people of Idumea were descended from Esau. Therefore, Herod was not a Jew, although he was married to a

Jewish woman, Mariamne. Herod wanted to prove to Rome that he was loyal and at the same time could find favor among his subjects, the people of Israel. As a result, in the eighteenth year of his reign, he started a building project that would continue long after his death. He decided to rebuild the Temple.

Rebuilding the Temple

Since the Jews had learned their lesson about foreign gods, while they were in captivity, the Temple had become dear to them. Herod was aware of this and tried to stop their fears by having most of the materials for the work on the Temple in place before he began building. He even had one thousand priests trained to do stonework and carpentry, which would be necessary for the inner sacred parts of the Temple. No Gentile could enter there. In addition, he brought ten thousand workmen to help with the rebuilding project. This project began in 20 BC and was not completed until AD 64. It took eighty-four years to complete. It was finished only six years before the Romans completely destroyed it.

Herod wanted to increase the size of the Temple. In order to do this, he had to build a larger platform. To accomplish that, the builders constructed supporting walls. Then they filled in the area around the walls. They doubled the size of the mount. The Temple complex covered about thirty-five acres. On this platform they constructed the temple. The walls were made of white marble. Gold and silver were used to decorate the doors.

The Second Temple had been in the shape of a square. Now it was extended to take the shape of a rectangle. The Temple was doubled in size. The entire complex was contained within the Court of the Gentiles. Gentiles, or non-Jews, could only enter the Gentile section of the Temple area. They were forbidden to enter the holy section of the

RECONSTRUCTION OF HEROD'S TEMPLE

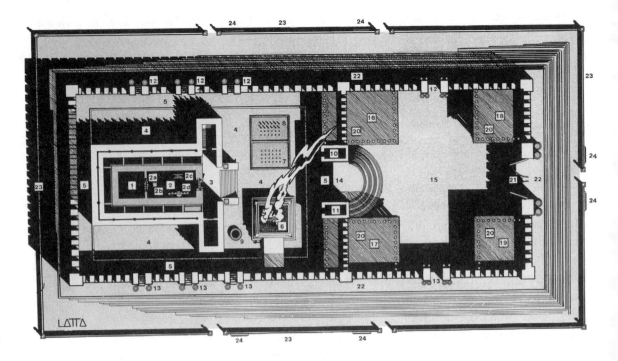

RECONSTRUCTION OF THE INTERIOR OF HEROD'S TEMPLE

Temple. Posted signs made it clear that any Gentile entering beyond the Court of the Gentiles would lose his life. Herod built a triple colonnade on the south side of the Temple. The colonnade extended eight hundred feet long. It was called the Royal Portico since it was the place where Solomon was crowned king.

The Court of Women was the only place where a Jewish woman was permitted to enter the Temple. From the Court of the Women, there were fifteen steps through the Nicanor Gate to the Court of the Men. Inside the Court of the Priests were the High Altar, the Laver, and areas to keep the animals for sacrifice. The priests would go up another set of steps into the Temple itself. It was divided into the Holy Place and Most Holy Place. The Holy Place contained the Table of Showbread, Great Menorah, Altar of Incense, and the Veil. The Ark of the Covenant was no longer present in the Most Holy Place. The Holy of Holies was empty.

Herod added the Fortress of Antonia to the northwest corner of the Temple. It housed a Roman guard unit. The Roman military tribune served as guards for the Temple complex. They stopped violence in the Temple area. The fortress was named after Mark Antony, who was a friend of Julius Caesar.

THE TEMPLE IN THE NEW TESTAMENT

Since the Temple was not yet built at the end of the Old Testament, we must turn to the New Testament for biblical events in Herod's Temple. Herod's Temple appears in many events in the New Testament. We will look at several examples of those events.

Early Events

Zachariah was an older priest who served in the Temple. He and his wife did not have any children. While he was doing service in the holy place, he had a vision from an angel. The angel told Zachariah that he and his wife would have a son.

As a sign of the promise of God, Zachariah would not be able to speak until the child was born. Zachariah's son was John the Baptist. The story is found in Luke 1:1–24; 67–79.

Jesus was in the Temple as a child. Mary and Joseph took Him to the Temple as an infant. Simeon and Anna blessed Jesus (see Luke 2:25–38). When Jesus was twelve years old, His parents took Him to Jerusalem. They went to the Temple, and He talked with the religious leaders. They were amazed at His understanding of the Scriptures at the age of twelve (see Luke 2:39–50).

Jesus' Ministry

When Jesus entered His ministry, He spent time in the Temple. He was there at the Feast of Tabernacles (see John 7). He was teaching the people. The Temple police tried to seize Him. They were not successful since it was not time for Jesus to be taken. Jesus again went to the Temple (see John 8). This time, the Scribes and Pharisees tried to trap Him. He taught from several locations in the Temple. One of His favorite locations was to teach in the areas of the treasury (see John 8:20).

In the final week of Jesus' ministry, Jesus went to the Temple. He became angry when He saw the money changers in the Temple. They were changing Roman coins into the Temple currency and charging the people unfairly to change the money. Others were making money by selling animals in the Temple. They had made the Temple into a market rather than a place of prayer. Jesus turned over their tables and drove them from the Temple. He accused them of making God's house a den of thieves (see Matthew 21:14).

Later, when Jesus was leaving the Temple, His disciples called His attention to the beautiful buildings in the Temple complex. In Matthew 24:2, Jesus said, "Don't you see all these things? I assure you: Not one stone will be left here on another that will not be thrown down!" Remember this prediction; we will look at it again.

Ministry of the Apostles

After Pentecost Peter and John were going into the Temple. They were near the gate called "beautiful." A man who was waiting for worshippers to enter the gate called to Peter and John, hoping to receive a gift. Peter and John told him to look at them. They told him that they did not have silver or gold, but in the name of Jesus he should take up his bed and walk. His ankles grew strong, and he was able to praise God for what had happened to him. The people were astonished and filled with awe (see Acts 3:1–10).

Another incident in the Temple occurred some years later. The apostle Paul went to the Temple to take a vow. This happened after his third missionary journey. Remember the warnings that were given concerning death to any Gentile who entered the Temple complex beyond the court of the Gentiles? He was accused by Jews in the Temple of bringing a Gentile convert with him from his missionary journeys. A riot broke out in the Temple. The soldiers had come from the Fortress of Antonia to rescue Paul (see Acts 21:26–36). As a result of that experience, Paul appealed to Caesar and was sent to Rome.

Attitude of the Jews toward the Temple

By the time of the New Testament, the Jews almost believed that something said against the Temple was a sin and could not be forgiven. They were disturbed when anyone was in the least way disrespectful of the Temple. They would rather die than allow something to be said against the Temple. They became angry at Jesus when He said in John 2:19, "Destroy this sanctuary, and I will raise it up in three days." While Jesus was referring to his body, the people believed that He was talking about the Temple. This was a sign of great disrespect. They could not forgive Jesus for this, and it was brought up again later in His life at the trial. The two witnesses that the high priest had paid to help them convict Jesus said in Matthew 26:61, "I can demolish God's sanctuary and rebuild it in three days." It seemed as if that would be enough to convict Him to die the death of a criminal. While He was dying on the cross, they insulted Him and shouted, "The One who would demolish the sanctuary and rebuild it in three days, save Yourself! If You are the Son of God, come down from the cross!" This is recorded in Matthew 27:40.

The same kind of anger was expressed against Stephen. Stephen preached about Jesus Christ and describes how the priests and others had caused the death of Jesus. Those who heard Stephen, dragged him to the Sanhedrin, which was the religious court of the Jews. There he was accused of blasphemy against Moses and against God. Finally, at his trial, they gathered false witnesses, just as they had done against Jesus. The false witnesses accused Stephen in Acts 6:13, "This man does not stop speaking blasphemous words against this holy place and the law." Just as in the case of Jesus, they accused Stephen of insulting the Temple. The way they saw the situation, speaking against the Temple could not be forgiven. It was not long before they dragged Stephen out of the court and picked up stones and began to stone him. There Stephen died.

DESTRUCTION OF THE TEMPLE

Recall the prophecy of Jesus from Matthew 24:2. Jesus said the Temple would be destroyed. In AD 66, Jews rebelled against Rome. There were groups of zealots who made the Temple their place of opposition to Rome. You will find additional information about this tragedy in a section entitled, "Bible geography."

THE ARCH OF TITUS

For four years, the Romans tried to stop the revolt. At first they were not successful. But with the greatest army that the world had seen to that time, the Romans worked to crush the rebellion. Finally in AD 70, Titus, the Roman general, led his troops to the Temple. They burned the wooden walls inside the Temple and destroyed the walls, block by block. They literally fulfilled the prophecy Jesus had made about not one stone standing on another.

It was customary for a successful Roman general to have his accomplishments put into stone in a commemorative arch. The Arch of Titus (see photo on previous page) stands in Rome near the Coliseum. On the inside walls of the Arch are displayed the items taken from the Temple in the successful campaign against the Jews. You can readily see the menorah that was captured and taken to Rome.

THE TEMPLE TODAY

The Temple is still loved today by the Jewish people. At the end of the Passover festival, the family repeats the phrase, "Next year in Jerusalem." The only remainder of the Temple is the Western Wall. It is still the most holy of places for the Jewish people. Many Jewish persons in the nation of Israel and outside of Israel would like to rebuild the Temple.

Bible Geography

The Bible is filled with references to specific geographical locations. From the earliest times in the Garden of Eden, geography has played an important role in the lives of people from the Bible times. As the story of the Bible became narrower and focused on the lives of Abraham, Isaac, and Jacob, the land still played an important part. The events of the Bible are located in specific places. The development of a culture—which includes the languages, the arts, music, science, literature, philosophy, and even religion—is closely tied to specific geographical locations. Towns and cities were formed and located according to the land formations. Everyday life in these ancient civilizations was directly related to the geographical features of the lands of the Bible. In order to understand the Bible and the customs of the Bible, it is essential for the student of the Bible to understand the geography.

For God's chosen people Israel, the Promised Land between Egypt to the south and Syria to the north has always played an important role. Abraham would have lived some time around 2000 BC. The Promised Land of Palestine was part of the covenant between God and His people. This covenant was first made between God and Abraham. It was renewed for his sons, Isaac and Jacob. Then it continued to be renewed for later generations.

Civilization in the ancient world started long before Abraham and the patriarchs. It is clear that the cradle of this early civilization lies along the area of land known as the Fertile Crescent. This is the land that stretches from the Persian Gulf and northwest along the Tigris and Euphrates Rivers. Then it turns southwest through Palestine and the Sinai peninsula. It ends in the land of Egypt, along the Nile River. From long before Abraham, as early as 3300 BC, the Middle Eastern nations of the Fertile Crescent dominated the ancient world. This continued until the rise of the European Greek civilization in 336 BC, when Alexander the Great assumed the title "King of Macedon." By the time of his death in 323 BC, Alexander had conquered the entire Fertile Crescent, and his armies had extended his kingdom as far east as the Indus River.

By 200 BC a new European power emerged in the ancient world. This power was Rome. The Romans continued to conquer the lands that had been under the control of the successors to Alexander the Great. By 63 BC Pompey conquered all of Palestine for Rome. Roman domination of Israel continued until AD 70, when Titus destroyed Jerusalem and the Temple. This brought an end to the Jewish state. The Jews were scattered throughout the ancient world. Rome continued in control of its Empire until overthrown by the Germanic tribes about AD 600. Greater detail on the historical geography of Palestine through Bible times can be found in the geography section of the *Parent/Teacher Handbook, Volume 1: The Bible,* pages 110 ff.

The Jewish state was reestablished in 1968. Today Israel coexists alongside the Palestinian state. The friction between these two groups is often in the news today and will probably continue well into the future. The ancient lands of Assyria and Babylonia are located in present–day Iraq and Persia is the present-day Iran. Both lands have come back into the news in the modern world.

In this section of Bible geography, we will examine the Empires outside of Israel with whom God's people interacted throughout biblical history, including Egypt, Phoenicia, Philistia, Assyria, Babylonia, Persia, Greece, and Rome. We will provide a brief background of the particular culture and history. Then we will examine the interaction between the people of Israel with the particular foreign culture. In addition to the material found in this section, you may want to consult an encyclopedia and Bible atlas or Bible encyclopedia for further detail on these countries from the ancient world.

Egypt is an important country in the history of the Bible. It is located in the northeast corner of Africa. It runs from the first waterfall on the Nile River to the Mediterranean Sea in the north. It is about 540 miles in length. Egypt has a temperate climate, which means that the temperature in the winter hovers around 50°, while the temperature in the summer is around 80°. The air is dry, and that allows things to be preserved and not deteriorate from the dampness, as happens in other areas. The Nile River overflows its banks each year. As a result, new earth is deposited on land every year. The land is able to produce good crops. The ancient Greek historian Herodotous described Egypt as "the gift to the Nile." The Egyptians developed an early form of writing, called hieroglyphics. This kind of writing uses small pictures instead of words, as we do in English. For many years the meaning of hieroglyphics was not understood, but today we are able to translate hieroglyphics.

Today Egypt is a heavily populated country, and the population continues to grow. Egypt is mainly a Moslem country. It is at the heart of the Arab world. For centuries there has been a small Christian population of Coptics. The Copts date back to the early days in Christianity.

Many Egyptians are still poor farmers with almost no modern equipment. Many have to search for work outside of the country. Cairo is the capital of Egypt today. It is a city of about fifteen million people. While many rich people live in comfortable homes, most Egyptians are poor.

Early Egypt

The Egyptians apparently descended from Ham, as described in Genesis 10:6. Archaeologists have discovered villages that date much earlier than 3000 BC. But we know that the civilization of Egypt dates from about 3000 BC. Menes was king in 3100 BC. He united the northern part of Egypt with the southern part to create the Egyptians state. He formed the first national government and founded his capital at Memphis. The Egyptian priest Manetho described about thirty families that ruled Egypt between the years 3000 to 300 BC. Some of these families were very strong and led the kingdom well, while others were weak. It is possible to divide the history of Egypt into three kingdom eras. The Old Kingdom extended from 2700 to 2200 B.C. The next period was the Middle Kingdom lasted from 2000 to 1800 BC. This would have been the age in which the patriarchs, from Abraham to Jacob, were described in Genesis. Finally, the New Kingdom era occurred from 1570 to 1100 BC. Following the rule of the pharaohs, other nations ruled Egypt. These included Libya, Ethiopia, Persia, Greece, and finally Rome.

The Old Kingdom (2700–2200 BC)

During the Old Kingdom period, the government of Egypt was strong. The rulers of the country became known as pharaohs. The pharaoh was a king, and he was believed to be a god. The pharaoh was the high priest, military commander, and judge. It was expected that the pharaoh would marry his sister. When they had a son, he would become the next pharaoh. Pharaoh appointed the government officials, who helped him rule the country.

During the Old Kingdom period, the Egyptians constructed the large pyramids. The largest of the pyramids covers the size of an area that would hold thirteen football fields. It is located in Giza. When the Nile River overflowed its banks, many of the farmers worked on the construction of the pyramids since they could not do any farming. The Egyptians also used slave labor to help with the building of their projects.

The Egyptians worshipped several different gods. The king of their gods was *Amun*. They believed he had the power to make crops grow, animals produce young, and people have children. His head was like a ram, while his body was like a person. *Bes* was the god of marriage and happiness. He was very ugly. *Ptah* was the god of crafts and the arts. He was very kind. He was married to *Sekhmet*. *Sekhmet* was the goddess of war. She was bloodthirsty. *Ptah* had to protect people from her evil ways. They did not believe in the One True God, Jehovah.

The Egyptians believed in life after death. The pyramids were constructed to hold the bodies of the pharaohs who had died. Their bodies were wrapped with strips of cloth soaked in special liquids to preserve the body as a mummy. Then they were placed in mummy cases, and their bodies were placed in the tomb in the pyramid. Food and drink were also placed in the tomb, along with many of their possessions in life. It was believed that they would need these in the spirit world. They believed that they took a journey after death.

Pressure from the priests and other government officials caused the Old Kingdom to decline. The Old Kingdom continued until about 2200 BC. The rulers for the next two hundred years caused the kingdom to become less powerful.

The Middle Kingdom (2000–1800 BC)

The Middle Kingdom began around 2200 BC. Amenemhet, one of the leaders of southern Egypt, took the throne of Egypt. He moved the capital to a city near Memphis. Amenemhet and the pharaohs who followed him restored the power of Egypt. They worked hard to increase trade with Palestine and Syria. This was a productive time in the life of Egypt. The end of the middle Kingdom took place in 1786 BC.

During the next one hundred years, the kings of Egypt were weak. As a result, groups of people from Asia settled in the Delta region of the Nile River. They brought with them more powerful means for fighting. They used horse-drawn chariots and more powerful bows. They controlled the Nile River delta region. They established their rule from the city of Avaris. To the native Egyptians, they became known as Hyksos. During the time these foreign kings ruled northern Egypt, there was an Egyptian pharaoh who ruled southern Egypt from Thebes.

It is possible that Joseph became the second in command to the pharaoh during the rule of the

Temple of Ramses II at Abu Simbel

Hyksos (see Genesis 41:39–45). These people came from a similar background to Joseph. The people of Israel continued to stay in Egypt for the next four hundred years.

During that period of time, a powerful pharaoh arose. He was Ahmose I. He drove the Hyksos out of Egypt. To do this, many Egyptians and many of the Hyksos died. But Ahmose I succeeded in 1554 BC. The Hyksos were driven into Palestine. It is possible that the new kings are described in the Bible as "a new king, who had not known Joseph, came to power in Egypt" (see Exodus 1:8). The Egyptians now brought the people of Israel into slavery.

The New Kingdom (1570–1100 BC)

The next five hundred years brought the period of the New Kingdom in Egypt. During that time Egypt became one of the first world powers. They worshipped the god *Re*, who later became *Amun-Re*. The leaders of Egypt now adopted the military approaches brought by the Hyksos. Thutmose I was able to take his troops as far as the Euphrates River. Thutmose's daughter, Queen Hatshepsut, was also a powerful leader. Egypt reached the height of its power during the reign of King Thutmose III. He extended the rule of Egypt into Asia and into Africa. The Egyptians brought slaves from other parts of Africa.

Amenhotep IV changed the direction and fortunes of Egypt. He worshipped the sun god, *Aten*. He even changed its own name to Akhenaten. *Aten* replaced *Amun* as the chief of gods. But he kept the god *Re*. He moved the capital to Akhetaten, about 175 miles north of the city of Thebes. This became a creative period in the life of Egypt.

One of the kings who followed Akhenaten took *aten* out of his name and became known as Tutankhamun or King Tut. Several pharaohs followed. Seti I and his son Ramses II attempted to restore the great power of Egypt. They made successful military campaigns into Asia.

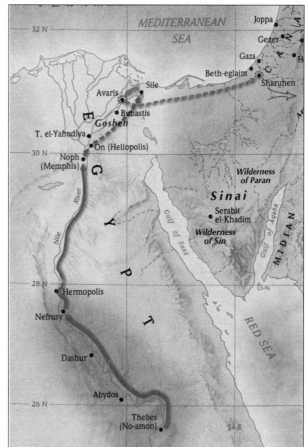

MAP OF EGYPT

But the next dynasty of pharaohs was not able to stop the bitter fighting among the nobles and the priests. Egypt lost many of its conquered territories. New invaders came to Egypt. Control of Egypt for the next seven hundred years went to these foreign invaders. These included foreign nations from Africa, Assyria, Persia, and later Alexander the Great from Greece. As we look at some of these foreign powers, the role of Egypt continued. But it never reached the power it had achieved during these earlier dynasties.

The Philistines

A small but powerful group of people settled on the Mediterranean coast of southwest Palestine. They were known as "sea peoples." It is believed that they came from the island of Crete or even mainland Greece. Many of these "sea peoples" invaded Egypt around the time the Israelites made their Exodus from Egypt. The Egyptians turned the "sea peoples" back. Then many of them settled in what became known as Philistia. Rather than a unified country, it was a series of city-states, with a local ruler. Philistia included the cities of Ekron, Ashdod, Ashkelon, Gaza, and Gath. They used iron for weapons to fight and tools for farming. The people of Israel did not know how to use iron for either of these purposes. As a result, the Philistines were very effective in fighting against the people of Israel. They also made the Israelites come to them to make farm tools and sharpen the tools.

The Philistines often fought against the people of Israel. Recall the story of Samson, which took place in Philistia (see Judges 13–16). The tribe of Dan was located next to the Philistine cities. It was threatened by the Philistines. The tribe moved to the north

(see Judges 18:11, 29). King Saul was not able to stop the Philistines. He lost his life in the fighting against them at Mount Gilboa (see 1 Samuel 31:1–13). King David was finally able to control some of their power (see 2 Samuel 5:17–25). Find the kingdom of Philistia and its city-states on the map from the kingdom of David and Solomon.

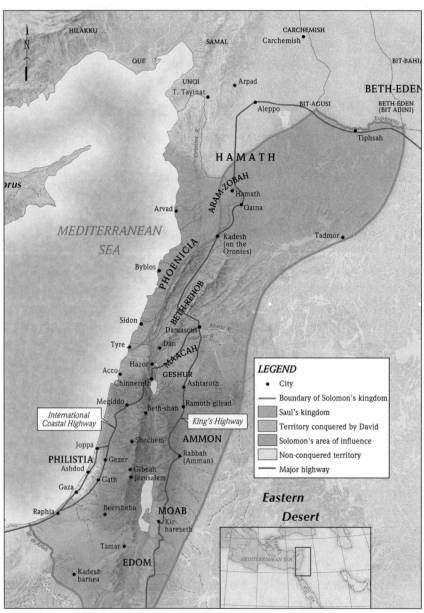

MAP OF THE KINGDOM OF DAVID AND SOLOMON

The Phoenicians

The Phoenicians were a group of people who came from the old Canaanite tribes that were settled in Palestine before Joshua conquered the land for the people of Israel. The word *Phoenicia* came from the Greek word, which means "purple". This is probably a reference to a dye they produced from the murex sea snail. It took about sixty thousand shells to make only one pound of the dye. Later the Romans would only allow members of the royal family to wear robes that were made of purple.

You may find their location of Phoenicia on the previous map to the northwest of Israel. They were located in what is present-day Lebanon. The Phoenicians were a seafaring people. With their rich supply of cedar, they built ships that traveled across the Mediterranean Sea. They were effective traders. They established trade with Greece, Africa, and Asia by sea. They not only used the sea, but they also established caravan trade routes through Israel in Judah and across the Fertile Crescent. They were most successful from about 1200 BC to about 300 BC. They lost their power after Alexander the Great conquered them. One of their most famous settlements was Carthage on the northern coast of Africa. The Roman wars with Carthage were decisive in pushing the Romans to become the masters of the world.

The Phoenicians did not conduct war against the people of Israel. But they do appear in a number of places in both the Old and New Testaments. Solomon's Temple was lined with cedar from the forests of Lebanon (see 1 Kings 5:8–10). Phoenician religion participated in the cults of the Baals and the Asherah. The Phoenician princess Jezebel brought Baal worship to Israel. She wanted to have Elijah killed. Instead God protected the prophet Elijah, and eventually she was killed in a violent death. But Phoenician religion brought idolatry to the people of God and in that way had an evil effect on Israel.

The Assyrian Empire

The Assyrian Empire was one of the first great world Empires of the Old Testament. Assyria played an important role in both Israel and Judah from about 855 to 625 BC. Assyria was located in the northwestern part of present-day Iraq. It is situated along the Tigris River. The climate there is warm during the summer and cold and wet during winter. The city of Ninevah is mentioned in the Bible as early as Genesis 10:11–12. Assyria had a long history that dated back at least to 1900 BC. The ancient Code of Hammurabi was the basis for their laws. The people of Assyria worshipped several gods, mostly from nature. One of their main gods was Assur, who was the god of war. The king was the chief priest for their god. The king was absolute. The people of Assyria were almost constantly at war. Most of the men served in the military forces.

During the reign of Tiglath-pileser I, 1115 to 1077 BC, the Assyrians moved west with their armies to the Mediterranean Sea. But Tiglath-pileser I was assassinated. His death brought an end to Assyrian expansion. Under the kings that followed, Assyria became less powerful in the Middle East. For Israel, there was a great struggle between the kings of Assyria and the kings of Aram-Damascus.

Aram-Damascus was located just north of Israel in present-day Syria. With the combined kingdoms of David and Solomon, Aram-Damascus was under the control of Israel. Apparently this kingdom broke away around the time that Israel and Judah split into two kingdoms. The kings of Aram-Damascus fought against their neighbor to the south, Samaria. For example, King Ahab of Israel fought against Ben-hadad II. He also fought with Ben-hadad II against the common threat of Assyria in 53 BC. As Assyria became stronger, the challenge for Israel to remain independent became more difficult.

Before this time countries like Egypt or Aram-Damascus would attack another country and take away the things they found. The weakness of Israel and Judah allowed Pharaoh Shishak to attack both Judah and Israel. His army stole all they could and then returned to Egypt. But, under Tiglath-pileser III, who ruled from 744 to 727 BC, Assyria became a world power. Assyria now took people from their own homeland and moved them to another of their conquered lands. They moved people around like pieces on a chessboard. As a result, it was much easier for the Assyrians to control the peoples they conquered. The conquered peoples were now just trying to survive in their new land.

Tribute

A tribute is a payment of gold and silver given from a country that was weaker to a more powerful country. It often caused the weaker country to become even less able to fight against the greater power. Both Israel and Judah were often required to pay tribute to the more powerful countries around them. This would certainly have included Assyria. Refusal to pay was considered rebellion against the more powerful king. It usually brought military action against the smaller country. This practice was common in the ancient world.

A group of nations joined together, including King Rezin of Damascus and Pekah of Israel, to try to stop Tiglath-pileser III. Tiglath-pileser III is called Pul in the Bible. They wanted Ahaz, king of Judah, to join together with their forces. Ahaz decided to appeal to the Assyrian king for help. The prophet Isaiah counseled the king against asking Tiglath-pileser III for help. Ahaz did it anyway. From this time on, Ahaz was required to pay a large yearly tribute to the Assyrian king. Judah was also forced to engage in some of the pagan Assyrian religious practices (see 2 Kings 16). Aram-Damascus no longer was a threat to Israel

because Tiglath-pileser III destroyed Aram-Damascus in 733 BC and killed their king, Rezin. Many of the people were taken from their land and resettled elsewhere. At the same time, Tiglath-pileser III reduced the size of Israel for its participation in fighting against Assyria.

Shalmaneser V ruled from 727 to 722 BC. Although we do not know a lot about Shalnaneser V, he did force Hoshea, king of Israel, to pay a large tribute each year. When Hoshea received promise of help from Egypt in opposing the king of Assyria, Hoshea decided not to pay the tribute (see 2 Kings 17:1–5). This brought the anger of the Assyrian king upon Israel. He brought his troops to Samaria, capital of Israel. They surrounded the city and would not allow any help to come from the outside. This lasted for three years. In 722 BC the city of Samaria fell to the Assyrians. Israel ceased to exist as a nation from that point onward.

A Colossal Stylized Bull with Human Face from the Time of Sargon II of Assyria

Sargon II, 722 to 705 BC, claimed the victory of Shalmaneser over the Northern Kingdom of Israel. He had many of the people of Israel carried into captivity and they were resettled in other lands. He also claimed Israel as part of the Assyrian kingdom. The Philistines from Gaza and Ashdod wanted to revolt against Sargon. Hezekiah, king of the Southern Kingdom of Judah, wanted to join the revolt against Assyria. Isaiah warned him not to participate (see Isaiah 18). Meanwhile, the king of Babylonia also wanted to revolt. He sent for help from King Hezekiah.

Sennacherib ruled from 704 to 681 BC. The whole kingdom seemed to be in revolt. Hezekiah of Judah joined the revolt. Sennacherib brought the full military power of the Assyrians and destroyed forty-six walled cities. He captured over 200,000 persons and took them into captivity. King Hezekiah was captured and placed in a cage. Sennacherib marched against Egypt. Isaiah encouraged King Hezekiah to continue to oppose the Assyrian king. The Bible tells us that an angel of the Lord protected Judah (see 2 Kings 19:35–36). The Greek historian Herodotus described a plague of mice. It is possible that an outbreak of the plague may have caused the defeat of the mighty Assyrian army. Sennacherib also engaged in many building projects in Ninevah. The anger of Sennacherib against Babylonia resulted in destroying that great city in 689 BC. Several years later Sennacherib was murdered by his own two sons (see 2 Kings 19:37).

Esarhaddon, 681 to 669 BC, replaced Sennacherib. He began to rebuild Babylon. The people of Babylonia became supporters of the Assyrian king. In 671 BC Esarhaddon invaded Egypt. The pharaoh went to Memphis, where the Assyrian king followed and conquered Memphis. Esarhaddon tried to return to Egypt after the Pharaoh rebelled against the Assyrians. Esarhaddon died on the way to Egypt.

His son, Ashurbanipal II, 669 to 627 BC, ruled over Assyria at the height of its power. With the help of twenty-two of the kings that served the

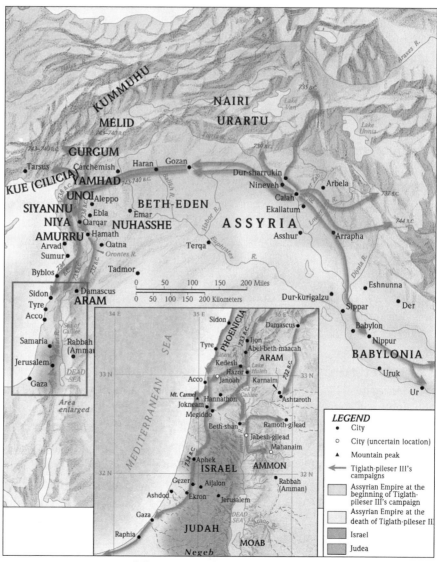

MAP OF THE ASSYRIAN EMPIRE

Assyrian king, he invaded Egypt. Among those who helped the Assyrian king was Manasseh of Judah. Only ten years later, the Egyptians were again in revolt against Assyria. Ashurbanipal II died in 627 BC.

Only a year or so after his death in 626 BC, Nabopolassar became king of Babylon. The days of Assyrian power were quickly coming to end. Under King Josiah, Judah was able to rebel as well. They stopped paying tribute money to Assyria. The combined power of the Medes and Babylonians was able to destroy the capital and several of the major cities of Assyria. In 610 BC the Babylonians marched on Haran. A small force of the Assyrian army, led by its general, combined with help from Egypt to oppose the Babylonians from the city of Haran. But it was too little and too late. The Empire of Assyria was completely destroyed.

The Babylonian Empire

The city of Babylon was ancient. It is mentioned in Genesis 10:10 and 11:9. Before 2000 BC it was a cultural center in the ancient world. Their ancient writing was known as cuneiform. The Babylonians wrote on small clay tablets. Babylon, or the Hebrew name Babel, is located about fifty miles south of the city of Baghdad. The climate of this area of the world is very hot. The famous Code of Hammurabi was developed by the king of old Babylon around 1700 BC. Yet it took another thousand years for Babylonia to emerge as a world power.

When we come to the biblical story of the rise of Babylon against Judah, Babylon had been under the control of its Assyrian neighbors to the northwest for over two hundred years. Refer back to the map of the Assyrian Empire. The new Babylonian Empire lasted from 626 to 539 BC. In 626 BC. Nabopolassar seized control of Babylon. Nabopolassar had strong ambitions to make Babylon a world power. In order to accomplish this, it would be necessary to destroy the Assyrian power to the north. He set out by establishing a partnership with Cyaxares, king of Media to the

northeast (see the map of the Medo-Babylonian Empireon the next page). Together Nabopolassar of Babylonia and Cyaxares of Media destroyed the city of Ninevah in 612 BC. This brought an end to the Assyrian Empire.

The Kings of Babylon

Nabopolassar's son, Nebuchadnezzar, led the Babylonian forces against the Egyptians. Nebuchadnezzar decisively defeated the Egyptians at the Battle of Carchemish in 605 BC. It was probably during this time that Nebuchadnezzar took Daniel and his three friends to Babylon. Nebuchadnezzar was unable to follow up his victory further south in Palestine because his father died. It was necessary for him to return to Babylon to take his place as the new king.

Nebuchadnezzar reigned as king of Babylon from 605 to 562 BC. During the next two years, 604 to 603 BC, Nebuchadnezzar conducted campaigns along the Palestinian coastal regions. He was interested in cutting off the trade routes, which led to Egypt. Pharaoh Neco of Egypt wanted to stop Nebuchadnezzar. Judah was caught in between the superpowers of Babylon and Egypt. After the death of King Josiah in a battle with Egypt, Pharaoh Neco removed Josiah's son Jehoahaz as king. He replaced him with another son, Jehoiachim. At this point, Jehoiachim switched his allegiance from Egypt to Babylonia. This occurred between 604 to 601 BC. Jehoiachim was forced to pay tribute money to Babylon. In spite of the warnings from Jeremiah to avoid siding with Egypt, Jehoiachim refused to pay any further tribute money.

At first it seemed as if Nebuchadnezzar would not respond. But in the year 597 BC Nebuchadnezzar brought his army and besieged Jerusalem. Jehoiachim died during this siege. The new king of Judah was Jehoiachin. He surrendered Jerusalem to the Babylonians. The Babylonian army tore through the city of Jerusalem and stole treasures from the Temple. Another group of prisoners was taken

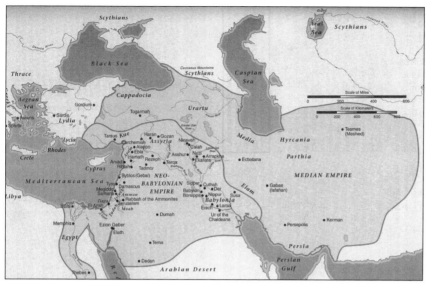

MAP OF THE MEDO-BABYLONIAN EMPIRE

(see Jeremiah 39:3). Labashi-Markduk was king for just three months in 557 BC, when he was murdered. The last king of Babylon was Nabonidus, who reigned from 556 to 539 BC. We do not know a lot about Nabonidus. He was more interested in the moon god Sin than in the god Marduk. Whether for that reason or some other, he did not live in Babylon. Belshazzar was the regent for Nabonidus in Babylon.

to Babylonia, and these included Jehoiachin, his family, and the prophet Ezekiel. Nebuchadnezzar replaced Jehoiachin with a new king, Zedekiah.

Zedekiah reigned as King from 596 to 586 BC. Some small victories by the Egyptians encouraged Zedekiah to rebel against Babylon. Jeremiah again tried to tell the king that rebelling against Babylon was foolish (see Jeremiah 27–29). But Zedekiah would not listen. Nebuchadnezzar returned with his army and laid siege on the city of Jerusalem from 588 to 586 BC. This time the Babylonians completely destroyed the temple and the city of Jerusalem. Zedekiah was taken before Nebuchadnezzar where he was forced to watch the execution of his sons. He was blinded and taken in chains to Babylonia as a prisoner.

Nebuchadnezzar was the greatest king of Babylon. He was not only strong as a military leader, but he also achieved a great deal in strengthening and building the city of Babylon. Evil Merodach freed Jehoiachin from prison and treated him with respect (see 2 Kings 25:27–30). He only reigned for two years, from 562 to 560 BC. Evil Merodach was followed by the son-in-law of Nebuchadnezzar, Neriglissar. He reigned from 560 to 558 BC. Neriglissar had been present at the fall of Jerusalem

Remember that fateful night in 539 BC, when Belshazzar held a feast for all the nobles in Babylon. He had his servants bring the golden and silver goblets from the Temple in Jerusalem. The story is told in Daniel 5:1–31. That night Belshazzar and his guests partied. They drank and sang praises to their idol gods. Suddenly, a strange hand wrote this message on the wall, *MENE, MENE, TEKEL, PARSIN.* Belshazzar turned pale. He called upon his magicians and wise men to interpret the meaning of this strange message. When they could not interpret its meaning, the queen remembered prophet from Judah, Daniel. Belshazzar called Daniel to interpret the meaning of the message on the wall. He told Belshazzar that the Babylonian reign was going to end. His kingdom would be taken by the Medes and the Persians. The end of the Babylonian kingdom came that very night.

The City of Babylon

It must have been a painful journey as the people of Israel made their way in chains from their homeland across the long miles to the great city of Babylon. While Jews would not have lived in Babylon, they likely spent time there. It was one of the wonders of the ancient world. The wife of Nebuchadnezzar was homesick for her homeland. The king had constructed the magnificent hanging gardens of Babylon. He had engaged in many large building projects, of which the gardens were only one.

Approaching the city, one would have crossed the Euphrates River and entered the enormous gate that led through the outer wall. Then one would have made his way through the inner wall. Inside the city it was necessary for the traveler to pass through the famous Ishtar gate. The gate

AN ARTISTS RECONSTRUCTION OF BABYLON

was covered with beautifully colored tiles, and the massive walls were lined with blocks of limestone. Inside the Ishtar gate was the great palace of the king. The palace was large and housed many buildings and rooms for the government. Beyond the palace was the huge temple to Marduk. It was in the form of the ziggurat and stood about three hundred feet square. They believed that this provided stepping stones for their god to come to earth. There were many other temples throughout the city. A visiting Jewish captive would have been awed by the site. Even after the fall of Babylon, the city served as a provincial capital for the next several hundred years into the future.

There is no evidence that the Jews were treated poorly. They were settled in a community on the Chebar River. This was about eighty miles south of the city of Babylon. Even though the people were surrounded by idols, they finally listened to the prophets and left their idols behind. They worshipped Jehovah God alone. Gradually they established a new life in Babylon. Scribes copied the holy Scriptures. They developed their own literature, such as the Babylonian Talmud. They built synagogues for the worship of Jehovah. They opened shops and built a life in their new homeland. They married and had families. As a result, they were able to maintain a separate life from that of the Babylonians and keep their worship exclusively to God. While many were able to develop a happy and meaningful life in Babylon, others felt the loneliness of being in a foreign land. They wanted to return to Palestine and to the holy city of Jerusalem. Many would have that opportunity when the Persian king invaded Babylon and encouraged many Jews to return to their homeland.

PERSIA

The people of Persia did not come from Mesopotamia. They were descended from peoples of Russia. They lived in present-day Iran, along the Black Sea coast. During most of the time, after they arrived in the second century BC, they were controlled by the Medes who lived north of them. Their Empire began in 539 BC and continued until the Greek Macedonian, Alexander the Great, defeated Persia in 331 BC. Cyrus the great, also known as Cyrus II, was born to Cambyses I, king of Persia, and Mandane, daughter of the Median king Astyages. Cyrus represented both Media and Persia.

Cyrus the Great

It is not surprising that Cyrus first united all of the Persian tribes. Then he took his troops north to the capital of Media, Ecbatana. Find Ecbatana in Media on your map. Cyrus had to help the Babylonians in this conquest. There he overthrew Astyages and took some of the wealth of the Medes in 550 BC. Cyrus moved north and west and conquered Lydia, which is present-day Turkey. This took place in the year 546 BC. With his success, Cyrus cut off the Babylonian trade routes. The Babylonian king, Nabonidus, left Babylon and appointed his son, Belshazzar, to rule in his place. The people of Babylon and the priests of their god, Marduk, could not accept this policy by their king. Cyrus took advantage of the unrest in this situation and invaded Babylonia. He conquered Babylon in 539 BC. This gave Cyrus control over all the former Babylonian Empire. The story of the defeat of Belshazzar is described in the Bible in Daniel 5.

Unlike his predecessors, either the Babylonians or the Assyrians, Cyrus encouraged the Jews to return to Palestine. The first migration back to Palestine took place under Ezra. Cyrus wanted the Jews to rebuild their Temple. He provided the means through the royal treasury to accomplish this. Cyrus is referred to as "His [God's] anointed" (see Isaiah 45:1). The story of these events is told in Ezra 1:1–4 and 6:3–5. A description of the requirements for peoples returning to their homelands may also be found on the "Cyrus Cylinder," which may be seen today in the British Museum.

At the death of Cyrus in 530 BC, his son Cambyses II took over the kingdom. He was not as effective as his father Cyrus had been. He is not mentioned in the Bible. But he was able to conquer Egypt in 525 BC. This took place three years before he died in 522 BC. Cambyses II was succeeded by another member of the royal line, Darius I.

Darius I

Darius I was an effective ruler from 522 to 486 BC. Early in his reign Darius had to stop revolts in Persia, Media, and Egypt. He divided the vast

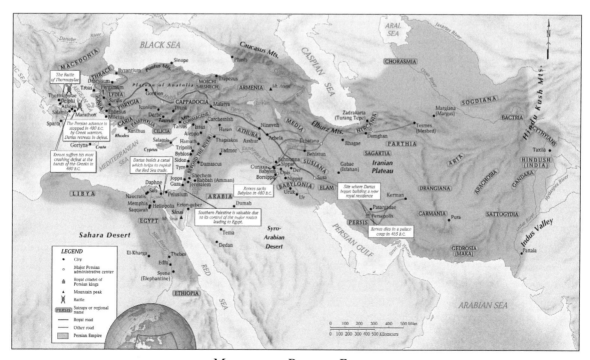

MAP OF THE PERSIAN EMPIRE

Persian Empire into twenty subdivisions, called satrapies. Each of the satrapies was ruled by a local ruler, known as a satrap. Darius established the royal postal system. He established his residence in the city of Persepolis. He built roads, like the major highway between Susa and Sardis. You might want to look for these cities on your map. The Greeks revolted against his rule in 499 BC. Darius was at first successful in his campaign against the Greeks. But his success in Greece did not last long. He was finally defeated by the Greeks at the Battle of Marathon in 490 BC. Darius died four years later, in 486 BC. Several of the countries that he ruled also revolted just before his death. Perhaps most important of these countries was Egypt.

PERSIAN KING DARIUS I

SEATED UPON HIS THRONE

The prophets Haggai and Zechariah preached during this period. You will recall that the prophet Haggai proclaimed God's message to the people of the importance of rebuilding the Temple in Jerusalem. Zechariah preached to the people of Judah that God would care for his people, if they continued to follow Him in obedience. During the time when Darius was king, the Temple was rebuilt and dedicated in 515 BC (see Ezra 6:13–15).

Xerxes I

Xerxes I was the son of Darius. Xerxes ruled from 486 to 465 BC. He continued to construct his capital at Persepolis. Xerxes had to establish his reign by stopping the rebellions that arose across the Empire. Most notably Egypt and Babylon were in revolt. After those revolts were stopped, Xerxes moved west to deal with the Greeks. He wanted to punish the Greeks for the defeat his father had experienced at Marathon. He succeeded in devastating Athens. But his fleet suffered defeat at Salamis in 480 BC. From this point Xerxes lost interest in further campaigns against the Greeks and returned home to Persia. When a revolt occurred in his palace, Xerxes was killed in 465 BC.

Xerxes is best known in the Bible by his Hebrew name, Ahasuerus. He was the king during the time of Esther. In the third year of Xerxes's reign, 483 BC, the king held a celebration at his palace in Susa, the city of Shushan in Esther. He invited all the nobles throughout the land to be in attendance. At the end of the days of celebration, Xerxes held a large banquet. He sent some of his servants to bring the beautiful Queen Vashti to the banquet. She refused to be put on display before these drunken people. The king became angry, and he removed her from being his queen (see Esther 1:1–21).

To replace the queen, Xerxes held a royal contest to find another beautiful woman who could replace Queen Vashti. Esther, the young Jewish girl, was chosen. This took place in the seventh year of the reign of Xerxes, 479 BC. The king loved her more than any of the other women in his court. He placed the crown upon her head and made her his queen. Then he held a great feast in her honor, and he had celebrations throughout the entire kingdom (see Esther 2:16–18).

Esther's uncle Mordecai discovered a plot against the king. He reported that plot to Esther. She told the king. The two men were executed. In 474 BC, the twelfth year of Xerxes's reign, Haman, one of the noblemen, hated the Jews and wanted them all killed (see Esther 3:7). With the help of her uncle Mordecai, Esther held a feast and invited the king and Haman to attend. She confronted Haman with his plan. The king had Haman put to death. The Jews were spared. They established a feast in honor of Esther, which continues today, the Feast of Purim. Mordecai was promoted to a position second only to the king.

Artaxerxes I

Artaxerxes is the last of the kings to be named in the Bible. He ruled from 465 to 425 BC. He succeeded his father Xerxes. He faced challenges from both the Greeks in the West and Egyptians to the south. Artaxerxes allowed Ezra and many of the priests, Levites, and scribes to return to Palestine under the king's protection in 458 BC. This was another opportunity for the Jews to return to Jerusalem and to rebuild their lives in the holy land. It was also evidence of the Persian policy and their desire to support the local peoples in their return to their homeland. The Jews did not have to serve the gods of Persia but were allowed to return and serve Jehovah.

Artaxerxes solved the problem of the Greeks, for a little while at least, by establishing the peace of Callias in 449 BC. The Persians agreed to keep their sphere of influence away from the Greeks. The Greeks did the same for their area of influence.

Artaxerxes became more concerned with Egypt. Another attempt to return to Palestine by the Jews, occurred when Nehemiah went to the king for help. Nehemiah was the king's cupbearer. This was an important position in the court of the king. The cupbearer protected the king from someone who might want to poison him. He drank from the wine first. Therefore, he was a trusted servant. Nehemiah became concerned about the walls in Jerusalem, which had broken down and allowed foreigners to hurt the people of God in the city. Nehemiah prayed to God for wisdom and success with the king to carry out the rebuilding of the walls of Jerusalem (see Nehemiah 1:1–11).

Nehemiah then went to the king and requested permission to return to Jerusalem to rebuild the walls (see Nehemiah 2:1–10). The king was concerned about Egypt. The request from Nehemiah came at the right time. It allowed the king the opportunity to strengthen his position in the lower part of Palestine by strengthening control over one of the major trade routes that led to Egypt. Artaxerxes wanted the support of the Jews in that area. So the king encouraged Nehemiah to carry out his request. This took place in about 444 BC.

Continuation of the Persian Empire

For the next ninety-five years six additional kings sat on the throne of Persia. None of these kings are mentioned in Bible. Xerxes II was the next in line of succession. He reigned for only two months in 423 BC. Darius II ruled from 423 to 404 BC. Darius carried on a war with Greece between 431 to 404 BC. As a result of that war, Persia regained some of the cities that it had lost in Greece. Artaxerxes II reigned from 404 to 358 BC. During his administration Egypt was able to free itself from Persian rule for a brief period of time. There was also an important revolt of the satraps between 366 to 360 BC. In 358 BC, a new king came to the throne, Artaxerxes III. He succeeded in bringing Egypt back under Persian rule in 342 BC.

But some events in Greece that occurred during his reign that would cause major problems for the Persians in years to come. In 359 BC Philip II of Macedon rose to power in Greece. Three years later in 356 Alexander the Great was born. Artaxerxes III reigned until 338 BC. He was succeeded by Arses from 338 to 336 BC. The last Persian king was Darius III, who ruled from 336 to 330 BC.

The end of the Persian Empire came at the hands of Alexander the Great. There were three major battles with the Greeks. The Greeks won all three. The first took place at Granicus. Look at the map of the Empire of Alexander the Great in the next section. While Granicus is not listed on the map, it is located on the promontory immediately south of Thrace in Asia Minor. The second battle took place at the river Issus. King Darius took his family with him to the battle. When the battle was over, the Persians had been defeated. Darius left his family to the mercy of Alexander, while he fled. Continuing east, Alexander and his army met the Persians again at Gaugamela in 331 BC. Gaugamela is located near the Tigris River, just west of Arbela. Again the Persians were soundly defeated for the third time. One year later Darius III was murdered by some of his own troops. This brought a complete end to the Persian Empire. Alexander then completed the task of finishing the Persian Empire by marrying the daughter of Darius III. Alexander assumed his right to take the throne of the Persia.

The Persians had treated the Jews with respect. They had helped Jews to return to their homeland. They had also allowed the Jews to rebuild the Temple and even provided the resources to accomplish this rebuilding. The Old Testament ended with the writings of the prophet Malachi. This probably took place around the year 458 BC. What happens next on the world scene is different from anything that has occurred before. The world political power shifts from the Asian East to the European West. While the Greek Empire is not directly discussed in the Scripture, it had a significant impact upon the Jewish people and prepared the way for the coming of Jesus Christ.

THE GREEK EMPIRE OF ALEXANDER THE GREAT

The time of the Greek Empire has become known as the Hellenistic period. The word for *Greece* is *Hellas* in the Greek language. The Hellenistic period changed the course of Western civilization. Greece had been a problem for the Persians. But Greece was not organized to face and defeat the Persian challenge. It had been a group of individual city-states. Athens and Sparta had competed with each other, along with the lesser cities in Greece. It remained for Philip II of Macedon to conquer the southern cities of Greece and to create a unified Greek state. This happened in 338 BC. The Treaty of Corinth came one year later when Philip and a confederation of Greek city-states agreed to bring revenge upon Persia. They were especially angry at the sacking of Athens by Xerxes in 480 BC.

Alexander the Great

Queen Olympias and King Philip had a son Alexander in 356 BC. He was educated by the Greek philosopher Aristotle. Revenge against Persia was a factor in Alexander's education. Alexander showed signs of great promise during his teenage years. He served as a Greek ambassador and also was able to lead his father's troops. These experiences prepared him well. At age twenty Alexander became king of Macedonia, when his father was assassinated.

Two years later Alexander was ready to do battle in the East. He crossed into Asia Minor with a small army. The Persians did not believe Alexander's small army was a threat. But Alexander's army was a more powerful force than they thought and quickly defeated all of the satraps in Asia Minor at the Battle of Granicas. Alexander then moved quickly across Asia Minor to Issus, located on the Mediterranean Sea. There he faced Darius III, king of Persia, and the entire Persian army. Darius thought that he would easily be able to defeat Alexander. He brought his

A SCULPTED HEAD OF ALEXANDER THE GREAT

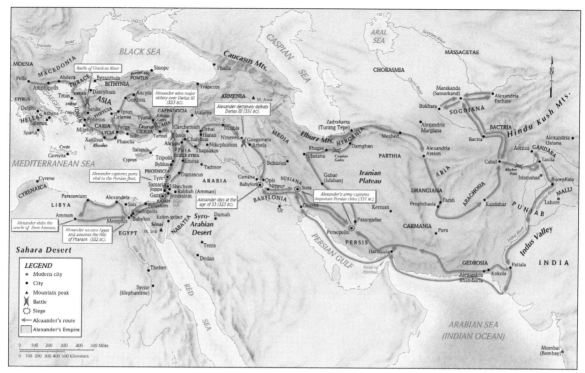

MAP OF THE EMPIRE OF ALEXANDER THE GREAT

family along with him. But when the battle went against Darius, the king left his family to his enemy Alexander. Alexander treated them kindly.

Alexander moved south. His next target was the city of Tyre. At that time the city was an island. Alexander built a causeway to the island and laid siege to the city for seven months. The people surrendered, and Alexander continued south. He destroyed the city of Samaria and had it rebuilt as a military outpost. He was apparently welcomed by the High Priest in Jerusalem, as he continued his march into Egypt. He quickly defeated the Egyptians and established the city of Alexandria within Egypt. Then he went to the Temple of Zeus at Ammon on the west side of Egypt. There he followed the local custom and proclaimed himself as a god.

Alexander then moved into the heart of the Persian Empire. At the Battle of Gaugamela in 331 BC, Alexander defeated Persia. He married the daughter of Darius III and claimed the throne of Persia. In the next year Darius was killed by some of his own troops. Meanwhile Alexander continued

his march to the East. He moved into northern India. His battle-weary troops refused to go farther, even though Alexander wanted to push farther East. His decision to march back through the desert led to the deaths of many of his soldiers, as they died of hunger or thirst. Alexander himself had suffered an injury in battle. When he finally reached the city of Babylon, he did not have the strength to continue on. On June 13, 323 BC, Alexander the Great died in Babylon at the age of only thirty-three. Alexander left no heir. His idea of establishing for himself a world Empire that he and his heirs would rule came to an end on that day in 323 BC.

The Empire that Alexander left resulted in fierce fighting among his generals. Four major divisions of the Empire resulted. Macedonia and Greece became one district. Thrace and Asia Minor were controlled by Antigonus. Syria and the East were taken by Seleucus. Palestine and Egypt came under the control of Ptolemy. During the years that followed, there was great unrest. While Macedonia and Greece did not figure in the political fortunes

PAINTING OF ALEXANDER THE GREAT FIGHTING DARIUS III AND AT THE BATTLE OF ISSUS IN 333 BC

of Palestine, the decisive battle of Ipsus with Seleucus and Ptolemy joining forces resulted in the death of Antigonus in 301 BC. Antigonus did not affect Palestine, but the Ptolomies and Seleucids did.

Hellenization

Hellenization was encouraged throughout the Empire Alexander created. Greek ideas and customs were mixed with the local culture. Large building programs—which included Greek temples, stadiums, and theaters all added to the breadth of culture. The classical ideal of a young man who was schooled in Greek ideals and developed a strong physical body was fostered throughout the Empire. The level of education increased during this period as well. Coins became standardized and were in use in the larger cities across the Empire. One of the most important assets of Greek culture was the common use of the Greek language, known as *koine* Greek. The language became the standard language for use in trade, politics, and the culture.

For the Jews Hellenization was not necessarily a good thing. Many Jews accepted Hellenization, and some of the ruling classes put aside their Judaism and became Hellenized. This caused great conflict between those who wanted to maintain traditional Judaism and those who wanted to be part of the new movement of Hellenization. Greek values were opposed to the Jewish religion and Jewish cultural values. The Greeks also fostered slavery, which was opposed by the Jews.

Rule of the Ptolemies

There was no political unity after Alexander died. This led to insecurity and in some cases great hardship among the conquered peoples. Palestine was located in between the Ptolemaic and Seleucid kingdoms. The Ptolemies established their capital at Alexandria in Egypt. They created the great lighthouse at Pharos. This lighthouse became one of the wonders of the ancient world. The Ptolemies were able to control Palestine for about one hundred years from 301 to 200 BC. They did not force Hellenization upon the Jewish people. Jews who held strongly to their religious faith were tolerated. But they did encourage Hellenization among many other Jews. The Ptolemies founded the great library at Alexandria.

Ptolemy II reportedly wanted a Greek translation of the Jewish Scriptures for his great library. According to legend, he invited seventy scholars from Palestine to complete the Greek edition of the Jewish Bible. They were set apart on the island of Pharos and completed the work in seventy-two days. This may have referred only to the five books of Moses. But we do know that the entire Old Testament, whether then or more likely at a later time, was translated into Greek by scholars in Egypt.

There was great conflict between the Ptolemies and the Seleucids. They fought several wars. In each case the Ptolemies were successful until about 200 BC. Antiochus III defeated Ptolemy V at Panias. This brought about a change in the political fortunes for Palestine. The Seleucids now took control of all of Palestine.

Rule of the Seleucids

Seleucus I developed his own city of Antioch in Syria as his capital in 300 BC. He also founded the Seleucid line of rulers. Antiochus III ruled from 223 to 187 BC. His success at Panias took Palestine away from the Ptolemies. Ten years later he met his own defeat at Magnesia in Asia Minor by the Romans. From that point forward, Antiochus had to pay a heavy tribute of money to Rome. To help pay use taxes, Antiochus tried to steal from the Temple at Elam. He was killed in the process.

His successor was Seleucis IV, who ruled from 187 to 185 BC. Seleucis had to raise the money that his father failed to pay to Rome. At this point the Jews were beginning to wish they were back with the Ptolomies. The land of Palestine was becoming rapidly divided into parties in favor of one group or the other. Seleucus sent Heliodorus to steal money from the Temple in Jerusalem. Heliodorus was not able to take the wealth from the Temple and returned to Antioch empty-handed. When the opportunity presented itself, he murdered Seleucus.

The next ruler was Antiochus IV Epiphanes. He was arrested by the Romans earlier and taken to Rome. There he learned about the might and power of Rome. Then he was sent to Athens, where he learned about the excitement of Greek culture and Hellenism. He came to believe that Hellenism would unite all parts of his kingdom. They would all worship one god, Zeus. With this in mind, he brought an army from Pergamum and killed Heliodorus. He then established himself as the rightful king in Antioch in 175 BC.

In the Temple at Jerusalem, there was a battle among several who wanted to be the High Priest. Large sums of money were paid to Antiochus IV to receive the honor. The one rightful priest, Onias, was assassinated. His brother Jason was a Hellenist and paid for the office of High Priest. But another man, Menelaus, paid a higher fee and was given the job by Antiochus. Then Menelaus helped Antiochus steal from the Temple, and the army went wild in the city of Jerusalem. When it was over, Antiochus made the Temple a place of worship to the Greek god Zeus. Jews were forbidden to practice their Jewish faith. Antiochus tried to remove all copies of the Torah. He had pigs sacrificed on the High Altar and forced the Jews to eat unclean food. Many Jews died for their faith in God, while some Jews accepted the worship of Zeus. This continued for several years. This was one of the worst experiences for God's people in Jerusalem. The prophet Daniel referred to this as the "Abomination of Desolation."

The Revolt of the Maccabeans

One of the older priests, Mattathias, had returned to his ancestral home in the town of Modein. He was there with his five sons. When Antiochus's agents tried to force the old priest and his sons to sacrifice to Zeus, Mattathias revolted. He killed the agent and tore down the altar. This took place in 167 BC. Mattathias and his five sons were joined by the religious group known as the *Hasadim*. These were the "pious ones." Even though Mattathias died a year later, the revolution against Antiochus IV Epiphanes had begun.

Judas the Maccabee, known as "the hammerer," succeeded his father as the leader of the rebellion. Judas and his followers hid in the mountains and were protected by the local people. They were able to make surprise attacks against the forces of Antiochus and quickly withdraw to safety. They had great success against a much larger army. Antiochus IV Epiphanes was killed during this time. His general, Lysias, was locked in a struggle for power. Judas was able to gain religious freedom for the Jews.

Then Judas was able to lead his troops into Jerusalem and force the Syrians to leave. By 164 BC the Jews were able to cleanse the Temple. This called for a great celebration. For eight days the people held the Festival of Lights, which was known as *Chanukah*. This has also become known as the Feast of Dedication. A miracle occurred during the celebration. There was only enough oil to like the lamps for one day, but miraculously the oil did not run out during the entire celebration. Jewish people still celebrate this holiday in December today.

But the struggle was not over. Fighting had to continue, as they had not completely rid Judah of the Syrian army. By 161 BC Judas was killed in battle. He was replaced by his brother Jonathan. Jonathan was very skillful. Unfortunately, by 142 BC he been captured by the Syrian king, and he was killed. The last son of Mattathias was Simon. Simon led the Jewish people to freedom from the Syrians. Now the land of Palestine was at last free in the year 142 BC.

The Hasmoneans

These events led to about eighty years of freedom from foreign rule. Simon was chosen as the High Priest and leader of the people of Judah. Simon started the line of the Hasmoneans. Jewish life was changed forever. The *Hasadim* began during this period and later became the group of strict religious Jews known as the *Pharisees*. Study of the Law increased. The Jews became sensitive about the

traditions of their ancestors and the Temple. Any threat to these was viewed as disloyalty. There was a strong sense of loyalty to the Jewish state. Hellenism became less of a threat to Judaism, although this was the time when the group known as the *Sadducees* began. They were not totally opposed to Hellenism. Many of the ruling political leaders of Palestine were among the *Sadducees*. The *Essenes* were a third group. They also began around this time. They believed in living strict and disciplined lives. They lived in communities that were looking forward to the coming of the Messiah.

The Hasmonean rulers continued until two Hasmonean brothers, Hyrcanus II and Aristobulus II, fought each other for control of Palestine. Aristobulus II ruled from 67 to 63 BC. His brother Hyrcanus II was able to gain help from Antipator, an Idumean, and defeat Aristobulus. The Idumeans were descendents of Esau. Remember the name Antipator. He and his son would figure into the events in Palestine for years to come.

Meanwhile, a larger threat to Palestine came from the Roman general Pompey. He appeared in Jerusalem on his way south from conquering Syria. Both Hyrcanus II and Aristobulus II appealed to Pompey for help. He was happy to help. Pompey entered the Temple but did not find anything worth taking. He made Hyrcanus II the High Priest and took Aristobulus II as a prisoner back to Rome. In 63 BC Palestine came under the control of the Romans. The freedom that had existed under the Hasmonean rulers came to an end.

ROMAN RULE IN PALESTINE

Rome played an important role in the world of the Bible. From 63 BC to AD 70. Rome dominated the Jewish state in Palestine. Rome continued to have a strong impact upon Jews for the remainder of the Empire. Rome also affected Christianity of the New Testament. Rome affected the birth of Jesus in Bethlehem by calling for a census from one's family of origin. Mary and Joseph had to go to Bethlehem. The Roman procurator Pilate was also responsible for making the final decision about the death of Jesus on the cross. While the Roman emperors paid no attention to these seemingly unimportant events, during the next three hundred years Rome did become aware of Christianity and the Christians. They believed the Christians angered their gods, and they persecuted the church until the time of the emperor Constantine. After Constantine, Rome played a major role in the growth and development of the Church. Roman civilization lasted for over 1000 years. It started in 753 BC and continued to about AD 476. We will briefly examine the beginnings of Rome and its development as a civilization. Then we will look at its relationship with both the Jews and Christians.

Early Development of Rome

According to legend, Romulus founded Rome in 753 BC. For the next 250 years seven kings ruled Rome. The kings were finally forced out of Rome. The Roman Republic, with its consuls, tribunes, and Senate, replaced rule by a king. The patricians or the wealthy land owners controlled the newly formed Roman Senate. The plebeians included all other citizens of Rome. Gradually, the plebeians gained power in the Senate. Originally, two consuls ruled. One could veto or stop actions that had been taken by the other. The Roman Senate was the most powerful political body. They made the laws. There was constant struggle between the patricians and the plebeians. This struggle continued, even while Rome enjoyed military successes in Italy and beyond.

Rome moved to conquer and occupy the rest of Italy. They won some of the battles and lost others. They persisted until they were finally successful. They learned a great deal about fighting through those years. These events helped the Romans to build the most effective fighting machine that the world had seen to that time. But then the Gauls from present-day France swept through and conquered Rome. But the persistence of the Romans allowed them to regain their city and to push the Gauls back. To move their military equipment and men, the Romans started building roads. The first was the Via Appia. Later, these roads became essential to trade and eventually of taking the gospel to cities across the Empire.

The Punic wars with Carthage were decisive in building the power of Rome. The question was, who would be the master the Mediterranean Sea? Rome did not do well against the land armies of Hannibal. But in the end the dogged persistence of the Romans resulted in the total destruction of Carthage. During the same period they fought against the Macedonians in Greece. Again they were successful and defeated the successors of Philip II and Alexander the Great in Macedonia, and Rome

EARLY DEVELOPMENT OF ROME	
Date (BC)	Events in Rome
1000–900	Latin tribes settled on the 7 hills of Rome along the Tiber River
753	Romulus founded Rome and the line of 7 kings
509	Tarquin II (534 to 509 BC) dethroned—Roman Republic begins
390	Gauls tear apart Rome
312	Construction of the Via Appia, first major Roman road—Roman control of the Italian peninsula
262–241	First Punic war with Carthage
218–202	Second Punic war with Carthage—Hannibal crosses the Pyrenees into Italy
214–205	First Macedonian War—to win Macedonia for Rome
200–196	Second Macedonian War—Philip V defeated
190	Antiochus III, the Seleucid, is defeated by Rome at Magnesia
171–167	Third Macedonian War—Macedonia divided into 4 districts
150–148	Fourth Macedonian War—Macedonia became a province
149–146	Third Punic War—Carthage destroyed—North Africa taken over by Rome
146	Rome destroyed Corinth

EVENTS LEADING TO IMPERIAL ROME

Date (B.C.)	Events in Rome
133–122	Land reforms of Tiberias and Gaius Gracchus
74	Bithynia and Cyrene taken by Rome
73–71	Revolt of Spartacus and 90,000 slaves
66–63	Pompey conquers Syria (64 BC) Palestine (63 BC)
60–53	First Triumvirate—Julius Caesar, Pompey, Crassus
58–51	Gaul conquered by Julius Caesar
48	Death of Pompey
46	Julius Caesar named dictator in Rome
44	Julius Caesar assassinated by Brutus and Cassius
42	Battle of Philippi—Mark Antony and Octavian defeat Caesar's assassins
42–31	Struggle between Mark Antony and Octavian for control of Rome
31	Antony and Cleopatra defeated at Actium by Octavian
27	Title of "Augustus" conferred on Octavian— beginning of the Roman Imperial period

Events Leading to Imperial Rome

Success in battle across the sea and over land did not solve the internal battles that were taking place within Rome. The wealthy patricians were getting richer, and the poor plebeians were suffering. The brothers Tiberias and Gaius Gracchus wanted to distribute state-owned land to the poor. The senate opposed this idea. Both brothers were assassinated. It remained for the former Roman general Lucius Sulla to become a dictator in 82 BC to bring peace. He soon retired in 79 BC. But Rome was ready for a dictator to bring peace to the city of Rome. Julius Caesar became the dictator.

Meanwhile the dispute between Hyrcanus II and Aristobulus II resulted in the Roman general Pompey marching through Syria and Palestine. He took both of these countries in the east for Rome. In the west, the warring tribes of Gaul had swept through Rome in 390 BC. Now Julius Caesar went to Gaul and conquered the people of Gaul.

Julius Caesar adopted his nephew, Octavian, and taught him well about gaining and holding power. At first Julius Caesar shared power with two other leaders. That soon changed, and he was named dictator. Two years later he was assassinated. Eventually, Octavian emerged as the first of the caesars, and that brought in the period of Imperial Rome which continued until AD 476.

Imperial Rome (27 BC–AD 284)

Imperial Rome lasted from 27 BC until AD 476. Throughout that five hundred year period, the emperors of Rome ruled as absolute dictators. The Senate, consuls, and tribunes still had some power, but Caesar had absolute power. Augustus Caesar did not push for greater power for himself. He was given the title of *Augustus* by the people. He was also given the title, *Imperator,* which meant "victorious general." But he preferred the title *Princeps*, which meant "First Citizen of the Roman state." He extended the boundaries of the Empire. He established colonies throughout the Empire to help in the administration of the Empire. He reformed the tax system and the judicial system. Perhaps his greatest achievement was the *Pax Romana* or the

RECONSTRUCTION OF FORUMS IN ROME

THE FAMOUS COLOSSEUM AT ROME

INTERIOR OF COLOSSEUM IN ROME

committed suicide. During the rule of some of the later emperors, violence in the city of Rome became a way of life. Rome reached its greatest extent around the year AD 150.

This was a time of great cultural progress, as well as growth in the Empire. Great writers like Virgil, Horace, Ovid, Livy, Martial, Juvenal, and Tacitus contributed to the Roman literature. Architecture and sculpture made important contributions. This was the time for the construction of the great chariot race courses, public baths, great amphitheatres, and the coliseum. The coli-seum was dedicated in AD 81. Along with culture and building, Roman law advanced during this time as well. Roman law became the basis for Western law and law in America.

Late Roman Empire (AD 284–AD 476)

In the later Roman Empire, the military command became more powerful. Emperor Diocletian became like an oriental tyrant. He forced people who wanted to meet with him to lie face down prostrate before him. Like many of the emperors, Diocletian saw himself as a god to be worshipped. He would no longer wear the simple robe of the princeps but wore a robe of purple, letting people know that he was head of the Empire and a god. The Senate no longer made laws. The Senate became a fashionable club. The Empire became so large that it was difficult to rule effectively. Diocletian divided the Empire into four units for more efficient administration. But competition among the four rulers created more problems than it solved.

Constantine the Great came to power as emperor. He led his troops into Rome victoriously conquering in the name of Jesus Christ. Constantine ruled both East and West. He established the Treaty of Milan in 313, which allowed Christians to have the same rights as other religions in the Empire. In 330 he moved the capital of the Empire to Constantinople. It was difficult to defend the

peace of Rome, which lasted for two hundred years.

Augustus did not want to establish a kingship. Tiberius was chosen by Augustus to become the next emperor. The next three emperors acted strangely. Caligula was believed to have been insane. Claudius was evil and cruel. Nero probably set the great fire of Rome. Then he blamed the Christians for the suffering it caused. He started the persecution of Christians. Finally Nero

Empire against the Germanic tribes that were attacking the Empire and Rome itself. As a result the East grew stronger, and the West grew weaker.

In AD 410 the Goths swept into Italy and tore Rome apart. By AD 455 the Vandals entered Rome, and they spent two weeks taking what they wanted from Rome. Finally, in AD 476 the German chieftan replaced the Roman emperor, Romulus Augustulus. From that point on, the German chiefs established little kingdoms, and the Roman Empire in the west had come to an end.

Herod the Great and His Family

Recall Antipator, the Idumean, from the last of the Hasmonean line of rulers. Antipator came to the aid of Julius Caesar, when Caesar was trapped in Alexandria. For this Antipator received Roman citizenship and a ruling title. Antipator acted quickly to install Herod as governor of Galilee. Herod's brother Phasael was installed as governor of Jerusalem. Herod was cruel and put down a Jewish revolt in Galilee in which many Jews were killed. Antipator was assassinated. Later Herod's brother Phasael committed suicide.

With them gone, in 40 BC Herod found an opportunity to go to Rome. With the help of Mark Antony and Octavian, Herod spoke to the Roman Senate. The Senate gave him the title of king of the Jews. Under the authority of Rome, Herod ruled in Samaria, Judea, and Idumea. He was king from 37 BC to 4 BC. He was just as cruel as king as he had been earlier. He did, however, engage in a large building program. He built amphitheatres, palaces,

EMPERORS OF ROME	
Dates	Emperors of Rome
27 BC–AD 14	Augustus Caesar
AD 14–37	Tiberius
AD 37–41	Caligula
AD 41–54	Claudius
AD 54–68	Nero
AD 69	Galba, Otho, Vitellius
AD 69–79	Vespasian
AD 79–81	Titus
AD 81–96	Domitian
AD 96–98	Nerva
AD 98–117	Trajan
AD 117–138	Hadrian
AD 138–161	Antoninus Pius
AD 161–180	Marcus Aurelius
AD 180–192	Commodus
AD 193–211	Septimus Severus
AD 211–217	Caracalla
AD 217–218	Macrinus
AD 218–222	Elagabalus
AD 222–235	Severus Alexander
AD 284–305	Diolcletian (East)
AD 286–305	Maximinian (West)
AD 312–337	Constantine
AD 337–361	Constantine's sons
AD 361–364	Julian the Apostate, Jovian
AD 364–379	Valentinian I Valens; Gratian Valentinian II
AD 379–392	Theodosius (East)
AD 395–423	Honorius

and other Roman buildings. His most ambitious project was building the Temple. It was one of the wonders of the ancient world. In addition to the Temple, Herod helped to make Palestine more Roman. The Jews hated Herod for his cruelty, even though he gave them a restored and enlarged Temple.

After his death three of his sons, a grandson, and a great grandson received responsibilities from Rome for ruling in the area. None of his descendents carried out the role that Herod filled. Roman leaders, such as Pilate, ruled over Jerusalem and Palestine.

The Jewish State and Rome

The Jews had to contend with both the cruelty of King Herod and the power of Rome. Many Jews revolted against both Herod and Rome. Many Jews were crucified. There were zealots among the Jews who took every opportunity to kill Roman soldiers. The Roman soldiers were garrisoned in the fortress of Antonia. They put down any uprisings that occurred in Jerusalem and the Temple.

During the reign of Claudius, the Jews were expelled from Rome (see Acts 18:1). There were also uprisings among the zealots during Claudius's reign. There was famine in Judea during these years as well. There was a Jewish revolt in AD 66. The revolt resulted in the siege of Jerusalem and its destruction by Titus in AD 70, while Vespasian was emperor. The arch of Titus, commemorating the destruction of the Temple, was dedicated in AD 81. Between

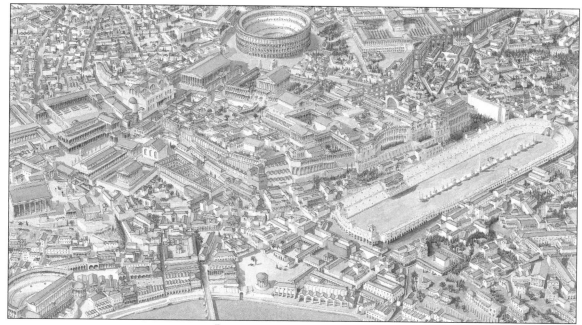

RECONSTRUCTION OF ROME

the years AD 115 to 117 under Trajan, there was a Jewish revolt in Cyrene, Egypt, and Mesopotamia. While Hadrian was emperor, from AD 132 to 135, Simon Bar Kokhbah led a rebellion that resulted in Jerusalem being destroyed and rebuilt as a Roman colony of Aelia Capitolina.

Christians and Rome

Jesus was born during the reign of Augustus Caesar. Tiberius was emperor when Jesus conducted His public ministry and was crucified. He was also emperor during the time Pentecost occurred and when Paul was converted. Rome took no official notice of these events.

Claudius was emperor when James was martyred. The first and second missionary journeys of Paul took place during Claudius's reign. It remained for the reign of Nero for the Roman state to pay attention to the Christians. During his reign Paul carried out his third missionary journey. Paul was sent to Rome and imprisoned there. He wrote his prison letters there. After the great fire in Rome, persecution of Christians was supported by the

Roman state. Both Paul and Peter were martyred. Nero committed suicide in AD 68.

Persecution against Christians continued. Many Christians lost their lives in the coliseum by the gladiators or being torn apart by wild animals. Persecution was heavy at some times and relaxed at others. It increased during the reign of Domitian. John was imprisoned on the island of Patmos and wrote the Revelation in AD 95. Domitian was assassinated in AD 96. Under Emperor Trajan and his successor Hadrian, persecution of Christians also increased.

It was not until Constantine the Great, who ruled from AD 312 to 337, that persecution stopped. The Edict of Milan in AD 313 brought an end to the killing of Christians. Julian the apostate tried to bring it back. His reign only lasted from AD 361 to 364. He was not successful. Christianity had finally triumphed. The control of the church during the Middle Ages followed.

Lesson Plans

INTRODUCTION

The most important book we have is the Bible. It tells us how the world was formed. It tells us how we were created. It tells us how sin entered the world. It tells us how to find peace with God and forgiveness of sin. It tells us about our future.

Children need to be introduced to the Bible early in life. They need more than just listening to isolated Bible stories. The Bible writers, under the inspiration of the Holy Spirit, gave us the entire story of God's redemption in Christ. Children need to learn the significance of stories like Daniel in the Lon's Den but as part of the entire story of God's history of redeeming man from sin.

Programs like the Core Knowledge Foundation series have clearly shown that children are capable of learning good, comprehensive material. This material will provide them with a solid foundation for their future. If we do not develop this foundation in the elementary school years, they are unlikely to learn it during the teenage years. Their interests turn elsewhere during adolescence.

Significant advances have been made in the last two decades in the science of learning and how the mind works. It is clear from what we know about the mind today that prior knowledge is essential to further learning. This prior knowledge base must be built during the elementary years.

This handbook is designed to introduce children to God's redemptive relationship to mankind. It is important to help children gain this understanding and appreciation early in life. This book and its activities can be used for several years. A variety of activities can be used at different age levels.

At this stage children deal with the concepts of time and place more easily. Before that time you will need to help them see how the specific Bible stories relate to their own time and place. The world in which we live is secular and postmodern. We must run against the tide and not capitulate to the postmodern point of view. If we do not, we will lose the next generation.

Children need to learn basic content. Their knowledge of God's Word will stay with them throughout their lives if they learn it now. They need to learn the major themes of the Bible—God's creation, sin and the fall, God's chosen people, salvation in Jesus Christ, God's new humanity in the church, and God's Word, the Bible. This book will help your child explore these great issues.

COURSE OVERVIEW

We have tried to provide all that you will need to teach your children the Bible.

The course is divided into 15 lessons. Lessons 1–7 guide you through the Old Testament. Of those, lesson 1 is an introduction to the Bible.

Lessons 8–14 will lead you through the New Testament. Lesson 8 reviews the Old Testament and introduces the New Testament.

Lesson 15 is a lesson on Bible geography. If you wish to cut down on the number of lessons, you might consider integrating lesson 15 into the other parts of the total study of the Bible, lessons 1–14.

For each lesson a variety of activities are presented. (Activity sheets follow each lesson and may be enlarged and duplicated. The answers for these sheets are found in the back of the book.) You will need to pick and choose those activities that will stretch each child. If they are going to go deeper later, they will need to learn the content now. The curriculum should spiral back on itself as the child grows older. It is not a problem to return to the material in this volume as the child moves a year ahead. You can recycle through this material again as your child grows and use activities that will appeal to the older child.

It is important to allow children to memorize Scripture. Research has shown that children have an amazing facility to memorize. We lose that ability as we grow older. Children understand much of what they are memorizing at their level, even if the full import of the Scripture is not gained until later. But if they do not memorize the Scripture when they are young, they will not be able to more fully appreciate the meaning later.

SUGGESTIONS FOR PREPARATION

1. Study the handbook in advance. Read the material you need to cover from the handbook with your child. Read the passages of Scripture from a modern translation, such as the Holman Christian Standard Bible®.

2. Read the objectives for the lesson you plan to teach. Examine the identifications so that you will be able to help your child understand new concepts, persons, or geographical locations.

3. With the objectives in mind, read through the learning activities. Think about which activities will best suit your child at his or her level of learning. Star those activities that you want to include in the lesson. Prepare a simple lesson plan that will include objectives, Scripture to be studied, identifications, content, and the particular activities you will use. You need only a sentence or phrase to identify what you will do. Most of the work is already done for you. The lesson plan is important since it becomes a road map for where you have been. You will want to refer back to it when you are ready to take your child to the next phase.

4. Locate any additional resources you might need. You do not need to go beyond the materials available at a stationary store or that you may already have at home. Still you may want to look in your church library, public library, or on Web sites and supplement what is suggested. A word of caution is in order concerning videos and other media. Make sure the content maintains fidelity with the biblical account. Some videos take liberties with the text and can change the meaning, giving your child a false understanding of the biblical revelation as God gave it.

5. Do background studies where appropriate. Study background information for Egypt, Babylonia, Palestine, Persia, Rome, and Greece. Your child will benefit in his or her studies at school as well. Take field trips. Expose your children to as many good experiences as possible. This will help them have interest and develop a love for God's Word and His people.

6. Keep records of what you have covered and test the children periodically. Suggested activities have test-related items, such as crossword puzzles, fill-in-the-blanks, etc. Find out what they are learning and emphasize or reteach (if necessary) concepts, persons, or places as necessary. Keep records of progress. You will also want to keep samples of the children's work for good examples.

7. Stress the whole. Do not get caught up in minutiae. An analogy that is significant here is the difference between the individual tree versus the forest. It is all too easy to see the individual tree and miss the forest. For example, if you teach the story of David and Goliath, it is easy to perceive this as a superhero story. Your child may miss the essential concept that this was God's way of dealing with the Philistine, who was defying the armies of God. He or she may also miss the role that story plays in the rise of David to become accepted by the people as God's anointed king over Israel.

8. Try to select activities that are age appropriate.

9. Have fun with your children! Learning should be fun. Keep in mind that your own attitude is important. You can inspire your children to enjoy their learning experiences.

TO PARENTS

You have a special opportunity to teach and lead your children to love and understand God's Word! Don't miss the opportunity. Sometimes it is easy to become discouraged and allow the child to do something else, rather than engage them with the Bible and Christian experiences.

When you are tempted to discouragement, recall the experience of Moses.

By faith Moses, when he had grown up, refused to be called the son of Pharaoh's daughter and chose to suffer with the people of God rather than to enjoy the short-lived pleasure of sin. For he considered reproach for the sake of the Messiah to be greater wealth than the treasures of Egypt, since his attention was on the reward. (Hebrews 11:24–26)

Remember where Moses learned about the people of God? It was not through being chosen by Pharaoh's daughter to live in the palace. It was through the instruction he received from his mother as a child. As a parent, you can make a difference in the life of your child as well.

Read to your child. Read aloud to him or her from God's Word. Talk about your faith in Christ. Learn along with your child. Select learning activities you can do by simply modifying them to use with your child. If you are homeschooling, you might want to invite other children who are being homeschooled to join you and your family for the study of the Bible.

We are praying for you!

To Teachers
You have a God-given opportunity to make a difference in the lives of the children whom God has entrusted to your care. It is essential to teach the school subjects, but you have a particular opportunity to teach them the eternal truth of God's Word. It is clear from the history of Israel that teachers were an essential part of the early teaching of the faith for children. Even today Jewish children attend Hebrew school to learn not only the language but also their Hebrew faith.

They memorize large portions of Scripture. Jesus, Himself, went through this kind of preparation. It is not surprising that He was prepared by age twelve to talk with the religious teachers in the Temple. He amazed them! When we next see Jesus in the Gospels, He is baptized and moves directly to the wilderness and the temptation experiences. Remember how He responded to Satan? In each case Jesus quoted from the Word of God. Can we do any less for our children?

While this passage comes from a period when teaching was more primitive, the principle still holds. One of the unique opportunities for the Christian school is to teach in the light of God's revelation.

Listen Israel: The LORD our God, the LORD is One. Love the LORD your God with all your heart, with all your soul, and with all your strength. These words that I am giving you today are to be in your heart. Repeat them to your children. Talk about them when you sit in your house and when you walk along the road, when you lie down and when you get up. Bind them as a sign on your hand and let them be a symbol on your forehead. Write them on the doorposts of your house and on your gates. (Deuteronomy 6:4–9)

There are a number of activities from which to choose. You should have enough to design your curriculum as you choose.

May God grant you wisdom and guidance as you minister to the precious lives of your children.

We are praying for you!

Unit One: Old Testament Review and Poetry and Wisdom Literature: Lessons 1–6

UNIT SUMMARY

This set of lessons will provide the learner with a review of the background in the Old Testament and an understanding of poetry and wisdom literature of the Old Testament. They will also help the student develop a lifelong love for God's Word through the Bible.

OVERVIEW

Objectives

By the end of this unit, the learner should be able to:

- Recall the significant persons who are identified and described in the Old Testament and be able to describe their contribution to the fulfillment of God's purposes,
- Understand and appreciate the significant events that occur in the Old Testament in the chronological development of God's dealing with humankind from Adam to the end of the Old Testament and into the period between the Old and New Testaments,
- Develop an understanding of Hebrew poetry and Old Testament wisdom literature, and
- Develop a lifelong love and appreciation for God's Word, the Bible.

Content Summary and Rationale

There is a wealth of content in the Old Testament, which is often ignored or overlooked. Yet God's redemptive activity in the New Testament cannot be fully understood without a clear understanding of His activity in the Old Testament.

It is essential to review the material from the Old Testament that will help us relate effectively to the New Testament. This includes material from the Book of Genesis. It gives us insight into the origin of humankind, the origin of sin, and the human dilemma that sin caused. The Book of Genesis also shows us how God extended His love to a sinful and stubborn humanity with the intent to win a fallen humanity back to Himself.

The content of this Old Testament unit leads the learner to see the hand of a loving God in history. When God calls one to faith in Himself and the achievement of His purposes in history, we are not called blindly to believe. There is a long history of God's relationship with humankind, and a clear picture is presented. Failure to believe and trust God leads to disastrous consequences and ultimately death. But for all those who believed and trusted God, there were long-term positive consequences. These who followed God experienced His blessing and ultimately to life.

We then turn to the wisdom and poetic literature of the Old Testament. Of all the books in the Bible, only the Psalms consistently teach us how to respond to God. The Psalms help us worship. They provide understanding of how to tell God about our needs and longings. They can help us deepen our relationship with God.

In the Proverbs there is wisdom—God's wisdom—for living a godly life in this sinful and corrupt world. We can learn about how we need to fear God. There is wisdom for parents in bringing up children in this world. Song of Solomon has one clear message for our culture, that marriage is between a man and a woman.

Ecclesiastes describes the meaning of life from the human perspective. Without God life does not have meaning. Job tells us about suffering. We do not know why we suffer in this world. There may be reasons, such as those that Job discovered, of which we may not be aware and may not be able to explain. One day we will understand, but in the meantime we need to live our lives in accordance with God's desires for us.

Key Concept

God provides wisdom for all of life. He made us and understands us. He wants us to come into a relationship with Himself. He has given us the means for finding fellowship with Himself through praise, adoration, confession, and expressions of love. He has given us wisdom for living today in this world. He has provided wisdom for facing the temptations that may be experienced in today's world. He guides us to trust in Him, whatever our circumstances in life.

Prior Knowledge Needed

During the early elementary school years, children can learn more than a superficial knowledge of stories, like David and Goliath. By third or fourth grade they can begin to understand time sequences. We need to provide them with the chronological understanding of the events that occurred in the Old Testament. If your child did not study the material in volume 1 of this series, you may want to spend more time with the review section of the Old Testament in lessons 1 and 2 in this volume. If your child did study the material in volume 1, you may simply want to review lessons 1 and 2 of this volume.

This unit does not presuppose that the child has any more than a superficial knowledge of the other parts of the Old Testament that are not included in the historical sections. During these years the child's understanding is in the process of developing.

Future learning will be built upon what the child learns during these years. Therefore, it is essential to guide the child's understanding of God and the Old Testament in ways that will provide opportunity for the child to grow toward a comprehensive and healthy understanding of who God is and what God requires of all who will love and serve Him. This unit will help develop the child's understanding of God and His purposes, as found in His revelation of Himself in the Old Testament.

Resources for Teachers and Students

- Buchanan, Edward, *Parent/Teacher Handbook The Bible, Volumes 1 and 3* (Nashville, Tenn.: Broadman & Holman, 2003).

- Butler, Trent, ed., *Holman Illustrated Bible Dictionary* (Nashville, Tenn: Holman Bible Publishers, 2003).

- Dockery, David, ed., *Holman Bible Handbook* (Nashville, Tenn.: Holman Bible Publishers, 1992).

- Hastings, Selina, *The Children's Illustrated Bible* (New York, N.Y.: DK Publishing, 1994).

- Holman Interactive *Bible Navigator* CD-ROM version available at your local LifeWay Christian Store.

- An encyclopedia—*World Book, Funk and Wagnalls, Britannica*, etc. (may use CD-ROM).

LESSON 1: PREHISTORY THROUGH THE JUDGES

Readings from the Parent/Teacher Handbook: The Bible, Vol. 3: "Review of the Old Testament"— "The Beginnings of the Human Race" through "Major Jewish Festivals"

OBJECTIVES
By the end of lesson, the learner should be able to:
- Sequence the events of the Old Testament and continue through the period between the Old and New Testaments,
- Recall the creative acts of God and the way sin entered the world,
- Explore the lives of Noah and the patriarchs,
- Review the life of Moses and the events of the Exodus,
- Review the lives of the Judges, and
- Identify each of the Ten Commandments.

IDENTIFICATIONS
Concepts
- *Covenant*—agreement between God and Abraham
- *Plagues of Egypt*—judgment of God upon the Egyptians
- *Ten Commandments*—moral law to be obeyed, even today

People	Materials Needed
• *God:* Creator of the universe and the one who cares about us enough to send His Son to die on the cross so that we may find God and salvation through Him	• *Parent/Teacher Handbook: The Bible, Vol. 3*
• *Adam and Eve:* first parents of the human race	• Activity Sheets for Lesson 1 *(Activity sheets located at the end of each lesson.)*
• *Noah:* saved from the Flood in the Ark	• Crayons, markers, and stickers
• *Abraham:* father of the Hebrew nation	• Blank sheets of white paper for drawing
• *Moses:* the leader God chose to lead the people of Israel out of Egypt	• Shoe boxes
	• Masking tape, plastic tape, and plastic adhesive
	• Lined paper for writing
	• Shelf paper, butcher paper, or newsprint

LEARNING ACTIVITIES FOR LESSON 1

Activity 1—Time Line for Bible History

Develop a time line for the history of the time periods covered by the Old Testament. You will want to extend this in the New Testament section later. In the text from the patriarchs, you will find a list of approximate dates. (We do not know the dates before the patriarchs.)

Use a sheet of shelf paper or butcher paper that will stretch to about six feet in length and write significant dates along the lower margin. Allow enough space for your children to draw pictures of the biblical events as you come to them in reading in the handbook. For example, you will want to do a section on the period before history begins. The children could draw pictures showing Creation, the creation of Adam and Eve, the Fall, Adam and Eve driven from the Garden of Eden, Cain and Abel, Noah and the Flood, and the Tower of Babel. The dates begin with the Period of the Patriarchs—Abraham to Joseph. You may create the chart in sections by attaching the patriarchs to the prehistory. If you place them on the wall, use masking tape or plastic adhesive (obtainable at a stationary store) that will hold the paper to the wall but not leave marks on the surface.

This activity will be ongoing as you move through the materials in the handbook for the Old and New Testaments.

Activity 2—Posters of the Creative Acts of God

Read the appropriate section from the handbook.

Divide your students into smaller groups. Have each group make one poster of one of the days of creation. If you are working individually, make a booklet of the days of creation.

Label each of the days and draw pictures to illustrate each of the events. Write captions under each of the pictures to describe what it must have been like. Here are the days of creation:

Beginning—Heavens and the earth

Day 1—God created light.

Day 2—God separated the water from the sky.

Day 3—Dry land was separated from the sea and created plants and trees.

Day 4—Sun and moon appeared to create day and night and seasons and years.

Day 5—Sea life as fish and birds to fly in the air were created.

Day 6—Animal life and human beings were created. Humans were different. Humans were created in the image of God and told to rule over the animal kingdom.

Day 7—God rested from His creation.

Activity 3—Plot the Story of Noah

Usc Activity Sheet 3 at the end of this lesson. Distribute a copy to each student.

Read the story in the handbook and in Genesis 6:5–8:22. Have the children consider each of the three groups: Noah, People, and Noah's Family. What was the reaction of each group? What did each group think about what Noah was doing? How did each group respond after the rain started?

When the children have finished writing their answers on the activity sheet, discuss the responses.

Activity 4—Wordfind on the Patriarchs

Use the Wordfind from Activity Sheet 4. The following names will be found in the Wordfind:

Abraham—father of the Hebrew people

Sarah—wife of Abraham

Isaac—son of Abraham and Sarah

Esau—first son of Isaac and Rebekah

Jacob—son of Isaac and Rebekah, who carried the Hebrew line

Joseph—favored son of Jacob and Rachel

Benjamin—favored son of Jacob and Rachel

Ephraim—son of Joseph

Manasseh—son of Joseph

Reuben—son of Jacob and Leah

Simeon—son of Jacob and Leah

Levi—son of Jacob and Leah

Judah—son of Jacob and Leah

Issachar—son of Jacob and Leah

Zebulun—son of Jacob and Leah

Naphtali—son of Jacob and Bilhah, along with son, Dan

Asher—son of Jacob and Bilhah, along with son, Gad

When your students have completed the Wordfind, talk together about the different persons who were represented in the Wordfind.

Activity 5—Filmstrip Story of Moses's Life

Duplicate copies of the filmstrip paper and provide your children with copies of Activity Sheet 5. Your children will need colored markers for this activity. You will also need a shoe box and tape.

Ask your students to make a filmstrip that will tell the story of Moses's life. Have them develop the story in four parts:

1. His early life in the basket in the river and his life in Pharaoh's household
2. His middle life after he killed the Egyptian and went to the home of Jethro and his marriage to Zipporah
3. His later life in confronting the Pharaoh, the ten plagues and leaving Egypt
4. Going to Mount Sinai and wandering of the people of Israel in the wilderness

The first fact of the story is written and drawn in the first frame, etc. Use a shoe box or something similar with a hole cut for viewing in the front and a hole cut to allow light in the back. Wrap the filmstrip on two dowels (top and bottom). Tape the scenes together and tape them to the dowels.

Have the students view the filmstrip one frame at a time as they roll through the strip from bottom to the top.

Activity 6—Collage Posters of the Ten Commandments

Divide your class into five groups. Provide each group with old magazines. You may also provide old Sunday school curriculum materials that have pictures of Bible-related themes. Or you may choose to have the students draw their own scenes.

Assign two commandments to each group. Have them prepare a poster for each of their commandments. Each poster should illustrate one of their assigned commandments. They may use a collage of pictures to show how the commandment should be followed and/or how the commandment is disobeyed in our society today.

Tape the posters to the wall. Discuss the meaning of each of the commandments.

Activity 7—Judges Fill-in-the-Blanks

Review the judges of Israel. You will want to read the material in the chart about the judges from the handbook. Give each student a copy of Activity Sheet 7. Ask them to write their answers in the appropriate blank.

Conclude this activity by discussing the role and importance of the judges in Israel.

Activity 8—Bible Verse Memory Book

Make a Bible Verse Memory Book to keep all of the verses that your children memorize.

Cut a sheet of 12x18-inch construction paper in half for the cover.

Fold eight sheets of plain white paper in half and staple them inside the construction paper to form a booklet. You may want to cut pieces of lined paper at the bottom of each page in the booklet. Your class members may print each memory verse on the lined paper. At the top of the page have your students illustrate the Bible verse, using crayons, markers, and stickers. Begin the booklet with the first verse to memorize for this lesson—Joshua 1:8.

This book of instruction must not depart from your mouth; you are to recite it day and night, so that you may carefully observe everything written in it. For then you will prosper and succeed in whatever you do.

Continue to use the booklet throughout the entire set of lessons in this unit.

WORKSHEETS FOR LESSON 1

ACTIVITY SHEET 3: NOAH AND FAMILY

When God told Noah to build the ark, what was the reaction of each group? How did Noah respond? What did his family and the other people think about what he was doing? How did each group respond after the rain started?

Noah	People	Family

ACTIVITY SHEET 4: WORDFIND FOR PATRIARCHS

```
O V H N M X V V Q S H I J C I
U U A A A W S X L J Z F P Z L
L O G C D P X X D K X N Z B L
S M X G L U H E L J M R I G S
V Q Z G X H J T S N O E M I S
N A J B C T I S A A C U X W T
U O E J H W P R K L U B X O S
L G O K D C B T A V I E O F M
U D M A N A S S E H M N A A A
B K C T T H U H W I C J H R P
E Z J T A F D D A Z B A X E G
Z W N R F H L R X O R M S H U
C H A A V E H K C B P I E S Z
P S T P V P I A A M N N Y A I
P Q C I E Y J H P E S O J M A
```

Directions: Find the following words in the Wordfind above.

Abraham	Benjamin	Judah
Sarah	Ephraim	Issachar
Isaac	Manasseh	Zebulun
Esau	Reuben	Naphtali
Jacob	Simeon	Asher
Joseph	Levi	

ACTIVITY SHEET 5: FILMSTRIP STORY OF MOSES'S LIFE

ACTIVITY SHEET 7: THE JUDGES

1. _____ made a careless vow to God that he had to fulfill when he defeated the Amorites.

2. Shamgar used an ox goad to kill _____ Philistines.

3. _____ was the last of the judges and the first of the prophets.

4. _____ conquered a Canaanite city.

5. Samson was a _____ and very strong. He killed thousands of Philistines when he destroyed their pagan temple.

6. _____ and _____ sang a victory song after defeating the Canaanite king, Sisera.

7. Ehud judged Israel for _____ years and defeated the Moabites.

8. Gideon led three hundred soldiers to defeat _____ Midianites.

LESSON 2: THE UNITED MONARCHY TO THE PERIOD BETWEEN THE OLD AND NEW TESTAMENTS

Readings from the Parent/Teacher Handbook: The Bible, Vol. 3: "The United Monarchy over Israel," "The Divided Monarchy of Israel and Judah," "The Exile and Beyond," and "The Conclusion" of this section

OBJECTIVES
By the end of lesson, the learner should be able to:
- Differentiate among the characteristics of Saul, David, and Solomon,
- Identify and describe selected kings and prophets of Israel and Judah,
- Identify and describe the captivity of the prophet Daniel,
- Explain the returns from Exile, and
- Identify the three Jewish groups who developed between the Old and New Testament.

IDENTIFICATIONS
Concepts
- *United monarchy*—twelve tribes of Israel united in one kingdom
- *Divided monarchy*—kingdom divided into Israel (northern ten tribes) and Judah (southern two tribes)
- *Exile*—Judah taken into captivity in 586 BC by the king of Babylonia
- *Maccabean revolt*—revolt against Syria, began 168 BC
- *Hellenization*—corrupting Jewish culture with Greek culture
- *Pharisees*—zealous religious men who followed both the written and oral law
- *Sadducees*—wealthy ruling classes who followed only the Written Law
- *Essenes*—community of persons who shared possessions and lived in isolation, looking for the coming of the Messiah

People
- *Saul:* first king of Israel
- *David:* God's anointed king after Saul, whose line would continue
- *Solomon:* David's son and king over the united monarchy
- *Hezekiah:* good king of Judah, who restored worship of God and used the Psalms in worship
- *Josiah:* good king of Judah, who restored worship of God in the Temple

MATERIALS NEEDED
- *Parent/Teacher Handbook: The Bible, Vol. 3*
- Activity Sheets for Lesson 2
- Blank paper
- A roll of shelf or butcher paper
- Lined paper
- Drawing paper
- Crayons and markers
- 3x5-index cards
- Stapler
- Animal crackers
- Plastic or wooden floatable boat
- Paper or wooden blocks

LEARNING ACTIVITIES FOR LESSON 2
Activity 1—Looking at the Lives of Saul, David, and Solomon
Read the section "The United Monarchy of Israel" in the handbook.

Give each of the children a 3x5-index card with "Success" printed on the front. "Failure" should be written on the reverse side.

The teacher should read the following statements about each of the three kings of Israel. Students hold up their cards to indicate whether the characteristic was a "success" or "failure" by the king.

Saul

1. First king over Israel, called by God (Success)
2. Saul prophesies for God (Success)
3. Saul does not follow God's instructions about sacrifice (Failure)
4. Spirit of God left Saul (Failure)
5. Saul gave his daughter to David in marriage (Success)
6. Saul tried to kill David (Failure)
7. Saul died in battle with the Philistines (Failure)

David

1. Anointed by Samuel to be king over Israel (Success)
2. In the strength of the Lord, David killed Goliath (Success)
3. Fled from King Saul (Failure)
4. Crowned king of Judah (Success)
5. Crowned king over Israel (Success)
6. Conquered Jerusalem and made it his capital (Success)
7. God's covenant with David (Success)
8. Military victories over his enemies (Success)
9. Committed adultery with Bathsheba (Failure)
10. Had Bathsheba's husband killed in battle (Failure)
11. Confronted by the prophet Nathan (Failure)
12. Birth of Solomon (Success)
13. Absalom rebelled (Failure)
14. David restored as king (Success)
15. Sinned in taking the census (Failure)
16. Planned and prepared for building the Temple (Success)
17. David named Solomon as his successor (Success)

Solomon

1. Asked God for wisdom; God gave him wisdom, wealth, and honor (Success)
2. Solomon married daughter of Pharaoh (Failure)
3. Solomon taxed the people heavily (Failure)
4. Solomon built the great Temple to the Lord (Success)
5. Solomon wrote some of the psalms, proverbs, and Ecclesiastes (Success)
6. Solomon married many wives (Failure)
7. Solomon followed the false gods of his many wives (Failure)

Talk with your students about failure and success in our Christian lives today. We fail when we sin and do not trust and obey God, just as the kings of Israel did. We succeed when we trust God and follow His commandments and seek His will for our lives.

Close this activity in prayer by telling God we will obey and trust Him to guide our lives.

Activity 2—Kings and Prophets Trivia Game for Israel and Judah

Read the section "The Divided Monarchy of Israel and Judah" from the handbook. Pay particular attention to the charts. You might even want to duplicate the charts for the students as you engage in this activity.

Have your students divided into four smaller groups. Give each group one of the duplicated charts. One group will write the names of the kings of Israel. The second group will write the names of the prophets of Israel. The third group will write the names of the kings of Judah. The last group will write the names of the prophets of Judah.

On the face of a 3x5-index card, write the name of the king or prophet. On the reverse side indicate the following four characteristics: (1) king or prophet, (2) Israel or Judah, (3) good or evil, (4) what the king did or what the prophet taught.

After all the cards are prepared, shuffle the cards. Divide the class into two teams. Have the teams compete with each other to see how many characteristics they can remember about each of the kings and prophets.

When you have finished playing the game, put aside the cards. Have the students discuss what they learned about what made the kings good or bad. Have them also consider how the prophets tried to help the people understand how to follow God. Summarize the discussion.

Activity 3—Research two significant kings of Judah

Select several good students to research and prepare reports on two significant kings of Judah—Hezekiah and Josiah.

Have them first read the material in "The Southern Kingdom of Judah" from the handbook. Then send them to the library to read about these two kings in a Bible dictionary, such as the *Holman Bible Dictionary*. Ask them to prepare a report and tell the class about what they learned about these two godly kings.

Activity 4—Circumstances in the Life of Daniel

Use Activity Sheet 4 at the end of this lesson to fill in the blanks about the life of Daniel and his reaction to the events in his life.

Read the section from the handbook titled "The Babylonian Exile—586 to 539 BC." In addition the students may want to do further study on the life of Daniel. Your students can find help in a Bible dictionary, such as the *Holman Bible Dictionary*. You may also want to read the story from a Children's Bible, such as *The Children's Illustrated Bible*. The stories from that source would include: "The Golden Statue," "Belshazzar's Feast," and "Daniel in the Lion's Den."

Complete Activity Sheet 1. Discuss how Daniel obeyed God, even when it was not popular. God blessed him as a result.

Activity 5—The Return from Exile

Use Activity Sheet 5 at the end of this lesson to fill in the blanks about the return from Exile. You will find material on this study in the handbook, "The Return from Captivity—538 to 444 BC." In this section, note particularly the chart on the "Return from Exile."

After they have completed the activity sheet, have the students consider what it must have been like to leave their home in Babylonia, where they had grown up from childhood, and return to Palestine. The prophets and their elders told them about what life in the Promised Land had been like before they were taken into captivity. They did not have television, movies, or other means to visualize and understand what it had been like back in Palestine.

Activity 6—Matching Three Jewish Groups

Use Activity Sheet 6 at the end of this lesson. Match the three groups with the appropriate description. You will find material on this study in the handbook in the section entitled, "The Maccabean Revolt 168 to 63 BC."

These three groups are important in the life of the Jews in the New Testament. You may want to have several students research these groups in greater detail in a Bible dictionary, such as the *Holman Bible Dictionary*. Who were they, and what did they do? How did they affect the lives of the Jews in the period between the Old and New Testaments? How important were they during the ministry of Jesus and later in the life and ministry of Paul?

Activity 7—Memorize 2 Chronicles 7:14

Have each child commit to memory: "*If my people, which are called by my name, shall humble themselves, and pray, and seek my face, and turn from their wicked ways; then will I hear from heaven, and will forgive their sin, and will heal their land*" (KJV).

The children can write each of the words on a 3x5-index card and use these to practice the verse by putting the words in order.

Have each child try to recite the entire verse from memory, with the reference. Then have them write 2 Chronicles 7:14 in their Bible Verse Memory Books. They can illustrate the verse as well.

You may also want to review the verse, Joshua 1:8, that was learned in the last lesson.

ACTIVITY SHEET 4: THE LIFE OF DANIEL

Circumstances in Daniel's Life	Daniel's Reaction
1. Taken captive to Babylon with three friends	
2. Dream of Nebuchadnezzar	
3. Handwriting on the wall	
4. Order to bow down to King Darius	
5. Daniel and the Lion's Den	

ACTIVITY SHEET 5: THE RETURN FROM EXILE

First Return	Second Return	Third Return
When:	When:	When:
Leader:	Leader:	Leader:
Persian Ruler:	Persian Ruler:	Persian Ruler:
Events:	Events:	Events:

ACTIVITY SHEET 6: MATCHING THREE RELIGIOUS GROUPS OF THE JEWS WITH THE APPROPRIATE DESCRIPTION

Directions: Match the Group in the left column by drawing a line to the appropriate description in the right column.

1. Pharisees	A. Live in communities, share their possessions and devote time to study the Torah
2. Sadducees	B. Religious group who believes in the resurrection and supports the oral law
3. Essenes	C. Wealthy, ruling group who believe in the Written Law but do not believe in the resurrection

LESSON 3: THE PSALMS

Readings from the Parent/Teacher Handbook: The Bible, Vol. 3: "Psalms—Introduction," through "The Lord's Goodness (Psalm 23:5–6)"

OBJECTIVES
By the end of lesson, the learner should be able to:
- Define and give examples of parallelisms and the different types—antithetic, synonymous, and synthetic,
- Identify characteristics of the Psalms,
- Name different types of Psalms, such as pilgrimage, majestic, repentance, etc., and
- Explore selected psalms for their message and meaning.

IDENTIFICATIONS
Concepts
- *Parallelism*—chief characteristic of Hebrew poetry
- *Antithetic parallelism*—two lines expressing the opposite thought
- *Synthetic parallelism*—two lines, with the second line expanding the thought of the first
- *Synonymous parallelism*—two lines, with a similar meaning
- *Pilgrimage psalms*—used on the pilgrimage to the Temple

- *Majestic psalms*—expressing the beauty and majesty of God
- *Repentance psalms*—expressing sorrow for sin by the person who is repentant
- *Judgment psalms*—expressing the judgment of God
- *Teaching psalms*—psalms that instruct the hearer in the ways of God
- *Lament psalms*—Psalms expressing sadness

People
- *David*: author of the greatest number of psalms
- *Hezekiah*: king of Judah, who added to the Book of Psalms
- *Moses*: author of Psalm 90, the oldest psalm in the collection

MATERIALS NEEDED
- *Parent/Teacher Handbook: The Bible, Vol. 3*
- Activity Sheets for Lesson 3
- Crayons and markers
- Blank sheets of white paper for drawing
- Lined paper for writing

LEARNING ACTIVITIES FOR LESSON 3
Activity 1—Introduction to the Psalms
Read the appropriate section from the handbook called "The Psalms—Introduction."

Distribute copies of Activity Sheet 1 for this lesson. This sheet is found at the end of this lesson.

Ask each student to fill in the blanks on the worksheet from the Introduction to the Psalms. After they have finished, discuss their findings. Share each of the psalms with them that are related to each of the characteristics.

Activity 2—Types of Psalms
Read the appropriate section from the handbook, "The Psalms—Introduction."

Distribute copies of Activity Sheet 2 for this lesson. This sheet is found at the end of this lesson.

After each student has finished reading the psalms indicated, have the students unscramble the letters for each of the different types of psalms. Ask them to fill in the appropriate word in the blank to describe the psalms indicated.

Activity 3—Parallelisms in Hebrew Poetry

Read the appropriate section from the handbook, "The Psalms—Introduction."

Hebrew poetry has both meter and stanzas. Meter is the pattern of stressed and nonstressed syllables. Unfortunately, meter does not always translate into English from the original Hebrew. Stanzas set thought patterns apart from one another in the poetry.

But the most characteristic form of Hebrew poetry that can be observed, even in English, is the *parallelism*. A parallelism may be found in two or three lines. The thought expressed in the first line is related to the thought in the next line or two lines.

There are three types of parallelism. (1) In a *synonymous parallelism*, the thought of the first line is expressed to mean the same thing as the thought in the second line. (2) In an *antithetic parallelism*, the thought of the second line is opposite in meaning to the thought of the first line. (3) In a *synthetic parallelism*, the thought of the second line enlarges on the thought of the first line.

To help your students gain an appreciation for the different types of parallelism, duplicate Activity Sheets 3a and 3b for this lesson. Ask the students first to discover the meaning of *parallelism* and each type of parallelism. Then using the definitions from Activity Sheet 3a, have the students identify which parallelism is found in each of the examples that follow in Activity Sheet 3b.

As you continue to study the Psalms, look for additional examples of parallelisms.

Activity 4—Psalm 1

Read the appropriate section from the handbook titled "Selected Psalms." Also read Psalm 1 in your Bible.

In advance of this lesson, duplicate Activity Sheet 4. Have the students place the appropriate descriptions under "Tree" (Way of Life) or under "Chaff" (Way of Death) to compare the godly with the ungodly person.

Conclude this lesson by asking the students to talk about ways in which they can *meditate* on God's Law, as counseled in this psalm. *Meditate* means "to concentrate on and think over and over in your mind." For example, you might suggest that students could meditate on who God is. They could meditate on the greatness of God and/or a verse of Scripture they have memorized.

Activity 5—David's Need for God's Protection (Psalm 3)

Read "Selected Psalms" for Psalm 3 in the handbook. Either read it to your students or have the students read it for themselves. Read Psalm 3 in your Bible.

Give each student a copy of Activity Sheet 5. Ask each student to write the ways by which God was a shield to David at a time in his life when he was afraid for his life.

After the students have finished, discuss how God helped David in his time of need. How does God help us today in our time of need? What can we do to receive God's help? Suggest things like trusting in Jesus, prayer, and relying on God's Word.

Activity 6—The Good Shepherd (Psalm 23)

Read Psalm 23 in your Bible. Then read the description in the "Selected Psalms" section for Psalm 23 in the handbook. This is probably the most loved psalm in the entire Scripture.

Use Activity Sheet 6 to compare the characteristics of the shepherd and the sheep. Draw lines to the correct description. Conclude this activity by discussing with the students how we are often like sheep and how God is our Good Shepherd today.

Activity 7—Memorize Psalm 23

Have the children memorize this psalm and include the verse in their Bible Verse Memory Books. They can illustrate the verse as well. You may also want to review the verses that were learned in the last lessons.

Psalm 23

The LORD is my shepherd;
there is nothing I lack.
He lets me lie down in green pastures;
He leads me beside quiet waters.
He renews my life;
He leads me along the right paths
for His name's sake.
Even when I go through the darkest valley,
I fear [no] danger,

for You are with me;
Your rod and Your staff—they comfort me.
You prepare a table before me
in the presence of my enemies;
You anoint my head with oil;
my cup overflows.
Only goodness and faithful love will pursue me
all the days of my life,
and I will dwell in the house of the LORD
as long as I live.

WORKSHEETS FOR LESSON 3

ACTIVITY SHEET 1: INTRODUCTION TO THE PSALMS

Directions: Fill in the blanks. Note: You may use an answer more than once.

1. The longest book in the Bible _____

2. The longest chapter in the Bible _____

3. The shortest psalm _____

4. The middle chapter of the Bible _____

5. The middle verse of the Bible _____

6. The most quoted Old Testament book
   in the New Testament _____

ACTIVITY SHEET 2: TYPES OF PSALMS

Psalm Type in Scrambled Letters	Examples	Type of Psalm
1. YSMNH	Psalms 37, 100; Express thanks	_____
2. SWMDOI	Psalms 1, 119; Leading godly lives	_____
3. EGNATACHI	Psalms 78; Instruction	_____
4. PRNCNTEEAE	Psalms 32, 51; Sadness for sin	_____
5. GMLGIREAPI	Psalms 134; Going up to Jerusalem	_____
6. NTALME	Psalms 3; Longing for God's deliverance	_____
7. EJTMICSA	Psalms 96, 97; Express the greatness of God in the New Testament	_____

Activity Sheet 3a: Parallelisms in Hebrew Poetry

Directions: To help you better understand Hebrew poetry, we will first define the meaning of parallelism. This is the most important characteristic of Hebrew poetry. Then define each type of parallelism.

1. Parallelism: _____

2. Synonymous: _____

3. Antithetic: _____

4. Synthetic: _____

Activity Sheet 3b: Identifying Examples of Parallelisms

Directions: Using your definitions, choose the correct type of parallelism.

1. Psalm 3:1 _____ *Lord, how my foes increase! There are many who attack me.*

2. Psalm 49:3 _____ *My mouth speaks wisdom; my heart's meditation [brings] understanding.*

3. Psalm 1:6 _____ *For the Lord watches over the way of the righteous, but the way of the wicked leads to ruin.*

4. Psalm 37:21 _____ *The wicked borrows and does not repay, but the righteous is gracious and giving.*

5. Psalm 104:16 _____ *The trees of the Lord flourish, the cedars of Lebanon that He planted.*

6. Psalm 133:1 _____ *How good and pleasant it is when brothers can live together!*

Activity Sheet 4: Psalm 1

Directions: From Psalm 1 and the list of characteristics below, select those that apply to the godly person and check the appropriate description. Do the same for the characteristics of the ungodly person.

	Tree *solidly planted*	Chaff *wind drives away*
1. Listens to the advice of classmates who do not honor God.		
2. Follows directions of classmates who do things that take you away from church.		
3. Joins a group that makes fun of going to church and being good.		
4. Enjoys going to Sunday school and church.		
5. Thinks about God and what He has done for you.		
6. Finds the instruction of God's people helpful through his/her life.		
7. Tells others about Jesus and His love for them.		
8. Does things that have eternal value rather than satisfying selfish desires.		
9. Is constantly focused on self and selfish desires.		
10. Does not look forward to eternity with God.		
Write one word for each that describes the result of the actions:		

ACTIVITY SHEET 5: PSALM 3

Directions: After you have read the description of Psalm 3 in the handbook, "Selected Psalms," on the shield, list the ways David trusted God in the midst of his personal crisis in running from his son, Absalom.

ACTIVITY SHEET 6: PARALLELISMS IN HEBREW POETRY

Directions: Draw a line from each of the characteristics to the shepherd or to the sheep, as appropriate.

Characteristics:

1. never leaves sheep
2. quiet
3. knows each sheep
4. not fighters
5. tender and loving
6. needs help finding food
7. carries rod and staff to protect
8. needs help finding still water
9. looks for lost sheep
10. needs protection from wild animals
11. followers
12. finds water and food

Shepherd

Sheep

LESSON 4: PSALMS AND THE SONG OF SOLOMON

Readings from the Parent/Teacher Handbook: The Bible, Vol. 3: "Psalm 32" through the end of the Song of Solomon

OBJECTIVES
By the end of lesson, the learner should be able to:
- Explain selected psalms for their meaning,
- Discover the sequence from selected psalms,
- Write a praise psalm, and
- Explore relationships, such as husband and wife and Christ and His church.

IDENTIFICATIONS
Concepts
- *Repentance*—turning away from sin and feeling sorry for that sin
- *Maskil*—teaching Psalm
- *Praise psalm*—a song or hymn to glorify God
- *Magnificat*—praise to God by Mary before Jesus was born (see Luke 1:46–55) compared with Psalm 98
- *Wisdom psalm*—a psalm that provides wisdom for the young
- *Acrostic*—stanzas that follow the alphabet; Psalm 119 follows the Hebrew alphabet

- *The Great Hallel*—great hymn of praise
- *Litany*—a form of prayer that is sung to God
- *Repentance psalms*—expressing sorrow for sin by the person who is repentant
- *Judgment psalms*—expressing the judgment of God
- *Teaching psalms*—psalms that instruct the hearer in the ways of God
- *Lament psalms*—psalms expressing sadness

People
- *David:* author of many of the psalms
- *Levites:* leaders of worship in the Temple after King Hezekiah

MATERIALS NEEDED
- *Parent/Teacher Handbook: The Bible, Vol. 3*
- Activity Sheets for Lesson 4
- Crayons and markers
- Pens or pencils
- Blank sheets of white paper
- Chalkboard or dry erase board

LEARNING ACTIVITIES FOR LESSON 4
Activity 1—A Prayer of Repentance (Psalm 32)
To find forgiveness with God for sin is important. Read the Psalm 32 section in the handbook. Also read Psalm 32 in your Bible. David knew what it meant to ask for and receive the forgiveness of God. After reading the material from the handbook and this psalm, ask class members to order the steps for repentance and forgiveness that are found in Activity Sheet 1 for this lesson.

Follow this activity with Activity 2, the crossword puzzle, before you discuss this psalm in detail.

Activity 2—Crossword Puzzle (Psalm 32)
Provide each student with a copy of the crossword puzzle from Activity Sheet 2 for this lesson. Have the students read the appropriate section in the handbook for Psalm 32. Also read Psalm 32 in the Bible.

Have the students fill in the correct answers on their crossword puzzle.

Discuss the meaning of this psalm to help us ask God for forgiveness for the times when we sin against Him.

Activity 3—Write a Psalm of Praise (Psalm 47)
Read the material in the handbook for the section on Psalm 47. Read Psalm 47 in your Bible.

Prepare the students to write a psalm of praise to God. Have them suggest ideas about the holiness and goodness of God. You may follow the outline from Psalm 47 by grouping the student suggestions under

(1) God is an awesome God; (2) God is to be praised; and (3) God is sovereign, and we can celebrate in joy that He reigns. List their suggestions on the chalkboard or on a dry erase board.

Next, ask the students to work in small groups of three to five students to write a psalm hymn of praise to God.

Share their psalm hymns and discuss the importance of praise and adoration of God. Close the session in prayer and hymns of praise to God for who He is.

Activity 4—*Learning from Israel's Past (Psalm 78)*

What lessons can be learned from Israel's past that could help the Israelites and that can help us today? Psalm 78 is identified as a *Maskil*. The best meaning for this term seems to be a "teaching psalm." Psalm 78 is a very effective teaching psalm. Read the material in the handbook for Psalm 78. Also read Psalm 78:1–17 in your Bible. (Note: We have only used the first seventeen verses. But you may choose to read further into the next one or more stanzas. They follow thematically a similar didactic pattern.)

Have the children work individually or in small groups. They should identify (1) what God did and (2) how Israel failed.

When the children have completed their study, have them share with the entire class. Write their contributions on the chalkboard or on the dry erase board so all can readily see.

From the first seventeen verses, be sure that they include the following points:

What God Did

- God established a testimony and set up a law in Israel to teach their children.
- God worked wonders in the sight of their fathers.
- God split the seas and brought them across on dry land.
- God led them with a cloud by day and a fiery pillar by night.
- God split the rock in the wilderness to give them drink.
- God brought streams out of the stone and made the water flow.

How Israel Failed

- The Ephraimite archers turned back on the day of battle.
- The people did not keep God's covenant and refused to live by His law.
- The people forgot what God had done for them.
- The people forgot the wonderful works that He had done for them.
- The people continued to sin and rebel against God.

Ask the students, "What was the purpose of all of this?" "What were the Israelites supposed to learn from this rehearsal of what God had done?" "What can we learn today from this psalm?" Focus your discussion on the goodness of God and how He cares for us even when we rebel and fail Him. But concentrate also on the fact that we can learn from the sins of the fathers in the past. We do not have to live like that in the world today. We do not have to follow the sin of the people we see in school, in our community, on television, or in the movies. We can become what God desires, and we can live according to the way He desires us to live. Our hope is in God. *"Because the One who is in you is greater than the one who is in the world"* (1 John 4:4b).

Activity 5—*The Word of God (Psalm 119:1–16)*

Psalm 119 is the longest chapter in the Bible. It is in the form of an acrostic, and it tells us about the wonder of the Word of God. Read the material in the handbook for Psalm 119. Read Psalm 119:1–16 in your Bible. (Note: We have only used the first sixteen verses. But you may choose to read further into the next one or more stanzas. They follow thematically the acrostic pattern.)

You may want to read the first sixteen verses aloud to the children. Duplicate Activity Sheet 5 and distribute copies to the members of your class. Ask them to look at Psalm 119:1–16 and find the words that mean the "Word of God." The letters are scrambled, and they are not in the same order in which they appear in this passage. You might consider giving a small prize to the one who correctly completes the task first.

Activity 6—A Litany (Psalm 136)

Psalm 136 is a beautiful psalm of praise. It was known as the "Great Hallel" or "The Great Psalm of Praise." Read the material in the handbook for Psalm 136. Also read this passage in your Bible. Become familiar with this great hymn of praise.

Talk to your students about the meaning of this psalm and its use as a litany. You will find the information that you need in the handbook. Be sure that you have sufficiently discussed this with the class so they know what a litany is and why it is used.

Give your students the opportunity to experience a litany firsthand. Try to set the stage for understanding the litany by talking about the litany at the important Jewish festivals. Recall for them Ezra 3:11 and 2 Chronicles 7:3.

Ask one of the children to read the first line of each verse in the psalm. Have the rest of the class respond with the rejoinder, "His love is eternal."

Activity 7—Characteristics of a Christian Marriage (Song of Solomon)

Read the material in the handbook under the section, The Song of Solomon—Introduction to Conclusion.

To help your children understand the importance of a Christian marriage, you may want to have them turn to Ephesians 5:22–33 in their Bible and read this passage. On the basis of this passage from the New Testament, have them respond to Activity Sheet 7 for this lesson.

Conclude this activity by helping the children understand how a Christian marriage differs from a marriage that does not honor Christ as the head of the home.

Activity 8—Memorize Psalm 100

One of the most beautiful hymns of praise in all of Scripture is Psalm 100. Down through the ages groups, like the pilgrims, sang this beautiful hymn of praise. This is one psalm that everyone should memorize. This psalm needs to be added in their Bible Verse Memory Books. They can illustrate the verses as well.

Psalm 100

Shout triumphantly to the LORD, all the earth.
Serve the LORD with gladness;
come before Him with joyful songs.
Acknowledge that the LORD is God.
He made us, and we are His —
His people, the sheep of His pasture.
Enter His gates with thanksgiving
and His courts with praise.
Give thanks to Him and praise His name.
For the LORD is good, and His love is eternal;
His faithfulness endures through all generations.

ACTIVITY SHEET 1: A PRAYER FOR REPENTANCE

Directions: Place the steps of repentance and forgiveness from Psalm 32 in the appropriate order (1–6).

_____ a. Desire to serve God with all your heart.

_____ b. Ask God to cleanse and forgive you for your sin.

_____ c. Confess to God the specific thing that you have done wrongly.

_____ d. God forgives your sin.

_____ e. Acknowledge your sin.

_____ f. Restore your fellowship with God.

ACTIVITY SHEET 2: CROSSWORD PUZZLE—WORDS FROM PSALM 32

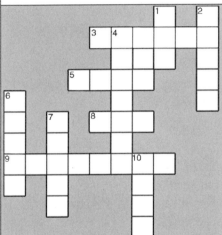

Across
3. thanksgiving
5. clean
8. ruler of life
9. happiness

Down
1. disobedience
2. God's forgiveness
4. reclaim
6. cleanse
7. center of one's life
10. white and clean

ACTIVITY SHEET 5: UNSCRAMBLE THE WORDS

Directions: Unscramble the letters to identify the words that are given in Psalm 119:1–16 that mean the "Word of God."

1. GMTDJEUNS _____

2. STMEOITINES _____

3. NCROSEDNIA _____

4. WLA _____

5. PPCTESRE _____

6. RWDO _____

7. MMDETNOSCAMN _____

8. TATSEUST _____

ACTIVITY SHEET 7: PRINCIPLES OF MARRIAGE

Directions: Choose the characteristics by placing a checkmark in front of those characteristics that should be present in a Christian marriage relationship.

_____ 1. Marriage is a lifelong commitment.

_____ 2. Each partner should point out the faults of the other spouse.

_____ 3. Each partner should do what he or she likes, even if the other doesn't like what is done.

_____ 4. Each partner should support the other.

_____ 5. Each partner should love and honor the other partner exclusively.

_____ 6. Husbands are to love their wives as themselves.

_____ 7. Wives are to respect their husbands.

_____ 8. A man must leave his mother and father and be joined to his wife.

_____ 9. In God's sight a husband and wife are one.

_____ 10. Husbands and wives should take separate vacations apart from each other.

Readings from the Parent/Teacher Handbook: The Bible, Vol. 3: "Proverbs"

OBJECTIVES

By the end of lesson, the learner should be able to:

- Discover the proverbs found in the Bible to help them in everyday life experiences,
- Define and write the distinct characteristics of a proverb,
- Examine the purpose of Proverbs from Proverbs 1:1–7,
- Explain "the fear of the LORD," and
- Identify several of the themes of Proverbs.

IDENTIFICATIONS

Concepts

- *Sage*—wise person who gives godly advice
- *Completing proverbs*—word *and* connects the first line with the second
- *Comparing proverbs*—word *than* is used to connect two ideas
- *Contrasting proverbs*—word *but* is used to contrast the first thought with the second
- *Fear of the LORD*—follow God's direction in our lives
- *Wisdom and understanding*—pay attention to wisdom and get understanding of life
- *Relationships*—theme of Proverbs that has to do with parents and children and family relationships
- *Use of words*—theme of Proverbs that relates to words that bless and do not hurt
- *Life and death*—significant theme of Proverbs that distinguishes between the two

People

- *Solomon:* king of Israel; author of Proverbs and Ecclesiastes; 1 Kings 4:29–34 states that he wrote 3,000 proverbs and 1,005 songs
- *Agur:* wrote Proverbs 30:1–33; we do not know much about him, except that he was a sage
- *King Lemuel:* wrote Proverbs 31:1–9; we do not know much about him, except that he also was a sage
- *King Lemuel's mother:* wrote Proverbs 31:10–31 about the virtuous woman; we do not know much about her

MATERIALS NEEDED

- *Parent/Teacher Handbook: The Bible, Vol. 3*
- Activity Sheets for Lesson 5
- Crayons and markers
- Blank sheets of white paper for drawing
- Construction paper
- Stickers
- 3x5-index cards

LEARNING ACTIVITIES FOR LESSON 5

Activity 1—Search the Internet for Proverbs

Proverbs are common in everyday life. Proverbs are sayings that capture ideas that are helpful to give us wise advice, and they are easy to remember. In preparation for this activity, read the section entitled, "Proverbs—Introduction," in the handbook.

Use your search engine on the Internet, such as www.google.com. Put the word *proverbs* in the search area. You will discover many resources for proverbs. Print out some examples to use with your class. Use the examples that you find along with some of the proverbs from the Book of Proverbs.

Have the students guess which proverbs are from the Bible and which are just wise sayings. Help them discover the difference between the wisdom of this world and the wisdom from the Bible. Note that the Bible gives us an understanding from Proverbs 1:7 that *"The fear of the LORD is the beginning of knowledge."*

Be sure to help the students understand that *fear* in this verse means "reverential awe" and "obedient respect." It does not mean anxiety from immanent danger, as we might think of fear in common discussion.

Use this activity as a springboard to discussion about proverbs and as an introduction to the study of Proverbs.

Activity 2—Bookmark Activity (Proverbs)

Your students will enjoy designing a bookmark for a proverb. Choose one proverb from the material in the handbook or one from the Book of Proverbs to write on a bookmark. Cut an 8 1/2x11-inch sheet of card stock in half. Then, fold the 4 1/2-inch sections in half. Finally trim 1 1/2 inches from the bottom. An example of a bookmark template can be found in Activity Sheet 2.

On the face of the bookmark, have your students write the proverb that they have selected. They can write the meaning of the proverb on the back of the bookmark. Have the children decorate the front of the bookmark with stickers or their own drawings.

Encourage them to use the bookmark for their schoolbooks and learn the verse and its meaning.

Activity 3—Types of Proverbs

There are three types of proverbs—completing, comparing, and contrasting. You will find information on these three types in the section entitled "Types of Proverbs" in the handbook.

Share with your class the information on the types of proverbs. In advance of this session, prepare copies of Activity Sheet 3.

Ask the students to read carefully the proverbs in the second column and draw a line from the proverb to the type it represents.

Discuss the types of proverbs and discuss the proverbs that are included on the chart. A lot of wisdom is included in these proverbs.

Activity 4—Themes of Proverbs

There are a number of themes in the Book of Proverbs. We have identified five of those themes: fear of God, wisdom and understanding, relationships, use of words, and life and death. Read about these themes in the section entitled "Themes of Proverbs" in the handbook.

Share your findings about these themes with your students. Prepare copies of Activity Sheet 4 for each student. Ask the students to find the themes included in the proverbs that are listed in the left column of the activity sheet. Place a number (or numbers) from the key provided that appropriately describes each proverb theme. Note that several proverbs relate to more than one theme, and as a result, there may be more than one number needed. The answer key will supply the correct answers. Go over the answers with your students. Don't forget to also look at the proverbs themselves.

Activity 5—Graphic Organizer (Proverbs 1:1–7)

Study the purpose of the Book of Proverbs from Proverbs 1:1–7. This passage is crucial to understanding the entire book. Read the material in the handbook under "Selected Themes and Teachings from Proverbs," Proverbs 1:1–7. Review this material with your class and read the passage of Scripture aloud to them.

Distribute 3x5-index cards to the students. Have them write their ideas about what the Book of Proverbs means and how students can use the proverbs in their lives today. Ask them to keep their single ideas separate. After they have studied this passage individually, have them join a group of three or four other persons and share their insights, adding to their notes.

Develop a concept map of major ideas, subtopics, and ideas that relate to one another. See the sample concept map for your use in Activity Sheet 5. Try to show how the ideas relate to one another. A concept map is an excellent graphic organizer to show the relationship among ideas. It is useful to show the relationships among the ideas presented in Proverbs 1:1–7.

Activity 7—Wisdom Theme

Read the section, "Theme: Wisdom and Understanding," in the handbook. Study the proverbs included under this topic. Share this information with your children. There is a move among some radical feminist groups to make Sophia or Wisdom a goddess. There is nothing in Scripture to warrant such ideas. But it is important for young people to understand the importance of wisdom, without going to excesses.

Assign several students to look up *wisdom*. They may use several sources: (1) a Bible dictionary, such as the *Holman Bible Dictionary*, (2) an unabridged dictionary, and (3) an encyclopedia.

Have them write a report and share it with the class.

Activity 8—Memorize Proverbs 1:7

The work of memorizing the previous two psalms was quite extensive. For this memorization task, there is only one verse. But this is an important verse. To remind the children what the theme of the entire Book of Proverbs is, have them memorize Proverbs 1:7.

The fear of the LORD
is the beginning of knowledge;
fools despise wisdom and instruction.

Have the children write this Scripture in their Bible Verse Memory Books and illustrate it. Also have them review the verses learned in the previous lessons.

WORKSHEETS FOR LESSON 5

ACTIVITY SHEET 2: BOOKMARK PATTERN

(fold)

Activity Sheet 3: Types of Proverbs

Directions: Match the Proverb with the appropriate type in the right column.

1. "The one who reveals secrets is a constant gossip; avoid someone with a big mouth." 20:19
2. "Then they will call me, but I won't answer." (1:28)
3. "Like vinegar to the teeth and smoke to the eyes." (10:26)
4. "Plans fail when there is no counsel, but with many advisers they succeed." (15:22)
5. "A wise man will listen and increase his learning." (1:5)
6. "A false witness will not go unpunished, and one who utters lies perishes." (19: 9)
7. "Better a meal of vegetables where there is love than a fattened calf with hatred." (15:17)
8. "The eyes of the LORD are everywhere, observing the wicked and the good." (15:3)
9. "Hatred stirs up conflicts, but love covers all offenses." (10:12)
10. "When pride comes, disgrace follows." (11:2)
11. "Better a little with righteousness than great income with injustice." (16:8)
12. "Guard your heart above all else, for it is the source of life." (4:23)
13. "A gentle answer turns away anger, but a harsh word stirs up wrath." (15:1)
14. "Idle hands make one poor, but diligent hands bring riches." (10:4)

| Completing |
| Comparing |
| Contrasting |

Activity Sheet 4: Themes of Proverbs

Directions: Place a number (or numbers) from the key that appropriately describes each proverb theme.

KEY: 1–Fear of God   2–Wisdom and Understanding   3–Relationships   4–Use of words   5–Life and Death

	Number(s)
1. My son, obey my words, and treasure my commands. (7:1)	
2. Truthful lips endure forever, but a lying tongue, only a moment. (12:19)	
3. The fear of the LORD prolongs life, but the years of the wicked are cut short. (10:27)	
4. Doing what is righteous and just is more acceptable to the LORD than sacrifice. (21:3)	
5. A man who finds a wife finds a good thing and obtains favor from the LORD. (18:22)	
6. Commit your activities to the LORD and your plans will be achieved. (16:3)	
7. The one who guards his mouth protects his life; the one who opens his lips invites his own ruin. (13:3)	
8. Genuine righteousness leads to life, but pursuing evil leads to death. (11:19)	
9. For the LORD gives wisdom; from His mouth comes knowledge and understanding. (2:6)	
10. Pleasant words are a honeycomb; sweet to the taste and health to the body. (16:24)	
11. The fear of the LORD leads to life; one will sleep at night without danger. (19:23)	
12. A foolish son is his father's ruin and a wife's nagging is an endless dripping. (19:13)	
13. The one who searches for what is good finds favor, but if someone looks for trouble, it will come to him. (11:27)	
14. A gossip goes around revealing a secret, but the trustworthy keeps a confidence. (11:13)	
15. The fear of the LORD is the beginning of wisdom, fools despise wisdom and instruction. (1:7)	
16. Don't plan any harm against your neighbor, for he trusts you and lives near you. (3:29)	
17. The path of the righteous is like the light of dawn, but the way of the wicked is like the darkest gloom. (4:18–19)	

ACTIVITY SHEET 5: CONCEPT MAP

Directions: Fill in the concept map for concepts that emerge from the study of Proverbs 1:1–7.

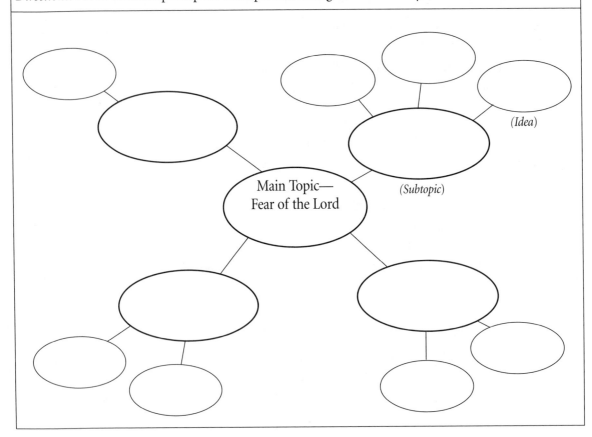

Readings from the Parent/Teacher Handbook: The Bible, Vol. 3: "Theme: Relationships" through the end of the Old Testament section

---

OBJECTIVES

By the end of lesson, the learner should be able to:

- Describe the importance of the things that we say,
- Contrast the two ways described by the author of Proverbs,
- Analyze other selected proverbs by theme and meaning,
- Construct your own proverb for right living,
- Describe the meaning of Ecclesiastes, and
- Explain what Job learned about suffering from his three friends and from God.

IDENTIFICATIONS

Concepts

- *Life and death*—one of the themes of Proverbs that places the ultimate opposites across from each other
- *Vanity*—lack of usefulness or worth; expressed about life apart from God by Solomon in Ecclesiastes
- *Suffering*—pain and distress; for Job caused by conditions for which he had no understanding

People

- *Solomon:* king of Israel; writer of Proverbs, Ecclesiastes, Song of Solomon
- *Job:* man from the Old Testament, whom God tested; writer of the Book of Job
- *Eliphaz:* comforter of Job
- *Bildad:* comforter of Job
- *Zophar:* comforter of Job
- *Elihu:* comforter of Job

MATERIALS NEEDED

- *Parent/Teacher Handbook: The Bible, Vol. 3*
- Activity Sheets for Lesson 6
- Crayons and markers
- Construction paper
- Blank sheets of white paper for drawing
- Chalkboard or dry erase board

LEARNING ACTIVITIES FOR LESSON 6

Activity 1—Controlling the Tongue

Introduce this unit by reading the section, "Theme: The Use of Words," from the handbook. Read the three sets of proverbs to your class. Then turn to James 3:1–12 in your Bible for the perspective of the New Testament writer on the same subject.

Have the students consider their own use of words. Provide each of your students with a copy of Activity Sheet 1. Ask them to write their reactions to the Scripture from Proverbs and James and the material from the handbook.

Conclude this activity by asking for contributions from the members of your class on what they have written. Summarize the contributions on the chalkboard or on a dry erase board. Impress upon your students the importance of the tongue. Ask them to be careful as they interact with one another to control their tongues.

Activity 2—Construct Your Own Proverb

Provide your children with examples of proverbs. Now that they have had the opportunity to read many proverbs from the Book of Proverbs and you have shared with them proverbs that are available online, ask them to write a proverb. They first need to find a theme for the proverb. We have looked at many themes over the past two sessions. They may choose one of those or select a new theme.

Next, they need to write a brief saying that will help them summarize their thoughts in several sentences. Your children should probably work alone at first to develop their own ideas. Then they may want to work together in small groups of three to five persons to gain the benefit from the thoughts of others.

Finally, have the children write out their thoughts in a couple of short sentences. Have your children share their proverbs with the entire class. Let this be the concluding activity for your study of the proverbs.

Activity 3—Absolute Futility (Ecclesiastes 1:1–2:26)

Ecclesiastes is the only book of its kind in the Bible. When you read it, the book almost seems depressing. Solomon, Israel's wealthiest and most opulent king, tasted the best of what life had to offer. He tried it all! Yet he found that none of the good things he had were satisfying.

Read "Selected Passages from Ecclesiastes," from the handbook. Read also the passage from Ecclesiastes 1:1–2:26 in your Bible. Familiarize yourself with the things that Solomon identifies on his search for meaning in life.

In advance of this lesson, dupicate Activity Sheet 3 for each of your students. Ask the students to listen as you share your thoughts on the Book of Ecclesiastes. Then have them circle the things that Solomon said brings meaning and happiness to life.

Conclude your discussion of Ecclesiastes with a summary of what brings true meaning and happiness to life. Essentially, Solomon says that we can find true happiness only in God. Nothing else can lead to happiness. But we cannot enjoy the good things that God has allowed us to have by hoarding our possessions. We only have those things because God has allowed us to have them. He is the giver and He may take them from us. In either event we need to thank Him for His goodness to us. It is only in knowing God as the giver of life and good things that we find meaning and true happiness in life.

Activity 4—Only One Route to Happiness (The Maze of Life)

Follow up Activity 3 with the maze in Activity Sheet 4. You will need to duplicate a copy of the maze for each of the children in your class. Have them follow the maze from the beginning, "The Journey through Life," to the end, "Happiness and Meaning in Life."

Be sure to point out the dead-end paths that occur when we get our eyes off the Lord and on possessions, wealth, family, or success. Help them understand that happiness and meaning in life come from a deep and abiding relationship with Christ in life today.

Activity 5—Theme of Ecclesiastes Secret Code

The main point of Ecclesiastes is found in the last three verses of the book:

"But beyond these, my son, be warned: there is no end to the making of many books, and much study wearies the body. When all has been heard, the conclusion of the matter is: fear God and keep His commands, because this [is for] all humanity. For God will bring every act to judgment, including every hidden thing, whether good or evil" (Ecclesiastes 12:12–14).

The most significant phrase is "fear God and keep His commands." It is found in verse 13.

Have members of your class decode the secret message, which is found in Activity Sheet 5.

Discuss the meaning of this phrase. Focus again on the meaning of "fearing God." Help your students to memorize this phrase. It is essential to leading a good life.

Activity 6—Job's Attitude toward God (The Life of Job)

Reproduce a copy of Activity Sheet 6 for each of the students in your class. Read the section in the handbook on the life of Job.

Have your students complete the activity sheet as you tell the story of Job and his life.

Conclude this activity with the idea that we may have to suffer in life. As in Job's case, suffering may not be a result of sin.

Activity 7—Job's Friends

Copy Activity Sheet 7 and give one to each child. Read the material in the handbook on the life of Job. His friends had one stock answer to Job's dilemma, "Job had sinned."

Discuss God's response to Job and his three friends. Job had not sinned. What happened was something beyond his control. Job continued to trust God, and God blessed him.

Activity 8—Job and Suffering

Job's situation was not unique and is not unique today. Many people today who love God and live godly lives still suffer. Help your children try to discover ways by which they can help others who are suffering. Below are two sample situations to explore. Help them find ways by which they can help.

Situation 1: One of your friends at school loses a parent who was killed in an automobile accident. How can we help?

Situation 2: The father of one of your friends has lost his job and has been unable to find a new one immediately. The family must move from their nice home to an apartment. How can we help?

Activity 9—Memorize Proverbs 3:5–6

A proverb that you will want your students to memorize is Proverbs 3:5–6. If they follow this on a daily basis, it will bring them safely through life and into God's eternal kingdom. Have them memorize these two verses:

> Trust in the LORD with all your heart,
>   and do not rely on your own understanding;
> think about Him in all your ways,
>   and He will guide you on the right paths.

You may want to write each of the words on colored construction paper and mix them up on the floor. Mix up the words and have the students place them in correct order.

Add these verses to their Bible Verse Memory Books. They can illustrate the verses if they want.

WORKSHEETS FOR LESSON 6

ACTIVITY SHEET 1: THE RESPONSIBLE USE OF WORDS

Directions: Summarize what you have learned from the material in Proverbs and the description of the tongue from the letter of James.

_____

_____

_____

_____

_____

_____

_____

ACTIVITY SHEET 3: MEANING IN LIFE

Directions: As you listen to the material from the handbook, and the passage from Ecclesiastes 1:1–2:26, circle those things that Solomon discovered that bring true meaning and happiness to life.

Wisdom	Pleasure	Education	Buildings and gardens
Success	Wealth	Possessions	Slaves
Career	Singers	Power	Sensuality
Pleasing God	Sin	Hard work	Eating and drinking
Merriment	Sports	Television	Joy for peace with God
Godliness	Toys	Guns	Pets

ACTIVITY SHEET 4: THE MAZE OF LIFE

Start – Journey Through Life

Success

Possessions

Power

Family

Wealth

Finish – Happiness and Meaning in Life

ACTIVITY SHEET 7: JOB'S FRIENDS

Directions: What answer did Job's friends give to his question?

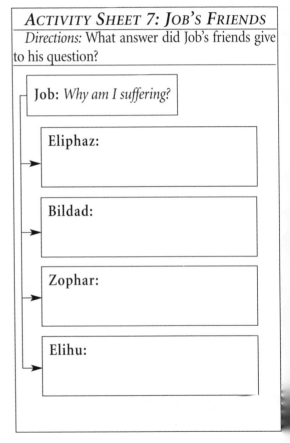

Job: *Why am I suffering?*

Eliphaz:

Bildad:

Zophar:

Elihu:

ACTIVITY SHEET 5: THEME OF ECCLESIASTES

The theme of Ecclesiastes is stated within the book. Can you decode the message?
Directions: Find the meaning of the message and the Book of Ecclesiastes.

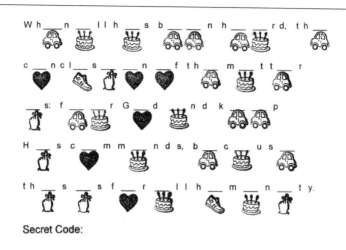

Secret Code:

ACTIVITY SHEET 6: THE LIFE OF JOB

Directions: Briefly summarize each stage of Job's life.

1. Job's life before God allowed Satan to test him.

2. Job's life after Satan tested him.

3. Job's friends come to comfort him.

4. God speaks to Job.

5. God gave Job a new life.

Unit Two: New Testament: Lessons 7–12

This set of lessons will provide the learner with background in the New Testament. Help the learner gain an understanding of the life and ministry of Jesus and the birth and growth of the early church of the New Testament. Help the learner examine the letters of the New Testament. Help the learner develop a lifelong love for God's Word to us through the Bible.

OVERVIEW
Objectives

By the end of this unit, the learner should be able to:

- Review the Old Testament study from the previous six weeks,
- Understand the significant persons identified and described in the New Testament and be able to describe their contribution to the fulfillment of God's purposes,
- Understand and appreciate the letters from the New Testament, which describe God's dealing with humankind,
- Understand how God dealt with sin in the New Testament and appreciate God's redemptive activity and His continuing redemptive activity in the New Testament and today, and
- Develop a lifelong love and appreciation for God's Word in the New Testament.

Content Summary and Rationale

After four hundred years between Malachi and Matthew, God's redemptive activity in the world continued with the birth of John the Baptist and reached its zenith in the life, ministry, death, and resurrection of God's own Son, Jesus Christ.

The Gospel writers tell us about the miraculous birth and sinless life of Jesus. But Jesus did not stop with a good life and ministry. He went to the cross of Calvary in order to redeem us from sin. No longer were sacrifices of animals necessary. ?'s Son, Jesus, died once and for all. God raised Him from the dead and demonstrated that God desires that all men should come to Him for salvation from sin here and now and eternal life in the hereafter. The prophecy of Jeremiah in the Old Testament came true. The Law of God was no longer only written on tables of stone but now upon the hearts of all who believe. Through Christ a person could come to know God and become part of God's family.

The apostle Paul became the first missionary to the Gentiles, those persons in other parts of the Roman Empire who were not Jews. Paul planted churches across the Roman world. Then he wrote letters to the churches to correct their failures and strengthen their ministry. The New Testament letters play a significant role in the development of the church. They provide us with understanding of theology and practical ways of living as a Christian.

Key Concept

God came to earth in the person of Jesus to win sinful man back to Himself. What happened to Adam and Eve at the Fall, when the relationship with God was severed, was now restored by God Himself coming to earth, living a sinless life of sacrifice and ministry, dying on the cross as a sacrifice for us, and being resurrected to a new life. This will one day be our experience also, if we accept the new life that Jesus provides. In the meantime the letters of Paul and the general letters give us practical guidance toward living as believers in Christ.

Prior Knowledge Needed

Similar to the Old Testament stories, most children, who have attended church through the kindergarten and preschool years, have heard many stories about Jesus. Their knowledge is limited. Most do not understand the importance of Jesus' life and death on the cross for our sin. Few have been exposed to the letters of the New Testament. This will be an opportunity to develop their understanding and appreciation for the instruction that may be found in the letters. They have been exposed to the Christian holidays of Christmas and Easter.

You can use their limited knowledge to enlarge their understanding. Help them develop a more comprehensive view of the life and ministry of Jesus. Help them develop an appreciation for the letters of the New Testament.

RESOURCES FOR TEACHERS AND STUDENTS
- Buchanan, Edward, *Parent/Teacher Handbook The Bible, Volumes 1 and 3* (Nashville, Tenn.: Broadman & Holman, 2003).
- Butler, Trent, ed., *Holman Illustrated Bible Dictionary* (Nashville, Tenn.: Holman Bible Publishers, 2003).
- Dockery, David, ed., *Holman Bible Handbook* (Nashville, Tenn.: Holman Bible Publishers, 1992).
- Hastings, Selina, *The Children's Illustrated Bible* (New York, N.Y.: DK Publishing, 1994).

- Holman Interactive *Bible Navigator* CD-ROM available at your local LifeWay Christian Store.
- *Holman Bible Atlas* (Nashville, Tenn.: Holman Bible Publishers, 1998).
- An encyclopedia—*World Book, Funk and Wagnalls, Britannica*, etc. (may use CD-ROM).

Additional Supplementary Resources for Teachers
- *The Visual Bible—Matthew*, A dramatization using the actual Scriptures. *Visual Bible—Matthew* may be used throughout the life and ministry of Jesus, lessons 9–13.
- *The Visual Bible—Acts* may also be used for the missionary journeys of Paul in lesson 14.

(Both series are available in VHS or DVD format. The DVD version provides access to the specific events that you may wish to show. The VHS version will have to be cued for the event that you wish to show).

LESSON 7: REVIEW OF THE NEW TESTAMENT

Readings from the Parent/Teacher Handbook: The Bible, Vol. 3: "Review of the New Testament," "The Coming of the Messiah—the Gospels," through "Why Did Jesus Have to Die?"

OBJECTIVES
By the end of lesson, the learner should be able to:
- Review the Old Testament study from the previous six weeks,
- Describe the miraculous events surrounding the birth of Jesus,
- Identify and describe several events from Jesus' ministry that illustrate what He did and taught,
- Identify the events of Holy Week, and
- Identify the persons to whom Jesus revealed Himself after the resurrection.

IDENTIFICATIONS
Concepts
- *Common Language*—Greek spread along with Greek culture through the Mediterranean world
People
- *Alexander the Great*: military genius, who

conquered lands from Greece to the northern part of India
- *Zealots*: group that opposed Rome and took every opportunity to kill Romans
- *Cyrus*: king of Persia, who sent many of the people of Judah back to Palestine
- *Pharisees*: Jewish religious group, who tried to maintain purity of the Jewish religion
- *Sadducees*: Jewish political group, who were part of the ruling class in Judah

MATERIALS NEEDED
- *Parent/Teacher Handbook: The Bible, Vol. 3*
- Activity Sheets for Lesson 7
- Crayons and markers
- White and colored construction paper
- Masking tape and plastic tape
- Shoe boxes
- Toothpicks
- Popsicle sticks
- Glue
- Lined paper

LEARNING ACTIVITIES FOR LESSON 7
Activity 1—Review of the Old Testament
To understand the New Testament, an understanding of the Old Testament is essential. The two parts of the Bible are closely related. Ask the students to recall whatever they can about the Old Testament that might have a bearing on the New Testament. Spend some time in brainstorming ideas that may get them started.

Then divide the class into smaller groups of three to five persons. Ask them individually to record things they recall from the Old Testament that may relate to the New Testament. Have them use Activity Sheet 1 to record their findings. These may include things discussed from the brainstorming session, but should go beyond those things. Creation, sin, and the fall of humankind, the deliverance from Egypt, the sacrificial system, the Tabernacle in the Wilderness, the Temple, the family of David, the finding of the Law in the Temple under Hezekiah, and the dispersion of the people of Judah into countries outside of Palestine are examples of events that have a direct relationship to the New Testament.

Discuss their findings. Share the importance of an understanding of the Old Testament for clear understanding of the New Testament.

Activity 2—*Show* The Visual Bible—Matthew *(Matthew 1–2)*
To display the background of the events of the birth of Jesus, you may want to use *The Visual Bible—Matthew* as an introduction to the events of this lesson. Remember that this is the version given by Matthew and does not portray the angels singing in chorus to the shepherds. It does give the narrative of the coming of the Magi or wise men and the escape to Egypt. You will want to view the biblical material through chapter 2. If you are using the DVD version, the place to begin is marked, but you will still have to carefully observe where to stop at the end of chapter 2.

After you have viewed the biblical material from chapters 1 and 2, you will want to review the sections titled "Birth of John the Baptist," "The Birth of Jesus," and "Jesus in Jerusalem" in volume 1 of the handbook series. Note the differences from the account of Luke. You will want to briefly talk about the things the children have been watching, before you begin to work on the activities for this lesson. Talk about how our understanding of the events is affected by the visualization of the events as opposed to the use of our imaginations in reading about the events described in these passages.

Activity 3—Diorama in a Shoe Box
In advance of this session, ask your students to bring shoe boxes to class. Have available popsicle sticks or craft sticks, glue, construction paper, etc. You can make figures out of construction paper. Create several scenes from the birth of Jesus, such as the following: Mary and Joseph traveling to Bethlehem, the birth of Jesus in the cow stall, the coming of the shepherds, the coming of the wise men, and the escape to Egypt.

You may divide the class into smaller groups and have each group work on a different scene. After each group has completed its diorama, have them study the Scripture from Matthew or Luke that relates to the particular diorama they created. Have your students briefly write the story that relates to their diorama.

When all are finished, have each group retell the story of the miraculous birth of Jesus, using their diorama and the story that they wrote.

Conclude this activity by discussing with the class how important the birth of Jesus is to our salvation.

Activity 4—The Baptism and Temptation of Jesus Crossword Puzzle
Provide each child with a copy of the crossword puzzle on Activity Sheet 4 for this lesson. Have the students read the appropriate section in the handbook titled "The Ministry of John the Baptist" through "Jesus' Public Ministry." Have the children fill in the correct answers on their crossword puzzle on the

activity sheet. Discuss the meaning of the baptism and temptation experiences.

Activity 5—The Life and Ministry of Jesus

Use Activity Sheet 5 at the end of this lesson. Distribute a copy for each child.

Read "Jesus' Public Ministry" through "Why Did Jesus Have to Die?" in the handbook. Have your students consider each of the three groups: beginning, middle portion, and end of Jesus' life and ministry. What were the events that occurred? What importance did each of the events have? How was Jesus' teaching affected?

When the children have finished writing their answers on the activity sheet, discuss the responses.

Activity 6—Acting Out the Miracles of Jesus

Divide your class into several groups. Assign each group one of the miracles of Jesus to act out. The rest of the class should try to guess the miracle that is being portrayed. You will find material on miracles in the handbook under "Jesus' Public Ministry" through "Why Did Jesus Have to Die?"

Here are some suggested miracles: The Wedding at Cana (John 2:1–11); Healing the paralytic (Mark 2:1–12); Feeding of the Five Thousand (Matthew 14:13–21); Jesus calmed the storm (Matthew 14:22–36); and Jesus raised Lazarus (John 11:38–44).

Discuss the meaning of these miracles. What did Jesus intend to accomplish? What did the disciples discover about Jesus? How did the people react?

Activity 7—Booklet on Holy Week and the Resurrection

Have each child prepare a booklet on Holy Week and the resurrection. You will find the chart in the handbook to guide you through this activity. Have them use one page for each day of Holy Week—Sunday through resurrection Sunday. For each day have them write what occurred and then draw a picture to illustrate the events.

Use colored construction paper to make a cover for the booklet. When they have finished, have several children share their booklets with the class.

Activity 8—Memorize John 3:1–21

To help your children understand the meaning of Jesus' ministry, have them memorize the interaction that Jesus had with Nicodemus in John 3:1–21. While this is a lengthy passage, the content will be valuable to the children now and for years to come.

There was a man from the Pharisees named Nicodemus, a ruler of the Jews. This man came to Him at night and said, "Rabbi, we know that You have come from God as a teacher, for no one could perform these signs You do unless God were with him."

Jesus replied, "I assure you: Unless someone is born again, he cannot see the kingdom of God."

"But how can anyone be born when he is old?" Nicodemus asked Him. "Can he enter his mother's womb a second time and be born?"

Jesus answered, "I assure you: Unless someone is born of water and the Spirit, he cannot enter the kingdom of God. Whatever is born of the flesh is flesh, and whatever is born of the Spirit is spirit. Do not be amazed that I told you that you must be born again. The wind blows where it pleases, and you hear its sound, but you don't know where it comes from or where it is going. So it is with everyone born of the Spirit."

"How can these things be?" asked Nicodemus.

"Are you a teacher of Israel and don't know these things?" Jesus replied. "I assure you: We speak what We know and We testify to what We have seen, but you do not accept Our testimony. If I have told you about things that happen on earth and you don't believe, how will you believe if I tell you about things of heaven? No one

has ascended into heaven except the One who descended from heaven—the Son of Man. Just as Moses lifted up the snake in the wilderness, so the Son of Man must be lifted up, so that everyone who believes in Him will have eternal life.

"For God loved the world in this way: He gave His One and Only Son, so that everyone who believes in Him will not perish but have eternal life. For God did not send His Son into the world that He might judge the world, but that the world might be saved through Him. Anyone who believes in Him is not judged, but anyone who does not believe is already condemned, because he has not believed in the name of the One and Only Son of God.

"This, then, is the judgment: the light has come into the world, and people loved darkness rather than the light because their deeds were evil. For everyone who practices wicked things hates the light and avoids it, so that his deeds may not be exposed. But anyone who lives by the truth comes to the light, so that his works may be shown to be accomplished by God."

The children should place these verses in their Bible Verse Memory Books and illustrate them.

WORKSHEETS FOR LESSON 7

ACTIVITY SHEET 1: RECALLING THE OLD TESTAMENT

Directions: What do you recall from the Old Testament that will help you understand the New Testament?

_____

_____

_____

_____

_____

_____

ACTIVITY SHEET 4: BAPTISM AND TEMPTATION OF JESUS

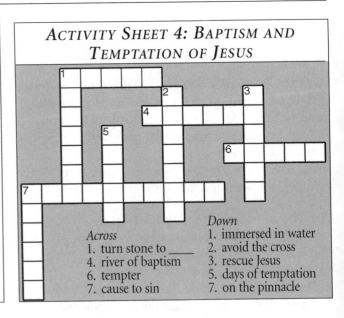

Across
1. turn stone to _____
4. river of baptism
6. tempter
7. cause to sin

Down
1. immersed in water
2. avoid the cross
3. rescue Jesus
5. days of temptation
7. on the pinnacle

ACTIVITY SHEET 5: THE LIFE AND MINISTRY OF JESUS

Directions: List and describe the events that occurred in Jesus' life and ministry.

Beginning	Middle	End

Readings from the Parent/Teacher Handbook: The Bible, Vol. 3: "Review of the New Testament"

OBJECTIVES

By the end of lesson, the learner should be able to:

- Describe what happened to the followers of Jesus after He ascended to heaven,
- Contrast the Jewish holiday of Pentecost with the Christian holiday of Pentecost,
- Explain the importance of Peter's visit to Cornelius,
- Identify the events in the life of the apostle Paul, and
- Explain the three missionary journeys of Paul and the trip to Rome.

IDENTIFICATIONS

Concepts

- *Pentecost*—Jewish feast that was the occasion for the coming of the Holy Spirit on Christian believers
- *Roman centurion*—leader of 100 Roman soldiers
- *Missionary*—one who is sent to bring the good news of the gospel
- *Conversion*—coming to faith in Jesus Christ as Savior and Lord

People

- *Peter:* disciple of Jesus, who preached at Pentecost and won the first Gentile convert, Cornelius

- *Cornelius:* Roman centurion who came to faith in Christ
- *Paul:* apostle, who was a Pharisee and came to Christ on the road to Damascus
- *Barnabas:* missionary who accompanied Paul on his first missionary journey
- *John Mark:* missionary who went with Paul and Barnabas on the first journey
- *Silas:* missionary who accompanied Paul on his later missionary journeys
- *Timothy:* young man, whom Paul nurtured in the faith and took on his missionary journeys and to whom Paul wrote two letters

MATERIALS NEEDED

- *Parent/Teacher Handbook: The Bible, Vol. 3*
- Activity Sheets for Lesson 8
- Crayons and markers
- Blank sheets of white paper for drawing
- Masking tape and plastic tape
- 3x5-inch index cards
- Lined paper for writing
- Posterboard
- *The Visual Bible—Acts* (optional)

LEARNING ACTIVITIES FOR LESSON 8

Activity 1—The Visual Bible—Acts

Before you begin this session, view *The Visual Bible—Acts*. You may want to view scenes from the first disk of the Book of Acts that would include "Receiving the Promised Gift," "Ministry of Peter and John," "The Story of Stephen," "The Story of Saul," and "Peter and the Gentiles." On the second disk you will need to be selective from Paul's missionary journeys. From the first missionary journey you might choose "Barnabas and Saul Sent from Antioch." From the second journey, you might select "Paul's Vision of the Man from Macedonia," "Lydia's Conversion in Philippi," "Paul in Corinth," and "Gallio Will Not Try Paul." From the third journey you might select "The Riot in Ephesus." From Paul's trip to Rome, you might select "Paul Is Arrested," "Paul Sails for Rome," "The Shipwreck," "Paul Preaching in Rome Under Guard," and "Epilogue."

Then you will want to review the material in the handbook for "The Coming of the Holy Spirit at Pentecost" through "The Journey to Rome."

This is an exciting story of the birth and growth of the early church. Your children should be enthralled with these developments. Help them to see that these developments are an extension of the resurrection of Jesus Christ, as the church expands from Jerusalem to the entire world.

Activity 2—Contrasting the Jewish Holiday of Pentecost with the Christian Holiday of Pentecost

Help the children understand the significance of the festival of Pentecost—first from the perspective of the Jewish celebration and second from the perspective of the birth of the Christian church. Below are some pertinent facts about Pentecost. Use these facts to teach about the meaning of Pentecost.

Jewish Festival of Pentecost—

The instructions for the first Pentecost celebration are given in Leviticus 23:15–21. It was literally the feast of seven weeks or fifty days (from which we get *pente*) from the second day of Passover celebration. It began during the forty years of wilderness wanderings of the Hebrew people.

During the Sefira or the first thirty-three days, there is a time of mourning for thousands of Jews who died of the plague during the second century. No weddings or dancing is permitted.

Pentecost was the celebration of the barley harvest. It was the first thanksgiving celebration. It celebrated the Exodus in the wilderness (see Exodus 19–20). It also marked the giving of the Law on Mount Sinai (see Deuteronomy 29:13–14).

The purpose of the celebration is a reminder to the Jewish adults about their heritage and to instruct the young in their Jewish heritage.

Christian Celebration of Pentecost—

At the first Pentecost celebration in Jerusalem after the resurrection of Jesus, the Holy Spirit came upon the Christian believers (see Acts 2:1–21). Christians received the power of the Holy Spirit to proclaim the good news of the gospel to the world as Jesus described in Acts 1:8.

Contrast the giving of the Law from the Jewish celebration with the infilling of the Holy Spirit on Christian believers in the Christian celebration (see Galatians 3:24 and 5:1).

After the period of the New Testament, the early church continued the Jewish practice of using Pentecost to teach both old and new believers. In today's church we have somewhat moved away from the use of holidays as a time of remembering and teaching. We need to reclaim our heritage of commemoration and teaching.

Activity 3—Paul before and after Conversion (Acts 9:1–31)

Read the appropriate material from the handbook for "The Coming of the Holy Spirit at Pentecost." Concentrate on the conversion of Paul. You will also want to read Acts 9:1–31 in your Bible.

Enlarge the Venn Diagram from Activity Sheet 3 and distribute copies of the diagram to the members of your class. Ask them to write the characteristics of Paul (Saul) before his conversion in the left circle. Write the characteristics of Paul after his conversion in the right circle. In the middle at the intersection of the circles, write those characteristics that were true for the apostle both before and after conversion.

Brainstorm characteristics for each of the three groups. On the left side you might include things like: Pharisee, zealous for his Jewish faith, persecuted Christians, etc. On the right side you might include things like: love for Christ, zealous for Christian faith, preached the gospel across the world, etc. At the intersection, you might include Jewish-Christian, Pharisee, Roman citizen, etc.

Activity 4—Questions and Answers about the Story of Cornelius

Read the appropriate material for the conversion of Cornelius in the handbook for "The Coming of the Holy Spirit at Pentecost." Also read Acts 10:1–11:18 in your Bible.

Share the story of Cornelius with the children. Point out that this is the first time the Holy Spirit came upon Gentile believers. This was an important occasion for the growth and development of the church.

Have the students use Activity Sheet 4 to review the story of the Holy Spirit coming to the Gentiles.

Activity 5—Results of Paul's Missionary Journeys

Read the appropriate material for the missionary journeys of Paul in the handbook for "The Three Missionary Journeys—Acts 13:1–21:26."

Divide your class into three groups. Have each group study one of the missionary journeys of Paul. Each group will need to read the appropriate Scripture and try to determine what the results were for that journey. Be sure to have the students look at the map for their journey and familiarize themselves with the places visited. Activity Sheet 5 includes the results from all three of the missionary journeys. They are scrambled. Ask each group to select the ones that are appropriate to the journey they studied. The answers are included below along with each of the journeys.

Group One—The First Missionary Journey (Acts 13:4–14:28)

The results were the following:

- Conversion of Sergius Paulus at Paphos, Crete
- Conversions and riot at Antioch (in Pisidia)
- Churches founded and established in the Galatian cities and elders appointed
- Report of the missionary journey to the church in Antioch (in Syria)

Group Two—The Second Missionary Journey (Acts 15:36–18:22)

The results were the following:

- Conversion of Lydia and the jailer at Philippi, where the church was founded
- Church at Thessalonica founded
- Conversion of Dionysius and Damaris at Athens
- Church at Corinth founded

Group Three—The Third Missionary Journey (Acts 18:23–21:14)

The results were the following:

- Church at Ephesus was established and became a center for evangelization of Asia
- Instruction to the Ephesian elders regarding official responsibilities

Activity 6—Paul's Trip to Rome

Read the appropriate material for the trip to Rome by the apostle Paul in the handbook for "The Journey to Rome—Acts 21:27–28:31."

Tell your students that they are each reporters for the *Roman Times* newspaper. They have been assigned by the newspaper to do a story on Paul the apostle. He has been creating a stir among the population for his witnessing about Christ. Tell them to take the following incidents and write them as a story for the paper.

Provide a copy of the chart in the handbook for "The Journey to Rome—Acts 21:27–28:31." You may read or tell the story, while the students take notes. Each child will need two sheets of lined paper. On the first sheet they will take notes on the trip to Rome. On the second sheet they will write their newspaper story.

Include the following facts about Paul's journey to Rome:

- Arrested in the Temple and accused of bringing a Gentile into the sacred area
- Paul's defense before the people
- Paul tells the commander at the fortress of Antonia that he is a Roman citizen
- Paul taken to Caesarea
- Paul before Felix and Festus; appeals to Caesar
- Sailing for Rome

- Shipwrecked in the storm at sea
- Paul on Malta; bitten by a snake but not killed
- Paul guarded by Caesar's guards, under house arrest; many become Christians

Activity 7—Memorize Acts 2:41–42

Have the children commit Acts 2:41–42 to memory: *"So those who accepted his message were baptized, and that day about 3,000 people were added to them. And they devoted themselves to the apostles' teaching, to fellowship, to the breaking of bread, and to prayers."*

Write each of the words on a 3x5-inch index card and keep practicing the verse. Put each word in order. Try to recite the entire verse from memory, with the reference.

Have the children write Acts 2:41-42 in their Bible Verse Memory Books and illustrate the verse as well. You may also want to review the verse that were learned in the last lesson.

WORKSHEETS FOR LESSON 8

ACTIVITY SHEET 3: VENN DIAGRAM—PAUL BEFORE AND AFTER CONVERSION

Directions: Write the characteristics of Paul (Saul) before conversion in the left oval and after conversion in the right oval. Write the characteristics of both at the intersection of the ovals.

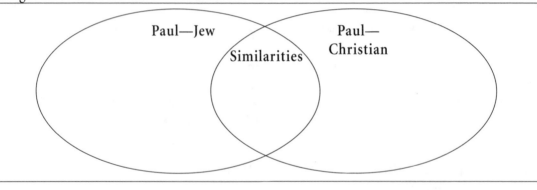

Paul—Jew

Similarities

Paul—Christian

ACTIVITY SHEET 4: PETER'S VISIT TO CORNELIUS

Directions: Write your answers to the questions about Cornelius on the lines provided.

1. Who was Cornelius?

2. How did God tell Cornelius what to do?

3. How did God tell Peter what to do?

4. What happened next in the story?

5. What happened after Peter preached to Cornelius and his family?

6. What did Peter tell the church at Jerusalem?

ACTIVITY SHEET 5: THE RESULTS OF PAUL'S MISSIONARY JOURNEYS

Directions: In the space at the left, write a 1, 2, or 3 in front of the results for the first, second, or third missionary journeys of Paul.

1. _____	Church of Ephesus was established, and it became a center for evangelization of Asia
2. _____	Conversions and riot at Antioch (in Pisidia)
3. _____	Conversion of Dionysius and Damaris at Athens
4. _____	Church at Corinth founded
5. _____	Report of missionary journey to the church in Antioch (in Syria)
6. _____	Conversion of Lydia and the jailer at Philippi, where the church was founded
7. _____	Instruction to the Ephesian elders regarding official responsibilities
8. _____	Conversion of Sergius Paulus at Paphos, Crete
9. _____	Church at Thessalonica founded
10. _____	Churches founded and established in the Galatian cities and elders were appointed

LESSON 9: LETTERS OF PAUL—GALATIANS, 1 AND 2 THESSALONIANS, 1 AND 2 CORINTHIANS, AND ROMANS

Readings from the Parent/Teacher Handbook: The Bible, Vol. 3: "Letters of the New Testament" and "The Missionary Letters of Paul"

OBJECTIVES

By the end of lesson, the learner should be able to:
- Identify and describe the cities to which Paul wrote,
- Identify and describe the problems that Paul addressed in each letter, and
- Explain justification by faith.

IDENTIFICATIONS

Concepts
- *Apostle*—sent one to carry the good news of the gospel
- *Gospel*—good news that Jesus came and died for our sins
- *Reconciliation*—making things right between God and the sinner
- *Faith*—belief and trust in Christ as Savior and Lord
- *Justification by faith*—made righteous before a holy God

People
- *Paul*: author of the missionary letters
- *Jesus*: Savior and Lord

MATERIALS NEEDED
- *Parent/Teacher Handbook: The Bible, Vol. 3*
- Activity Sheets for Lesson 9
- Crayons and markers
- Blank sheets of white paper for drawing
- 12x18 construction paper
- *The Visual Bible—Acts* (optional)

LEARNING ACTIVITIES FOR LESSON 9

Activity 1—The Visual Bible—Acts

View *The Visual Bible—Acts* rendering of the missionary journeys of Paul. In advance of this lesson, check the passages in Acts and be selective in the events that you view with the class.

Emphasize the cities to which these letters were written. From the first missionary journey, stress the cities of Galatia—Antioch (in Pisidia), Iconium, Lystra, and Derbe. From the second missionary journey, focus on Thessalonica and Corinth. From the trip to Rome, emphasize Rome.

Activity 2—The First Missionary Journey in Galatia

Read the section on Galatians in the handbook. In a Bible dictionary, such as the *Holman Bible Dictionary*, read about Antioch (in Pisidia), Iconium, Lystra, and Derbe. If you have a copy of the *Holman Interactive Bible Navigator* CD-ROM, you may also find these cities in the *International Standard Bible Encyclopedia* (ISBE).

Locate significant facts about each of the cities. Set up your room with four tables around the room. Using what you have learned about each of the cities from the Bible dictionaries and from the first missionary journey (see Acts 13:1–21:26) list the important characteristics for each city. Divide the class into five groups. Have each group study the city and what happened in their city. Ask them to sit at one of the tables representing their city. Have the fifth group serve as Paul and his companions. Ask them to go around to the tables and interact with the persons from each city.

When you have finished, ask the children to summarize information about the city and what happened in that city on a sheet like the one in Activity 2 for this lesson. They should complete four sheets for the four cities of Galatia. This will become part of a notebook on the letters of Paul.

Activity 3—The Letter to the Galatians

For this activity continue your study of Galatians. The major problem toward which Paul directed his letter was the work of the Judaizers. These were men who tried to take the Christian faith away from the persons in Galatia by forcing them to keep all of the Jewish laws along with the practices of their Christian faith. The Judaizers did not believe that one could only be saved by faith in Jesus Christ alone.

You should have already read the section on Galatians in the handbook. Use the puzzle in Activity Sheet 3 to point out the evil work of the Judaizers.

The puzzle should read as follows: Jewish religious leaders who want Christians to be zealous to follow every Jewish regulation as well as Christian practices.

Activity 4—Research Cities with Churches to Which Paul Wrote

The cities with churches to which Paul wrote in his missionary letters were important commercial centers. There are three letters to be studied in this context. Each came from the missionary correspondence. They are Thessalonica, Corinth, and Rome.

Divide your class into three groups. Have each group research one of the cities. They will find material in a good Bible dictionary, such as the *Holman Bible Dictionary*. You can also find material on the *Holman Interactive Bible Navigator* CD-ROM. Ask each group to prepare a report for the class on the city to which they were assigned. Make the report an oral report.

Have the rest of the students take notes on the city for their notebook on the cities to which Paul wrote his letters. Each student should have the sheets from Activity 2 and add sheets for Thessalonica, Corinth, and Rome.

Have the students prepare covers, using 12x18-inch construction paper. Fold the construction paper in half and insert the pages. Using crayons and/or markers, have the students decorate their covers.

Activity 5—Thessalonians Wordfind

Read the section on 1 and 2 Thessalonians in the handbook. Try to grasp the themes of these two letters. Then read the letters through at one sitting. Be prepared to discuss the letters with your students.

This activity is a wordfind from Paul's letters to the Thessalonians and is found in Activity Sheet 5. The words are taken from the Holman Christian Standard Bible®. Have your students take turns reading through 1 and 2 Thessalonians. Look at the words in the wordfind and try to place them in context, even if you are using another version of the Bible.

Conclude this activity by looking at the themes of these two letters. Ask the students what they can learn from these two letters.

Activity 6—Problems in the Church at Corinth

There were many problems in the church at Corinth. Read the section on 1 and 2 Corinthians in the handbook.

Let us focus on only one of the problems—Meat Sacrificed to Idols found in 1 Corinthians 8–10. In Paul's day the meat was brought to the pagan Temple. There it was butchered. The priests would burn the insides and sell the fresh meat. Many Christians were upset by this practice. They did not want to buy meat that had been in a pagan temple and blessed by the priest. Other Christians said that the idols are only that—dumb idols of wood or stone—and they could see no reason for not eating the meat. The idols did nothing to it. This dispute created a great deal of hard feeling among the Christians who disagreed with one another.

It is interesting to note that this problem is still with us today. In the Buddhist temple in Taipei, Taiwan, the pagan population still buys their meat from the priests in the temple. It still causes a struggle for the Chinese Christians. Some have no problem with the practice, while others will not buy meat in the temple.

The apostle Paul responded by stating the problem in chapter 8 of 1 Corinthians. He provided the biblical basis for answering the problem in chapter 9. In chapter 10 he gave practical advice to the Christians who were troubled. His advice to those who are not troubled by buying the meat was to stop if it hurt another Christian.

Use Quads, which means Question, Answer, Details, in groups of four to deal with this problem. Use Activity Sheet 6 with your students to complete this exercise. Provide some background for the study from the material presented above. Divide your class in groups of four. Then have each student take the QUAD sheet and write his/her name in the space provided and write four different questions on the sheet. Cut the sheets in four parts and distribute the questions to other members of the group. Each student should have four questions to answer. Write the answers and return the questions to the person, whose name is on the sheet.

After the original writers have all of their questions returned, have the group read the questions and the answers. Are the answers correct? If they are not, seek to correct the answers. Then in a couple of words summarize the answer in detail.

Activity 7—Justification by Faith (Romans)

Read the section on the "Letter to the Romans" in the handbook.

From Paul's letter to the Romans, we learn that we are justified before the Law of God through faith in Jesus Christ. Jesus lived a sinless life. He died on the cross, and His death replaces our death when we place our trust in Him. *Justification* is a legal term that means "we have satisfied the demands of the Law." We have done this not through our own righteousness but through the righteousness of Jesus. We have done nothing to earn this righteousness. Therefore, God declares us righteous before Him. It is God's gift freely given to us. There is one essential condition to receiving that gift—faith. We must exercise faith. Faith is both believing that God has provided this gift and trusting in God to bring it to pass (see Romans 5:1–10).

Have your students work in small groups of three to five persons. Provide each student with a copy of Activity Sheet 7. From Romans 5:1–10 have the students record the cause and the effect of justification. The one condition is already included. The cause is God's love for us in sending His own son Jesus to die on the cross for us. Share their findings.

Activity 8—Memorize Romans 12:1–2

From Paul's letter to the Romans, have your students memorize two very powerful verses found in Romans.

Therefore, brothers, by the mercies of God, I urge you to present your bodies as a living sacrifice, holy and pleasing to God; this is your spiritual worship. Do not be conformed to this age, but be transformed by the renewing of your mind, so that you may discern what is the good, pleasing, and perfect will of God.

You will want to find a place in the Bible Verse Memory Books for these verses.

WORKSHEETS FOR LESSON 9

ACTIVITY SHEET 2: THE CITIES OF GALATIA

Directions: Briefly describe the city that you are studying: _____ (name of city)

_____

_____

_____

_____

ACTIVITY SHEET 3: THE JUDAIZERS

Directions: Fill in the blanks to find out the evil work of the Judaizers.

J _ _ _ _ _

_ _ _ _ _ _ _ _ U _

_ _ _ D _ _ _ _

who _ A _ _ _

_ _ _ I _ _ _ _ _ _

to be Z _ _ _ _ _ _ _

to follow E _ _ _ _ _

Jewish R _ _ _ _ _ _ _ _ _

as well as _ _ _ _ _ S _ _ _ _

practices.

ACTIVITY SHEET 5: WORDFIND ON 1 AND 2 THESSALONIANS

Directions: Complete the Wordfind by using the words on the right.

S	S	A	N	C	T	I	F	I	C	A	T	I	O	N
E	Y	C	O	M	I	N	G	Z	S	X	X	Q	F	S
S	F	A	I	T	H	W	N	J	K	S	M	B	X	S
S	I	Z	R	E	L	B	I	S	N	O	P	S	E	R
E	N	O	C	P	B	V	C	C	A	L	A	N	R	U
N	M	X	N	U	W	K	T	J	H	M	G	O	T	X
T	L	I	L	R	P	Q	E	U	T	V	N	I	F	F
I	C	R	Y	W	Q	X	W	D	L	C	I	T	Z	B
W	K	R	O	W	T	N	M	G	K	W	R	A	Z	A
E	K	P	E	U	V	B	Q	M	R	H	E	V	L	S
N	B	V	P	J	Q	F	X	E	G	L	F	L	G	C
D	O	K	W	V	O	L	T	N	O	J	F	A	E	B
L	I	D	F	C	P	I	L	T	M	B	U	S	C	K
T	V	O	V	O	S	R	C	O	F	N	S	C	E	H
Q	E	V	P	I	W	M	A	E	G	U	R	T	P	J

Coming
Faith
Judgment
Love
Pray
Rejoice
Responsible
Salvation
Sanctification
Suffering
Witnesses
Work
Thanks

ACTIVITY SHEET 6: QUADS

Name:	Name:
Question:	Question:
Answer:	Answer:
Name:	Name:
Question:	Question:
Answer:	Answer:

ACTIVITY SHEET 7: CAUSE AND EFFECT

Directions: From Romans 5:1–10, record the cause and effect of justification.

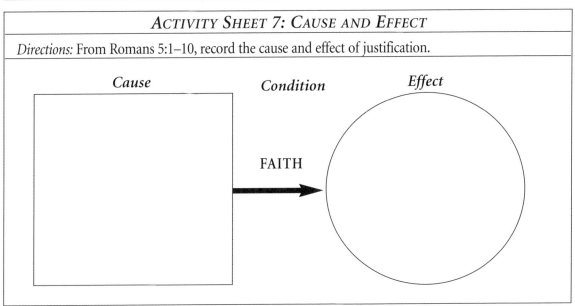

Cause   *Condition*   *Effect*

FAITH

LESSON 10: LETTERS OF PAUL—EPHESIANS, PHILIPPIANS, COLOSSIANS, PHILEMON, 1 AND 2 TIMOTHY, AND TITUS

Readings from the Parent/Teacher Handbook: The Bible, Vol. 3: "Letters of the New Testament" and "The Missionary Letters of Paul"

OBJECTIVES
By the end of lesson, the learner should be able to:
- Identify and describe cities to which Paul wrote in the prison letters and beyond,
- Identify the main objective for each of the letters, and
- Name lessons to be learned from each of these letters.

IDENTIFICATIONS
Concepts
- *Diana*—goddess worshipped in Ephesus
- *Parable*—story that contains a moral principle
- *Elders*—leaders in the church; Paul wrote to Titus about the elders

People
- *Paul:* author of the letters
- *Lydia:* seller of purple from Philippi, who became a Christian

- *Philippian jailer:* after the earthquake, Paul and Silas were still there, and the jailer and his family became Christians
- *Euodia:* Philippian woman who had a quarrel with Syntyche
- *Syntyche:* Philippian woman who had a quarrel with Euodia
- *Philemon:* slave who became a Christian and returned to his former owner in Colosse
- *Timothy:* friend and coworker with Paul
- *Titus:* Gentile companion of Paul

MATERIALS NEEDED
- *Parent/Teacher Handbook: The Bible, Vol. 3*
- Activity Sheets for Lesson 10
- Crayons and markers
- Blank sheets of white paper for drawing
- Roll of shelf paper or butcher paper
- Masking tape and plastic tape
- 4x6-index cards

LEARNING ACTIVITIES FOR LESSON 10

Activity 1—The Visual Bible—Acts

View *The Visual Bible—Acts* rendering of the missionary journeys of Paul. In advance of this lesson, check the passages in Acts and be selective in the events that you view with the class.

Emphasize the cities to which these letters were written. From the first missionary journey, stress the cities of Ephesus, Colossae, and Philippi.

Activity 2—Research Cities with Churches to Which Paul Wrote

The cities with churches to which Paul wrote in his missionary letters were important commercial centers. There are three letters to be studied in this context. Each came from the missionary correspondence. They are Ephesus, Colosse, and Philippi.

Divide your class into three groups. Have each group research one of the cities. They will find material in a good Bible dictionary, such as the *Holman Bible Dictionary*. You can also find material on the *Holman Interactive Bible Navigator* CD-ROM. Ask each group to prepare a report for the class on the city to which they were assigned. Make the report an oral report.

Have the rest of the students take notes for their notebook on the cities to which Paul wrote his letters. Each student should have the sheets from Activity 2 in lesson 9 and add sheets for Ephesus, Colosse, and Philippi.

Activity 3—Who Am I?

Read the section on the "The Prison Letters" in the handbook.

Below are descriptions of several people who were closely associated with the apostle Paul. Write their descriptions on 4x6-index cards, with the correct answer (shown in italics below) on the back side of the card. Have the children divided into small groups around a table. Have them guess the name of the person or persons from the description on the card.

1. I was converted under the ministry of Paul. The church met in my home. I had a runaway slave named Onesimus. My wife's name was Apphia. There is a letter written to me by Paul. *My name is Philemon.*

2. Paul was my teacher in the faith. My grandmother's name was Lois. Paul taught me what a leader should be like. Paul wrote two letters to me. *My name is Timothy.*

3. I was a Gentile companion of Paul. Paul wrote me a letter. I accompanied Paul and Barnabas to Jerusalem, probably in the relief effort. I am not mentioned in the Book of Acts. *My name is Titus.*

4. I was a slave who ran away and stole some property from my master. While in Rome, I became a Christian. Paul helped me. He sent me back to my master with a letter asking for forgiveness and that I might be returned to him. *My name is Onesimus.*

5. My wife and I were tent makers. We were put out of Rome when the Emperor Claudius forced Jews to leave Rome. We accompanied Paul to Ephesus. We helped start the church at Ephesus. *Our names are Priscilla and Aquila.*

6. I kept the prison where Paul and Silas were jailed. When the earthquake came, I was afraid of losing my job. I was about to commit suicide. But Paul and Silas would not let me do that. I became a Christian, and all of my family was baptized. *I am the Philippian jailer.*

7. I was converted and baptized in the city of Philippi by Paul. I was a businesswoman. I sold the purple dye that was used for royal robes. Paul and his companions stayed in my home. *My name is Lydia.*

8. I was sent by the Philippians to help Paul in Rome. I almost died in Rome. Paul used me to take the letter to the Philippians from his prison. Paul wanted to thank them for their help and warn them about false teachers. *My name is Epaphroditus.*

Activity 4—Silversmiths Riot in Ephesus (Acts 19:23–41)

Read the section on "Ephesians" in the handbook.

After having studied the city of Ephesus, you know something of the culture. As further background for the study of Ephesians, construct a "What's New?" chart like the one on Activity Sheet 4. Duplicate copies for each students. In your Bible, read Acts 19:23–41. Discuss this experience from Paul's missionary journey with them. Have them fill in the "What's New?" chart as you discuss the passage. You may also want to summarize each of the chapters from Paul's letter to the Ephesians. You will want them to discover the letter to the Ephesians.

As a result of this study, have your students consider what changes they need to make to be more Christlike and to be a more effective witness.

Activity 5—Letter to the Colossians and Philemon

Read the sections on "Colossians" and "Philemon" in the handbook. You will also want to read both Colossians and Philemon in the Bible.

In advance of this lesson, cut 9-inch squares from construction paper. Have the students fold the squares in half each way, so that you have four smaller squares. Then unfold the paper and fold from the corner to the center. This will give you four flaps with which to work.

Divide your class into five smaller groups. Have each group take one chapter from Colossians and the fifth group to use Philemon. On the outside flaps, write "Who?," "What?," "When?," and "Where?" Write the chapter and title on the inside. On the inside of the flaps, write answers to each of the four questions. Decorate the outside. These will make a good display on your bulletin board and capture the essence of Colossians and Philemon.

Activity 6—The Whole Armor of God (Ephesians 6:10–20)

Duplicate copies of Activity Sheet 6. Have the students complete the listing of the armor and its purpose. Tie this activity together with the next activity for memorization.

Activity 7—Memorize Ephesians 6:10–13

To help your children understand the importance of being protected to live a godly life, have them memorize Ephesians 6:10–13.

Finally, be strengthened by the Lord and by His vast strength. Put on the full armor of God so that you can stand against the tactics of the Devil. For our battle is not against flesh and blood, but against the rulers, against the authorities, against the world powers of this darkness, against the spiritual forces of evil in the heavens. This is why you must take up the full armor of God, so that you may be able to resist in the evil day, and having prepared everything, to take your stand.

You will want to find a place in your Bible Verse Memory Books for these verses. Illustrate also.

WORKSHEETS FOR LESSON 10

ACTIVITY SHEET 4: WHAT'S NEW?	ACTIVITY SHEET 6: THE WHOLE ARMOR OF GOD
Topic: Silversmith's Riot in Ephesus	*Directions:* Describe each part of the armor of the soldier of God and how it is used by the soldier. Read Ephesians 6:10–20.
What I Know:	
Paul was preaching in Ephesus	Helmet
People weren't buying idols of Diana, goddess	
	Chest or Breastplate
Silversmiths were angry with Paul	
What I'll Find Out:	Belt
	Shield
What I Learned:	Sword
	Feet

Readings from the Parent/Teacher Handbook: The Bible, Vol. 3: "Letters of the New Testament" and "The General Letters"

OBJECTIVES

By the end of lesson, the learner should be able to:

- Describe the superiority of Christ as a prophet, priest, and king,
- Understand the kinds of persons who received the letter to the Hebrews,
- Identify the major themes of James, and
- Describe the significance of Jude's letter.

IDENTIFICATIONS

Concepts

- *Prophet*—Jesus was the greatest of the prophets
- *Priest*—Jesus was the greatest high priest after the order of Melchizedek
- *King*—Jesus is our king
- *Melchizedek*—priest who Abraham gave a portion of his wealth (Genesis 14:17–20; Psalm 110:4)

People

- *James:* half brother of Jesus, author of James, and leader in the church at Jerusalem
- *Jude:* half brother of Jesus and author of Jude

MATERIALS NEEDED

- *Parent/Teacher Handbook: The Bible, Vol. 3*
- Activity Sheets for Lesson 11
- Crayons and markers
- Blank sheets of white paper for drawing
- Roll of shelf paper or butcher paper
- Masking tape and plastic tape

LEARNING ACTIVITIES FOR LESSON 11

Activity 1—Jesus—Prophet, Priest, King (Hebrews)

Read the sections on "The General Letters" in the handbook, especially Hebrews.

Have your students use a Bible dictionary and look up each of these three roles that Jesus assumed. Then have them write their findings on each of the three circles on Activity Sheet 1.

Discuss the student findings and the greatness of Christ.

Activity 2—The Greatness of Christ (Hebrews)

For this activity, duplicate copies of Activity Sheet 2. Have your students respond to the question posed on the sheet.

Your students should realize that Jesus was the Son of God and greater than all of these other created beings. Jesus was doing the creating of these other beings.

Activity 3—Points to Consider (James)

Read the sections on "The General Letters" in the handbook, especially James. Read the letter of James in the Bible.

Divide your class into several groups. Assign one or more problems to each group. Ask each group to read the passage in James and complete Activity Sheet 3 for each of the problems addressed in James.

Here are the problems:

- Trials and Maturity (James 1:2–18)
- Hearing and Doing the Word of God (James 1:19–27)
- Sin of Favoritism (James 2:1–13)
- Faith and Works (James 2:14–26)

- Controlling the Tongue (James 3:1–12)
- Wisdom from Above (James 3:13–18)
- Proud and Humble (James 4:1–12)
- Warning to the Rich (James 5:1–6)
- Truthful Speech (James 5:12)
- Effective Prayer (James 5:13–20)

Discuss the importance of each of the problems that James writes about and how his advice can help us in our everyday living.

Activity 4—Puzzle (Jude 24–25)

Read the sections on "The General Letters" in the handbook, especially Jude. Read the letter of Jude in the Bible.

One of the great benedictions in the Bible is found in Jude 24–25. Paste the puzzle template from Activity Sheet 4 on a sheet of cardboard. Write the words of these verses on each of the puzzle pieces. Mix up the pieces and have the children put them together.

Activity 5—Memorize James 1:2–4

One of the great sets of verses in James comes from 1:2-4. Have your students memorize these verses.

Consider it a great joy, my brothers, whenever you experience various trials, knowing that the testing of your faith produces endurance. But endurance must do its complete work, so that you may be mature and complete, lacking nothing.

You will want to find a place for these verses in your Bible Verse Memory Books. Write the verses in the booklet and illustrate them.

WORKSHEETS FOR LESSON 11

ACTIVITY SHEET 1: PROPHET, PRIEST, AND KING

Directions: After you have studied each of these offices that Jesus filled, summarize your findings in each of the circles below.

Prophet

Priest

King

Jesus

ACTIVITY SHEET 2: THE GREATNESS OF CHRIST

Why do you think that the Book of Hebrews tell us that Jesus was greater than angels, greater than Moses and Joshua, greater than any other being?

ACTIVITY SHEET 3: POINTS TO CONSIDER

Directions: Have one star sheet for each of the problems that was assigned. Write the problem in the center and list the points that James makes to respond to the problem.

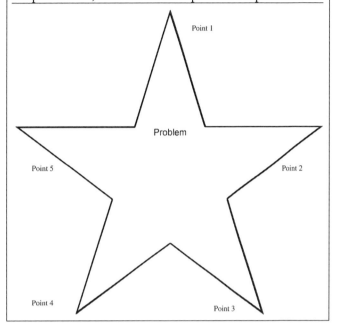

Point 1

Problem

Point 5

Point 2

Point 4

Point 3

ACTIVITY SHEET 4: JUDE 24-25

Directions: Write the words on the puzzle. Mix up the pieces and have the children put the puzzle together.

Readings from the Parent/Teacher Handbook: The Bible, Vol. 3: "Letters of the New Testament" and "The General Letters"

OBJECTIVES
By the end of lesson, the learner should be able to:
- Explain the importance of the resurrection and its significance for believers then and now,
- Recount the postresurrection appearances of Jesus to the women, the disciples, the two disciples on the road to Emmaus, and Thomas,
- Define and describe the Great Commission for disciples then and now, and
- Explain the ascension of Jesus from earth to heaven and describe the promise given by the angels.

IDENTIFICATIONS
Concepts
- *Salvation*—new birth to spiritual life in Jesus Christ
- *Holiness*—set apart to God
- *False teachers*—persons who would lead Christians astray from the truth
- *Day of the Lord*—God's judgment upon sin and sinners

- *Fellowship*—relationship among Christians around Christ
- *Chosen of God*—those who are called to new life in Christ

People
- *Peter:* apostle and leader in the early church, author of 1 and 2 Peter
- *John:* beloved disciple of Jesus and author of 1, 2, and 3 John

MATERIALS NEEDED
- *Parent/Teacher Handbook: The Bible, Vol. 3*
- Activity Sheets for Lesson 12
- Crayons and markers
- Blank sheets of white paper for drawing
- Roll of shelf paper or butcher paper
- Masking tape and plastic tape
- Reusable adhesive

LEARNING ACTIVITIES FOR LESSON 12

Activity 1—Biographies of Peter and John

Read the sections on "The General Letters," in the 1 and 2 Peter, and 1, 2, and 3 John in the handbook.

Have your students recall everything that they can about the apostle Peter and the apostle John. If they have difficulty, have them consult a good Bible dictionary or the *Bible Navigator* program. Have them record their findings on Activity Sheets 1a and 1b.

The biography will provide a good background for studying the letters of Peter and John. Both had a significant relationship with Jesus. This adds importance to the messages they wrote in these letters.

Discuss the findings with the entire class. Suggest that members of the class remember some of the findings here as they read the letters of 1 and 2 Peter and 1, 2 and 3 John.

Activity 2—Heaven from the Letters of Peter

What will heaven be like? This is an interesting question and one that will interest most children. Heaven is talked about in the letters of Peter. Have the children research the question of heaven. Ask them to consult a Bible dictionary. They may use the materials in the *Bible Navigator* program.

Have several students research the question and bring a report to the class. Be sure to end this class with the hope that heaven provides. Stress that it is not possible to get there at the end of life unless one has accepted Jesus Christ as personal Lord and Savior.

Activity 3—Wordfind (1, 2, and 3 John)

Some important words are used in 1, 2 and 3 John. Their meaning helps us understand the letters of

1, 2, and 3 John more effectively. Without an understanding of these words, one cannot hope to understand these letters. Here are a set of brief definitions for the words used in the wordfind.

- Truth—that which is revealed and open
- Light—God is light; we walk in light as believers in Jesus Christ
- Word—purpose and overall unity that underlies all of reality
- World—fallen nature of all created reality; it takes on an evil connotation
- Antichrist—anyone who is against Christ; but there is a specific person who is the Antichrist
- Love—agape love is total self-giving with no expectation of return; God's love
- Life—relationship that is characterized by fellowship
- Fellowship—*koinonia* is the true relationship among believers around Jesus Christ
- Confidence—boldness before God that comes through knowing Jesus Christ as Savior

Activity 4—Love and Truth

Read the sections on "The General Letters," 1, 2, and 3 John in the handbook.

Read 2 John with your students. Notice how important these two ideas are in this little letter. Use Activity Sheet 4 to examine the relationship between love and truth. Have the students draw a line from the characteristic on the left to the appropriate statement where the word belongs. Summarize their importance.

Activity 5—Memorize 2 Peter 1:3–8

Memorize 2 Peter 1:3–8. This passage of Scripture will guide your children to a deeper relationship with Jesus Christ. Have them memorize the entire passage. But help them focus upon the things that God has given us so we won't be useless in verses 5–7.

For His divine power has given us everything required for life and godliness, through the knowledge of Him who called us by His own glory and goodness. By these He has given us very great and precious promises, so that through them you may share in the divine nature, escaping the corruption that is in the world because of evil desires. For this very reason, make every effort to supplement your faith with goodness, goodness with knowledge, knowledge with self-control, self-control with endurance, endurance with godliness, godliness with brotherly affection, and brotherly affection with love. For if these qualities are yours and are increasing, they will keep you from being useless or unfruitful in the knowledge of our Lord Jesus Christ.

Finish this section by placing these verses in your Bible Verse Memory Books.

WORKSHEETS FOR LESSON 12

ACTIVITY SHEET 1A: THE APOSTLE PETER

Directions: Recall everything that you can about the apostle Peter. Who was he? Was he married? When was he with Jesus?

ACTIVITY SHEET 1B: THE APOSTLE JOHN

Directions: Recall everything that you can about the apostle John. Who was he? What did he do? What was his relationship to Jesus?

_____

_____

_____

_____

_____

_____

ACTIVITY SHEET 3: WORDFIND (1, 2, AND 3 JOHN)

Directions: Find the words above on the right that appear in the wordfind.

R V K N Y C U Z E Q Z P P R X	
M L O S B X K X R L G Q Z D H	Antichrist
M W S S L L O V E L T H G I L	Confidence
L E R E M Y Y R T I H W T C S	Fellowship
B C H N X A S A T F T D P B K	Life
P N S T F B Y N D E U Q B D T	
J E V I L H R T X L R L N R O	Light
U D D W X X D I R L T N R I A	Love
Q I T D X P V C M O B K N C N	Truth
N F R L R N L H D W D I S T J	
R N B R M W I R C S V Y D A P	Witness
R O Y O U E O I D H A N B H M	Word
D C X W S W V S X I I D V D A	World
Z I U I E A X T E P B N P S Z	
D L O D L E E T N E X O B M O	

ACTIVITY SHEET 4: LOVE AND TRUTH (2 JOHN)

Directions: Draw a line from the characteristics listed on the left to the appropriate statement where the word belongs.

	I was very glad to find some of your children walking in _____, in keeping with a command we have received from the Father.
LOVE	Anyone who does not remain in the teaching about Christ, but goes beyond it, does not have God.
	The one who remains in that teaching, this one has both the Father and the Son.
	Not as if I were writing you a new command, but one we have had from the beginning—that we _____ one another.
	And this is _____ : that we walk according to His commands.
TRUTH	If anyone comes to you and does not bring this teaching, do not receive him into your home.
	This is the command as you have heard it from the beginning: you must walk in _____.
	Many deceivers have gone out into the world; they do not confess the coming of Jesus Christ in the flesh.

Unit Three: Tabernacle, Temple, and Bible Geography: Lessons 13–15

UNIT SUMMARY

This set of activities will focus on the Tabernacle, Temple, and geography outside of the Holy Land. It will go back in time for several thousand years to the time of the patriarchs and come forward in time to the life and ministry of Christ and the apostle Paul, about two thousand years ago.

OVERVIEW

Objectives

By the end of this unit, the learner should be able to

- Understand the role of both the Tabernacle and the Temple,
- Understand the historical development of the nations surrounding Israel, and
- Describe the lands in which the Hebrews and later the Jews settled.

Content Summary and Rationale

Through this set of activities, the student will be able to discover the places of worship that were designed by God Himself—the Tabernacle in the Wilderness and the Temple in Jerusalem. Students will also gain an appreciation for the countries that surrounded Israel. They will come to appreciate the great world Empires that developed in other lands and discover how the people of Israel interfaced with these other peoples and cultures.

This set of activities is important because learners will discover that the peoples of the Bible were different from people who live in our context. Without moving across the time dimension and the space dimension, the student will not be able to grapple with the significant differences between then and now and between here and there. Both of these concerns will affect the way the learner is able to relate to Bible times and Bible people. The Bible lands, as we know them today, are still an area of heated tension for Jews, Christians, and Muslims.

Key Concept

The key concept for this study is the importance of the places of worship and the physical location of the Holy Land in its geographical context.

Prior Knowledge Needed

Basic understanding of time and distance are needed to appreciate this unit. You will introduce your students to the countries of Egypt, Babylonia, Persia, Greece, and Rome. You will also examine the countries that threatened the people of Israel from positions near them, such as the Phoenicians and the Philistines. You will want to call attention to the Middle East and its current place of prominence on the news each day.

RESOURCES FOR TEACHERS AND STUDENTS:

- Buchanan, Edward, *Parent/Teacher Handbook The Bible, Volumes 1 and 3* (Nashville, Tenn.: Broadman & Holman, 2003).

- Butler, Trent, ed., *Holman Illustrated Bible Dictionary* (Nashville, Tenn: Holman Bible Publishers, 2003).

- Dockery, David, ed., *Holman Bible Handbook* (Nashville, Tenn.: Holman Bible Publishers, 1992).

- Easley, Kendell, *The Illustrated Guide to Biblical History* (Nashville, Tenn.: Holman Reference, 2003).

- *Holman Bible Atlas* (Nashville, Tenn.: Holman Bible Publishers, 1998).

- Holman Interactive *Bible Navigator* program on CD-ROM, available at your local LifeWay Christian Store.

- An Encyclopedia—*World Book, Funk and Wagnalls, Britannica*, etc. (may use CD-ROM).

LESSON 13: THE TABERNACLE IN THE WILDERNESS

Readings from the Parent/Teacher Handbook: The Bible, Vol. 3: "The Tabernacle in the Wilderness"

OBJECTIVES
By the end of lesson, the learner should be able to:
- Match the five terms for the Tabernacle with their descriptions,
- Locate the furniture in the Tabernacle,
- Identify the meanings of the four coverings and the veil in the Tabernacle,
- Identify the five offerings used in the Tabernacle, and
- Describe the meaning of the sacrificial system and its relationship to Jesus Christ.

IDENTIFICATIONS
Concepts
- *Tabernacle*—the construction of a temporary place of worship as they traveled

- *Priests*—God called men to serve in the Tabernacle
- *High Priest*—from the line of Aaron, a hereditary office; conducted the Day of Atonement sacrifices
- *Levites*—assisted in the Tabernacle and its movement

People
- *Moses:* called by God to lead the Exodus and construction of the Tabernacle
- *Aaron:* Moses' brother, who worked with his associates in the Tabernacle

MATERIALS NEEDED
- *Parent/Teacher Handbook: The Bible, Vol. 3*
- Activity Sheets for Lesson 13
- Crayons and markers
- Blank sheets of white paper for drawing

LEARNING ACTIVITIES FOR LESSON 13

Activity 1—Matching the Names of the Tabernacle

Read the appropriate section in the handbook entitled "The Tabernacle in the Wilderness."

You will discover that there are five names for the Tabernacle. Each of these names expresses a different aspect of the Tabernacle. Duplicate Activity Sheet 1 and have your children match the descriptions with the appropriate name.

Bring this activity to a conclusion by discussing the importance of each of the names.

Activity 2—Placement of Furniture in the Tabernacle

Read the appropriate section titled "The Tabernacle in the Wilderness" in the handbook.

The design of the Tabernacle and the placement of the furniture were extremely important, since God Himself gave Moses the design and the furniture to place in the Tabernacle. The design helped the people of Israel understand the importance of redemption and how it was obtained. It later signified the role of Jesus' sacrifice on the cross for our sins and how that sacrifice made us clean in God's sight. Help your children to discover the importance of the design of the Tabernacle and the furniture that was placed in the enclosure.

After the children have completed Activity Sheet 2, discuss each of the items in the Tabernacle. Point out the sections of the Tabernacle: the Court, the Holy Place, and the Most Holy Place. Show them how Jesus was both our sacrifice for sin and our High Priest, who opened the veil to the presence of Almighty God.

Activity 3—Coverings of the Tabernacle (Sentence Completion)

Read the appropriate section on "The Four Coverings" in the handbook, "The Tabernacle in the Wilderness."

Along with the furniture and its placement, the four coverings were also important. Discuss with your class the four coverings and the veil from your reading in the handbook. Have the students complete Activity Sheet 3 to conclude this activity.

Activity 4—The Five Offerings

Read the appropriate section, "The Sacrifices of the Tabernacle" in the handbook in the section entitled, "The Tabernacle in the Wilderness."

Five offerings are listed in Scripture. They are among the more important responsibilities in the Tabernacle and later in the Temple. Sacrifices were offered for the entire community as well as for individuals. Two of the offerings were for sin—the trespass offering and the sin offering. But notice that neither of these offerings was made on behalf of a person who willfully sinned, knowing that what he did was wrong and yet he went ahead and did it anyway. We need to be careful not to engage in sin that is willful in our day either. You will want to point this out to the children in your class.

Before your class, duplicate classroom quantities of Activity Sheet 4. Help the children understand the sacrificial system. One type of offering paid the price for sin, and another offered to God an expression of thanksgiving for His goodness. We can do the same but without the necessity of killing an animal because Jesus was sacrificed on the cross for us and in our place.

Activity Sheet 4 will bring to remembrance the use of each of the offerings that were given in the Tabernacle.

Activity 5—Christ Our Sin Offering

In this activity the children need to see that God has provided a sin offering for us. Activity Sheet 5 is in the form of a puzzle. Provide copies for each member of the class, and ask them to fill in the puzzle.

Activity 6—Memorize John 1:1–14

One of the great passages of Scripture that describes the role of Jesus as our sin bearer is John 1:1–14. Memorize this great passage of Scripture.

In the beginning was the Word; and the Word was with God, and the Word was God. He was with God in the beginning. All things were created through Him, and apart from Him not one thing was created that has been created. Life was in Him, and that life was the light of men. That light shines in the darkness, yet the darkness did not overcome it. There was a man named John who was sent from God. He came as a witness to testify about the light, so that all might believe through him. He was not the light, but he came to testify about the light. The true light, who gives light to everyone, was coming into the world. He was in the world, and the world was created through Him, yet the world did not recognize Him. He came to His own, and His own people did not receive Him. But to all who did receive Him, He gave them the right to be children of God, to those who believe in His name, who were born, not of blood, or of the will of the flesh, or of the will of man, but of God. The Word became flesh and took up residence among us. We observed His glory, the glory as the One and Only Son from the Father, full of grace and truth.

Be sure to include this Scripture passage in your Bible Verse Memory Books. Also have the children illustrate these verses.

ACTIVITY SHEET 1: NAMES OF THE TABERNACLE

Directions: Place the number of the definition next to the letter for the appropriate name.

_____A. Sanctuary

_____B. Tabernacle

_____C. Tent

_____D. Tent of Meeting

_____E. Tabernacle of
     Testimony

1. Ten Commandments are located in this place of worship.

2. Conveys the idea of a home

3. Conveys the idea of the assembly or congregation between God and people

4. Dwelling place or habitation of God

5. Holy place or chapel

ACTIVITY SHEET 2: PLACEMENT OF FURNITURE IN THE TABERNACLE

Directions: Draw lines from the furniture to the place it fits on the floor plan of the Tabernacle. Then write the letter from the descriptions below on the line underneath the appropriate piece of furniture in the Tabernacle.

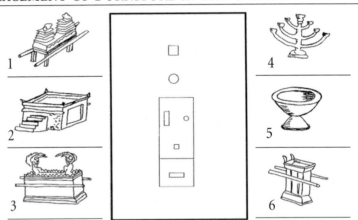

A. The Altar of Incense provided a sweet-smelling perfume. This represents the prayers of God's people that ascend to God. A person who is humble and prays acts like a sweet-smelling aroma before God. (Exodus 30:1–10)

B. The Table of Showbread held twelve loaves of bread. This meant that God provided adequately for each of the twelve tribes of Israel. Bread provided food for the priests and symbolized the dependence of the people on God. (Exodus 25:23–30)

C. The Golden Lampstand or Menorah had seven candles placed in holders. They showed God's care for His people and their dependence upon Him. (Exodus 25:31–40)

D. The Altar of Burnt Offering is a large altar that stood outside the Tabernacle. On the altar the animals were sacrificed. People had to bring animals that did not have any blemishes. They were sacrificed, and their blood was shed for the sins of the people. (Exodus 27:1–8)

E. The Bronze Laver was used for the purification of the priests before they went into the presence of the Lord. The priest had to wash his hands before he sacrificed the animals. Priests were offering sacrifice on behalf of the people and had to observe all of the regulations that God gave them. (Exodus 30:17–21)

F. The Ark of the Covenant was the most important structure in the Tabernacle. This was the place where God dwelt. A priest entered the Holy of Holies only once a year to place the blood of the goat on the Mercy Seat between the cherubim. The priest was tied with a golden cord, so that he could be removed if he died while inside the Holy Place. (Exodus 25:10–22)

ACTIVITY SHEET 3: SENTENCE COMPLETION

Directions: Complete the sentences as they relate to the coverings of the Tabernacle and the veil.

1. The first covering was easily observed by the priests as they carried out their work in the Tabernacle. As the priest looked up to the ceiling, he would see curtains of blue, purple, and scarlet. The blue is a reminder of heaven. The purple is a reminder of God as King. The scarlet helped the priest understand God's love for humans. In all there were ten curtains in this first covering.

The ten curtains were made of _____.

2. The second covering was coarse and black in color. While the inner coverings remind us of the majesty of God, this did not. Sin is ugly. It reminds us of sin and that sin must always be forgiven before a worshipper can have fellowship with God.

It was made of _____.

3. The third covering was dyed red. It reminds us of the blood that must be shed for the remission of sins.It was made of _____.

4. The fourth and final covering was to protect the Tabernacle from the weather. It symbolized the separation of the holiness of God from the world that surrounded the Tabernacle.

It was made of _____.

5. The veil was a curtain that separated the Holy Place from the Most Holy Place. It was handwoven and had cherubim woven into it. The cherubim are in the presence of a Holy God.

It was made of _____.

ACTIVITY SHEET 4: OFFERINGS

Directions: Match the offering below to the name of that offering by placing the correct number on the line next to its name.

___A. Burnt Offering   ___B. Meal Offering   ___C. Peace Offering   ___D. Sin Offering   ___E. Trespass Offering

1. This is not a sweet-smelling offering to the Lord. This offering atoned for sin committed by the individual. The blood was poured out on the Brazen Alter. Some of the blood was sprinkled on the Golden Altar of Incense in the Holy Place by the priest.

2. This is an offering given to God in worship. The person bringing the offering did so as an act of worship. A bull, cow, lamb, or goat might be given. The offerer and the priest both ate of this offering.

3. This offering is described in Leviticus 1. It was done every morning and evening. Its purpose was to atone for the sins of the people. Two lambs that were a year old and without blemish were sacrificed.

4. This offering is described in Leviticus 5. This offering emphasized sin against another person and required that the offerer pay for the damage done. For example, the offerer might have killed his neighbor's cow accidentally. This situation would require this offering.

5. This offering is described in Leviticus 2. This offering was a gift to be given to God. Leaven was allowed in this offering, and olive oil was often used. Some was consumed by the fire, and the remainder was eaten by the priests.

ACTIVITY SHEET 5: OUR SIN BEARER

Directions: Select the appropriate words from the list below, to fill in blanks on your answer sheet.

Jesus _____ _____ on the cross _____ my _____ and opened the _____ of Paradise for me.

for   gates   Christ   sin   died

LESSON 14: THE TEMPLE IN JERUSALEM

Readings from the Parent/Teacher Handbook: The Bible, Vol. 3: "The Temple of Solomon"

OBJECTIVES

By the end of lesson, the learner should be able to:

- Compare the Tabernacle and the Temple,
- Discover the differences among the Three Temples,
- Identify the Jewish festivals, and
- Identify events in the Temple in the New Testament

IDENTIFICATIONS

Concepts

- *Temple*—permanent replacement for the Tabernacle
- *Shekinah*—glory of God in the Temple of Solomon

People

- *Solomon:* built the great Temple to the Lord

- *Jeroboam:* kept the people of Israel from worshipping in the Temple in Jerusalem
- *Ezekiel:* prophet in captivity who had a vision of the new Temple
- *Zerubbabel:* built the Second Temple after captivity
- *Antiochus IV Epiphanes:* evil ruler of Syria, who sacrificed a pig on the High Altar
- *Mattathias:* Maccabean leader who led the revolt against the Syrians
- *Herod the Great:* rebuilt the Second Temple and enlarged the Temple

MATERIALS NEEDED

- *Parent/Teacher Handbook: The Bible, Vol. 3*
- Activity Sheets for Lesson 14
- Crayons and markers
- Blank sheets of white paper for drawing
- Lined paper

LEARNING ACTIVITIES FOR LESSON 14

Activity 1—Comparison of Tabernacle and Temple

Read in the handbook the sections, "The Tabernacle in the Wilderness" and "The Temple of Solomon."

Use a Venn Diagram to illustrate the similarities and differences between the Tabernacle and the Temple. Prepare Activity Sheet 1 in advance of this class meeting. Have the students complete the diagram and discuss the differences.

Activity 2—List the Differences among the Three Temples

Read the sections in the handbook entitled "The Temple of Solomon," "The Temple of Zerubbabel," and "Herod's Temple."

Have the students list the characteristics of each. In what ways were they similar? List the similarities among the Three Temples in the appropriate blocks on Activity Sheet 2. Then do the same for the differences in the appropriate boxes on the same activity sheet.

Activity 3—Jewish Festivals

You will find details on the major Jewish festivals in the *Parent/Teacher Handbook, Vol. 2*, pages 39–51. If you do not have volume 2, you may search the Internet and find the Jewish festivals. The three main festivals for which many people went on pilgrimage to Jerusalem and the Temple were Passover, Pentecost, and Tabernacles.

You will also want to read the section in this handbook, "The Temple of Solomon" and "Festivals of the Jewish Year."

Use Activity Sheet 3 to complete this exercise.

Activity 4—Act Out the Events of the Temple in the New Testament

Read the history of the events of the Temple in the New Testament in the handbook, the section entitled "The Temple in the New Testament."

Have your students form five groups to act out several of the New Testament events that happened in the Temple.

Situation 1—Zachariah and the promise of a son.

Zachariah was a priest, serving in the Temple. He had a vision from an angel that his wife would have a son. He was no longer able to speak until the child was born (see Luke 1:1–24, 67–79).

Situation 2—Jesus at twelve years of age.

Jesus was with His family in Jerusalem. Jesus met with the religious leaders in the Temple. They were amazed at His understanding. His parents found that He was not with them as they were traveling home. They returned to the Temple and found Him talking with the religious leaders. They were amazed (see Luke 2:39–50).

Situation 3—Jesus and the money changers in the Temple.

Jesus went to the Temple and saw the money changers were charging the people unfairly when they changed Roman coins for Temple money. Others were selling animals within the halls of the Temple. Jesus became angry. He turned over their tables and drove them out of the Temple (see Matthew 21:14).

Situation 4—Peter and John at the Temple Gate.

After Pentecost, Peter and John went to the Temple to preach about Jesus. They found a man at the gate, who was crippled. He was begging for money. They told him that they did not have money, but that in the name of Jesus he could get up and take his bed home (see Acts 3:1–10).

Situation 5—Paul went to the Temple to make a vow.

After his third missionary journey, Paul entered the Temple to take a vow. The Jews accused him of taking a Gentile convert into the inner part of the Temple. Gentiles were not allowed in that section. They would be put to death. A riot broke out in the Temple. Soldiers came from the fortress of Antonia to rescue Paul (see Acts 21:26–36).

Activity 5—Memorize 1 Corinthians 6:19–20

The Temple today is located in the hearts of those who follow Christ. Have your students memorize these two verses from 1 Corinthians 6.

Do you not know that your body is a sanctuary of the Holy Spirit who is in you, whom you have from God? You are not your own, for you were bought at a price; therefore glorify God in your body (vv. 19–20).

Have the children write these verses in their Bible Verses Memory Books. You will also want to review the verses from past lessons.

ACTIVITY SHEET 1: VENN DIAGRAM COMPARISON OF TABERNACLE AND TEMPLE

Directions: Compare the Tabernacle and the Temple. Place characteristics of the Tabernacle that are only related to it in the left circle. Do the same for the Temple in the right circle. Place characteristics that apply to both in the intersection of the circles.

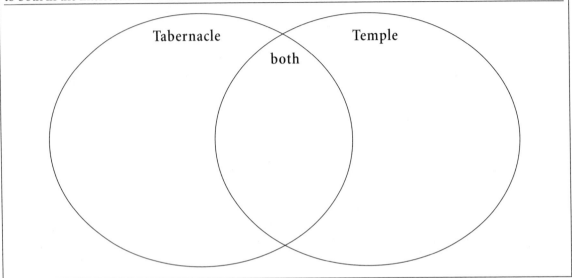

Tabernacle · both · Temple

ACTIVITY SHEET 2: SIMILARITIES AND DIFFERENCES AMONG THE THREE TEMPLES

Similarities among the Three Temples

Solomon's Temple	Second Temple	Herod's Temple

Differences among the Three Temples

Solomon's Temple	Second Temple	Herod's Temple

ACTIVITY SHEET 3: FESTIVALS OF THE JEWISH YEAR

Directions: From the description of the festival, identify it correctly by placing the number next to the appropriate name.

____A. Rosh Hashanah

____B. Yom Kippur

____C. Feast of Tabernacles

____D. Hanukkah

____E. Purim

____F. Pesach

____G. Shavuot

1. This joyful celebration follows inward assessment of sin committed during the year past. In this festival Jewish families live in booths or *sukkah* under the stars and appreciate the handiwork of God. This is a harvest festival.

2. This feast occurs fifty days after another major festival. It is called counting the omer. It is a harvest festival. But it also commemorates the giving of the Law. On this feast day Israel became a nation.

3. This is the Jewish New Year. It is not celebrated as we celebrate joyously the ringing out of the old year and the ringing in of the new. Rather, it is a solemn two-day holiday in which Jewish persons look back over the past year and think about those things that have broken their relationship with God.

4. This is the feast of Queen Esther, who saved the Jews from being killed by the wicked Haman in Persia. Her bravery is celebrated with joy. The feast comes toward the end of winter and the beginning of spring.

5. This is the holiest day of the Jewish year and comes at the end of the Ten Days of Awe after the New Year and before the Feast of Tabernacles. During the days of the Temple, the High Priest sacrificed a ram and placed the blood on the mercy seat in the Holy of Holies. Then the sins of the people were taken on the other ram, and he was put over a cliff, symbolically taking the sins of the people for the past year. It was commonly believed that until about AD 30 the scarlet cord on the ram's horn turned white when God accepted the sacrifice. (After AD 30 there was no need for the sacrifice because Jesus opened the Holy of Holies through His death on the cross.)

6. This feast has a *seder* or order of service which is different from most other feasts. This feast commemorates the Exodus from Egypt in the Old Testament. The foods that are eaten help Jewish families to remember what their founding fathers experienced as they were slaves in Egypt and then by the mercy of God were spared the angel of death. They escaped into the wilderness and then to the Promised Land.

7. This feast remembers the Maccabean Revolt against Antiochus IV Epiphanes, the Syrian ruler. Antiochus made the Temple a Temple to Zeus and sacrificed pigs on the altar each day. Mattathias and his sons believed that God would help them revolt against the evil Antiochus. They fought a war in which they were outnumbered but by God's grace victorious. They cleansed the Temple and restored worship of Almighty God. During the rededication of the Temple, they ran out of oil for the lamps, but the oil continued for the entire eight days of celebration.

Readings from the Parent/Teacher Handbook: The Bible, Vol. 3: "Bible Geography"

OBJECTIVES

By the end of lesson, the learner should be able to:

- Identify locations of events on the map,
- Explain the various Empires that arose during Bible times, and
- Recall the kings of the Empires during Bible times.

IDENTIFICATIONS

Locations

- *Egypt*—powerful Empire during Bible times; northeast corner of Africa, along the Nile River
- *Phoenicia*—country to the north of Palestine; interacted with the people of Israel
- *Philistia*—seafaring people along the western coast of Palestine, who carried out war with the people of Israel, until subdued by King David
- *Assyria*—powerful country to the north and east, present-day northern Iraq; cruel toward their enemies
- *Babylonia*—powerful country, led by Nebuchadnezzar to defeat Assyria and dominate the world of that day
- *Persia*—present-day Iran, who defeated the Babylonians and emerged as the dominant world power
- *Greece*—led by Alexander the Great, the Greeks defeated Persia and conquered the entire world of that day
- *Rome*—replaced Greece and dominated the world for about one thousand years

MATERIALS NEEDED

- *Parent/Teacher Handbook: The Bible, Vol. 3*
- Activity Sheets for Lesson 15
- Crayons and markers
- Blank sheets of white paper for drawing
- Lined paper
- Colored pencils

LEARNING ACTIVITIES FOR LESSON 15

Note: This unit will differ from the preceding units. If you spend adequate time on the activities listed, you will consume as much time as you would for the other lessons in this series. This is a valuable unit, since it introduces or deepens understanding of the world Empires that have emerged in history. This unit can be interdisciplinary, combining art, history, religious beliefs, political boundaries, language skills, and the Bible.

Activity 1—World Powers Map Exercise

Read the section, "Bible Geography" in the handbook.

Use Activity Sheet 1 and make sufficient copies for your students to have a map of each of the Empires. Using the maps from the "Bible Geography" section in the handbook, have each student develop a copy of the Empire. Shade the sections with colored pencils or markers. Include all of the geographical divisions and cities that are important to the Empires and the biblical relationships. Keep these with the reports in the next activity as well as part of the study of this unit.

Activity 2—Empires of the Past Posters

Read the history of the events of the Temple in the New Testament in the handbook under the section, "Bible Geography."

This activity can consume a good portion of your class time devoted to this unit. Divide your class into smaller groups. Assign each group with one of the major world Empires. Have them develop an extensive report about that country and report their findings to the entire class. They may report in the traditional way or they may be encouraged to use the overhead projector, slides, or develop a PowerPoint® presentation. This activity should span a period of three to six weeks in length. Encourage creativity and good effort in carrying out this task.

The countries and Empires to study are: Egypt, Phoenicia and Philistia, Assyria, Babylonia, Persia, Greece, and Rome.

In the report, include the following information:
1. Title and location of the country
2. Brief history of the country
3. People
4. Political development
5. Important people, such as kings and rulers
6. Cultural contributions
7. Economic growth and development
8. Downfall of the Empire
9. Interaction with the people of Israel
10. The country as it is today
11. Location, using maps from antiquity and today

You may also want your students to create posters for each of these countries to be displayed around the classroom.

Activity 3—Field Trips to Museums

Take your class on a field trip to one or more museums. Usually museums of history or art are best. You want your students to experience some of the early artifacts that have come from the cultures of the past. Usually there are self-guided tours that will help you focus on materials of particular interest. Carefully observe the exhibits on display. What has made them worthy of note? From what time period did they come? Compare objects of different time periods for similarities and differences. The museum can provide an excellent learning experience for children.

If you are located near a large city, such as New York, Chicago, Washington, D.C., Cleveland, or Los Angeles, there are excellent museums for artifacts from the past. The museum at the University of Chicago has Babylonian and Assyrian relics. The Metropolitan Museum of Art in New York City has a wealth of artifacts from Egypt, Mesopotamia, Greece, and Rome. Even smaller cities, like Minneapolis and Raleigh, have excellent art museums with artifacts from ancient cultures. Explore your community for the resources it has available.

ACTIVITY SHEET 1: OUTLINE MAP

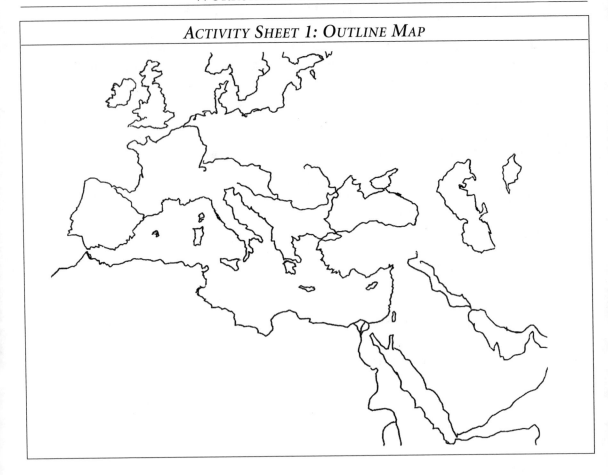

ANSWERS TO ACTIVITY SHEETS

LESSON 1

Activity Sheet 4

Activity Sheet 7
1. Jepthah
2. 600
3. Samuel
4. Othniel
5. Nazarite
6. Deborah and Barak
7. 80
8. 135,000

LESSON 2

Activity Sheet 6
1. B
2. C
3. A

LESSON 3

Activity Sheet 1
1. Psalms
2. Psalms 119
3. Psalms 117
4. Psalms 117
5. Psalms 118:8
6. Psalms

Activity Sheet 2
1. Hymns
2. Wisdom
3. Teaching
4. Repentance
5. Pilgrimage
6. Lament
7. Majestic

Activity Sheet 3b
1. Synonymous
2. Synonymous
3. Antithetic
4. Antithetic
5. Synthetic
6. Synthetic

Activity Sheet 4
Tree:
4, 5, 6, 7, 8
Result: Life
Chaff:
1, 2, 3, 9, 10
Result: Death

Activity Sheet 6
1. Shepherd
2. Shepherd
3. Shepherd
4. Sheep
5. Sheep
6. Sheep
7. Shepherd
8. Sheep
9. Shepherd
10. Sheep
11. Sheep
12. Shepherd

LESSON 4

Activity Sheet 1
5, 3, 2, 4, 6, 1

Activity Sheet 2
Across
3. praise
5. wash
8. God
9. gladness
Down
1. sin
2. mercy
4. restore
6. purge
7. heart
10. snow

Activity Sheet 5
1. Judgments
2. Testimonies
3. Ordinances
4. Law
5. Precepts
6. Word
7. Commandments
8. Statutes

Activity Sheet 4
The following
characteristics
should be
checked: 1, 4, 5,
6, 7, 8, and 9.

LESSON 5

Activity Sheet 3
1. Contrasting
2. Contrasting
3. Comparing
4. Completing
5. Completing
6. Completing
7. Comparing
8. Completing
9. Comparing
10. Completing
11. Comparing
12. Completing
13. Contrasting
14. Contrasting

Activity Sheet 4
1. 3
2. 4
3. 1, 5
4. 2
5. 3
6. 2
7. 4
8. 5
9. 2
10. 4
11. 5
12. 3
13. 2
14. 4
15. 1, 2
16. 3
17. 5

LESSON 6

Activity Sheet 5
Secret Code:
Ecclesiastes 12:13

LESSON 7

Activity Sheet 4
Across
1. bread
4. Jordan
6. devil
7. temptation
Down
1. baptism
2. worship
3. angels
5. forty
7. Temple

LESSON 8

Activity Sheet 5
1. 3
2. 1
3. 2
4. 2
5. 1
6. 2
7. 3
8. 1
9. 2
10. 1

LESSON 9

Activity Sheet 3
Jewish religious
leaders who want
Christians to be
zealous to follow
every Jewish
regulation as well
as Christian
practices.

Activity Sheet 5

LESSON 12

Activity Sheet 3

```
R V K N Y C U Z E Q Z P P R X
M L O S B X K X R L G Q Z D H
M W S S L L O V E L T H G I L
L E R E M Y Y R T I H W T C S
B C H N X A S A T F T D P B K
P N S T F B Y N D E U Q B D T
J E V I L H R T X L R L N R O
U D D W X X D I R L T N R I A
Q I T D X P V C M O B K N C N
N F R L R N L H D W D I S T J
R N B R M W I R C S V Y D A P
R O Y O U E O I D H A N B H M
D C X W S W V S X I I D V D A
Z I U I E A X T E P B N P S Z
D L O D L E E T N E X O B M O
```

Activity Sheet 4

1. Truth
2. Truth
3. Truth
4. Love
5. Love
6. Truth
7. Truth

LESSON 13

Activity Sheet 2

1—B
2—D
3—F
4—C
5—E
6—A

Activity Sheet 4

A—3
B—5
C—2
D—1
E—4

Activity Sheet 3

1. linen
2. goat hair
3. ram skins
4. sealskins or leather
5. cloth

Activity Sheet 5

Jesus Christ died on the cross for my sin and opened the gates of Paradise for me.

LESSON 14

Activity Sheet 3

A—3
B—5
C—1
D—7
E—4
F—6
G—2